HISTORY OF THE WESTERN WORLD

General Editor: John Roberts

The Age of Expansion
1848-1917

Overleaf: Workshop of the world. A
contemporary print places the Great
Exhibition of 1851 at the Crystal Palace in
London firmly in its place – as seen through
British eyes.

ALL THE WORLD GOING TO SEE THE GREAT EXHIBITION OF 1851.

The Age of Expansion 1848-1917

Marcus Cunliffe

G. & C. Merriam Company, Publishers
Springfield, Massachusetts

Designed by Margaret Downing

Library of Congress Cataloging in Publication Data

Cunliffe, Marcus.
    The age of expansion, 1848–1916.
    (History of the Western World, v. 5)
    Bibliography: p. 304.
    1. History, Modern- -19th century. 2. History
    Modern- -20th century. I. Title. II. Series.
D358.C8   940.2'8   73–18488
ISBN 0–87779–060–4

Manufactured in the United Kingdom

Contents

List of Maps

Introduction

Acceleration is the one obvious overriding trend in modern history. It stands out from the welter of themes which overwhelm the student. Its operation can be felt immediately. Whatever happens, happens more quickly; when changes occur, they occur more rapidly and the chain-reactions they start are more quickly apparent than ever before. In retrospect, this quickening of pace is observable a long way back. By now it has become so fast that, given the appointed biblical span of life of three-score years and ten, a modern man can expect the world to change radically during his lifetime. Indeed, he can confidently expect revolutions. This was already true of a lifetime covering the years of which Professor Cunliffe has written in this book. A man born in 1848 would have been sixty-nine in 1917. He would have begun his life in the year men called 'the springtime of the nations' and finished it when nations that had no political existence in that year were fighting the greatest war in history.

If the same man lived to the age of seventy which he might reasonably expect, he would have ended his life on the eve of the greatest triumph of the principle of nationality in history, in the peace-making which followed the end of the First World War. This suggests one of the unities and continuities of what follows. Within the boundaries of the Western world, the triumph of nationality was almost complete in these years; the non-national dynastic world all but disappeared. Yet to concentrate on this theme would leave out others just as full of revolutionary change. On the material plane this is the age also of the coming of electricity, anaesthetics, the internal combustion engine and the aeroplane. In the intellectual sphere it is the age of Karl Marx, Charles Darwin, Richard Wagner, Henrik Ibsen, Sigmund Freud and Ernest Rutherford – and the list could be continued by another six names equally celebrated.

This richness poses enormous difficulties of construction which cannot be solved within a conventionally narrative structure. Even the evolving unity at the heart of the book – the Western world – seems to threaten to disappear or else so expand as to be almost unmanageable. Professor Cunliffe's Western world transcends not only Europe, but also the Atlantic community which was added to the old Mediterranean nations to form the Western world in the seventeenth and eighteenth centuries and provides the intelligible unit of study of books chronologically antecendent in this history. This is not merely a matter of the well-known phenomenon of overseas imperialism (or, for that matter, of Russian overland imperialism) and the involvement with other continents and peoples which this implied. It is also because of a Western transformation of the non-Western world. It sucked alien peoples willy-nilly into the Western orbit.

This happened in many ways. If they were ruled directly by Western powers, they absorbed what the West brought through administrators, governors and teachers. If they kept their independence, non-Western peoples could only survive by adopting Western techniques, ideas and institutions which infected their cultures with alien elements. The final culmination of this came only very recently, when the nations of the former colonial empires shook off their rulers in the name of nationality and Marxism, two *Western* ideologies.

This means that even before 1917 the 'Western world' is a phrase which is still capable of new meaning. In the seventeenth century it transcended the Christian Europe from which it had emerged; in the nineteenth, it began to expand beyond the communities of European stocks which it had spread round the world and to manifest itself in the claims of nationalists, reformers and revolutionaries in China, Japan and India who sought to change their own societies to make them more like Europe or the United States. John Stuart Mill, Samuel Smiles, John Dewey, Ibsen – oddly assorted as the list now seems, they were names which lit the future for many a young Asian. Insofar as they did so, the West had once more extended itself. Thus it made its final and perhaps most successful conquests.

It is worth bearing this in mind to offset a sense of impending disaster; as readers of history we labour under the burden of knowing what is coming as 1916 approaches. That was the last year in which the great empires which had gone to war were intact. The Russian would collapse the next year, the German, Habsburg and Ottoman Empires the year after. When this happened, men would be shaken and confused; familiar landmarks would have been swept away. Yet they should not have been quite so surprised; so much had already changed. In 1848 there had been no German Empire in existence, nor a united Italy. The Habsburg Empire, too, had been a very different structure from that of 1916.

Only two of the victorious Great Powers of 1918 would be nations with old, settled constitutions which went back more than a century – the United Kingdom and the United States.

The presence of the United States marked one of the greatest changes of all, the entry on the historical stage of the first super-power. This fact was still masked in 1917; it eluded the comprehension of many people until 1941 and many of them were Americans. Though American participation would be decisive and though the Great War was righly called the First World War, its crucial battles were fought on a narrow strip of territory, for centuries a European cockpit, and in the sealanes which approached the British Isles. It was a war for European power. In 1939, Europe would go to war again. That war, too, would turn into a world war. But it would be fought in the Pacific and in North Africa as well as in Europe and those fighting would be as often the soldiers of non-European as of European powers. Then the nature of the different Western world which was already half-born by 1917, and whose shape can be discerned in this book, would be apparent.

JOHN ROBERTS

1 Prologue: The World in Motion

The Dynamic Societies

The years 1848 to 1917 yield us a richly varied set of events, an almost infinite profusion of piecemeal historical information. The question which must dominate both author and reader is how this plethora of activity can be shaped into a homogenous *world* history, as distinct from merely an account of the more prominent nations of Europe, plus the United States. One solution might seem to be offered by Karl Marx and Friedrich Engels, even if their *Communist Manifesto*, published in 1848 – the year of revolutions throughout Europe – and their other writings during the next decade remained almost unknown to the general public. For they offered a comprehensive explanation of what happened in 1848, why it had happened, and what must happen in the future. But there is no need to dwell upon the brilliant potency of the Marxist interpretation, to which we shall return later in the book.

We clearly cannot write world history with much insight if our viewpoint is entirely that of the West. Perhaps world history in the fullest sense cannot yet be written: none of us knows enough or has yet achieved enough detachment from the societies we try to chronicle. A thoroughly bourgeois version would be too smugly narrow. Yet a radical version, using Marxist ideas, might also present too blinkered, too Western a picture – as if non-European societies were simply 'barbarian', backward, awaiting their turn of the chronological wheel to progress through an essentially *European* sequence of development. This book is broken into three sections. The middle section tries to move out from the specifically European context into the rest of the world.

Non-Europeans may feel that that is a very small ration, and that the book is still much too Europe-centred. The balance of material, however, rests upon a conviction formed not only by writings in economic history but by those in almost every other field. One comes to the conclusion that for the period 1848–1917 the principal emphasis must be on the national societies recognized as leaders at the time – though with some regard for chronology, in order to deal with shifts in achievement, power and prestige

13

through the decades. This Europe-centredness – leaving aside for the moment what precisely may be meant by 'Europe' – would be unavoidable whether one were attempting a history of industrialization or of warfare, science, architecture, exploration, music, medicine, philosophy and so on. To argue thus is not to deny that many millions were living in other, very different communities; that some of their cultures had attained a high level in previous epochs; or that they remained fascinating in their own right, with considerable potential – witness Turkey, India, China, Japan – for new growth.

The striking fact is that by the nineteenth century some societies of the world had achieved general prosperity, and the power that flows from prosperity, over a relatively short span of time, while others had not. And in mid-century the gap between the rich and the poor societies was steadily widening. The beginnings of the process pre-date our era, but we can see its operation in full swing between 1848 and 1917. Perhaps we can modify and broaden the typology of the *Manifesto* by calling the more successful societies 'dynamic' in the dictionary sense of 'producing force related to motion'. Their key words nearly all have to do with activity, enterprise, change. These also, of course, often carry an unpleasant connotation, since the societies generated callousness and doubt along with bustling assurance. Thus the *opportune* moment, which people were urged to seize, might lead to *opportunism*. A shifting scene produced *shiftiness* in the weak: note the American remark, 'It's good to be shifty in a new country', where the word is highly equivocal. *Confidence*, essential to business, opened the door to the trickster, or *confidence-man*. The word *nervous* originally signified strength and muscularity. The strains of modern life altered its associations to those of timidity and anxiety.

Many members of advanced societies deplored change and did their best to resist it. According to a familiar story, Tsar Nicholas I, finding a reference to 'progress' in a government document, wrote in the margin: 'This word must be deleted from official terminology.' But change was irresistible. Even such temperamentally conservative and authoritarian figures as Count Bismarck in Prussia had to learn to cope with it, by seizing the initiative and introducing change in the minimal doses calculated to be efficacious, much as doctors began to prescribe inoculation with a disease as the means of preventing it. Change was not in itself a total rule of life. Few men were able to welcome change wholeheartedly. The businessman who had invested his capital in new machinery, vastly proud of his capacity to 'move with the times', became understandably dismayed when his equipment was superseded by some still newer process; and the consequences for employees thrown out of work by technological innovation were still more alarming. Or a person who was open to experiment in technology might be highly resistant to new religious or social theories. Nostalgia – regret for a vanished object or place once it has vanished – was one of the century's special emotions, and *Home, Sweet Home* one of its most archetypal songs. Railroads and steamships spelled travel, adventure, liberation; they also entailed separation, loneliness, distance. This was the other side of the coin of progressive ebullience. Uneasiness accompanied change; misgivings flourished along with optimism. The intellectual in Paris, London or New York was a new breed of man: a theoretical democrat who inwardly despised the masses, a city-dweller who simultaneously adored the metropolis and condemned the civilization that had made it possible. There was a swelling chorus of disaffection that paralleled the age's sonorous hymns to progress.

The Plan of the Book

The chief emphasis in the chapters that follow is therefore on the dynamic societies, and the reactions to them of the rest of the world. Our theme is motion, and the desire for motion.

Ideally, this ought to include motion through time; for history deals with development, and the most readable history is apt to be couched as narrative. There is, however, no suitable way of giving priority in our period to the time-dimension, in relation to the other dimension of space. An attempt at a comparative view of several civilizations obliges the historian to arrange his material thematically rather than chronologically. This may seem to involve some dodging backward and forward in time. But there are other, important advantages in aiming at breadth of vision. The book's final, brief epilogue, in recapitulating major themes, also indicates some chronological threads. Taken together, the nine principal chapters offer nine ways of looking at large questions or large areas of the world during a span of about two human generations, or one average lifetime. In a world of such variety and complexity, of course, the notion of an 'average' person, born in 1848 and dying in 1917, is hypothetical. If we imagine such a person, we can say

that he might have been born in Europe; that if his early life was
spent in the countryside, he might well die as a townsman; that he
might well serve as a soldier, and perhaps be involved in a war;
that he would be married, beget several children and see some of
them die in infancy; that he would start poor, and remain un-
wealthy, but nevertheless believe that he was better off than his
ancestors, not to mention the inhabitants of other 'uncivilized'
societies. He would probably justify this conviction by contrasting
the horse-drawn conveyances of his boyhood with the automobiles
and omnibuses of his latter years, or candlelight with gas and
electricity, or the quill pen with the typewriter, or the music-hall
with the cinema. He would probably be patriotic, and have a
portrait of royalty hanging on his wall. He would believe in
progress. He would also, with no sense of contradiction, probably
feel that the world was going to the dogs.

Part One

The European Dynamic

2 Machines

Faith in machinery is . . . our besetting danger; often in machinery most absurdly disproportioned to the end which this machinery . . . is to serve; but always in machinery, as if it had a value in and for itself. What is freedom but machinery? what is population but machinery? what is coal but machinery? what are railroads but machinery? what is wealth but machinery? what are, even, religious organizations but machinery? Now almost every voice in England is accustomed to speak of these things as if they were precious ends in themselves, and therefore had some of the characters of perfection indisputably joined to them.

Matthew Arnold, 'Sweetness and Light', in Culture and Anarchy, *1869*

The Situation at Mid-Century

In 1839 Dr Thomas Arnold, headmaster of Rugby School, for the first time in his life saw a railway train, puffing (or as he no doubt thought, hurtling) through a hitherto undisturbed English landscape. The experience seemed overwhelmingly significant: 'Feudality', he said, 'is gone for ever.' This sense that science and technology were transforming the world overnight pervades the writings of the time. Alfred de Vigny, visiting England in the same year, 1839, was appalled by the industrial grime of Birmingham. His poem *La Maison du Berger* set against the 'coal-black towns' a consolatory vision of pastoral calm. And the English poet William Wordsworth hated the noisy, smoky intrusion of the railroad in his beloved Lake District.

These misgivings will be explored in later chapters, but for our immediate purpose, the important things to grasp are the extent of the transformations that were being wrought, and the wealth and gratification they brought to the dynamic nations. In mid-century, for every person who was dismayed by industrialism, a score expressed either glowing enthusiasm or at least a manful readiness to face up to the consequences.

Two points are worth stressing. The first is that the industrial revolution was well advanced by mid-century. To begin the story at 1848 or 1850 would be like coming into an opera at the beginning of the second act. Steam, a revolutionary 'prime mover' in the days of Boulton and Watt, was by 1850 an established, in fact essential, source of power. Coal was being mined in abundance to provide fuel. The steam-engines themselves, thanks to a large increase in the production of iron and to sophisticated technological improvements, had become more and more reliable and powerful. Thus, compound or high-pressure engines were familiar if much admired features of industrial life. A character in Benjamin Disraeli's novel *Coningsby* (1844) commends a bank in Manchester as 'high-pressure to the backbone' – with the implication that it is not only active but safe. Iron was a major material, on the way to becoming as basic to existence in the leading nations as wood was in traditional societies. The railway, a novel means of transport in the 1820s, was by 1850 a proven system of incalculable potential. In Britain, where industrialization had gone furthest, just over half the population now lived in towns. Here and there, in Belgium, in northern France, in the north-eastern parts of the United States and patchily elsewhere, mid-century found numbers of men and women at work in large premises, producing textiles and other goods in mass quantities. Many of the devices on which large-scale mechanized production depended – accountancy, company and patent law, stock exchanges, banking, insurance, postal and telegraph services – were also well past their infancy. Indeed the textile and coalmining industries had fixed their essential technology and were to undergo little change in the next few decades. Many inventions that subsequently altered other industries, or brought new ones into being, were already grasped in theory and merely awaiting perfection through the process – sometimes short, sometimes frustratingly protracted – of technological experiment. Scores of resourceful engineers were busying themselves with the construction of machine tools: machines, that is, to make machines. No wonder that some observers felt machinery had human, or rather superhuman, attributes, and tended to personify it. In England, said the American Ralph Waldo Emerson (*English Traits*, 1856), steam was a member of Parliament.

The second point is that, having launched the industrial revolution, Britain was in 1850 unquestionably the world's greatest industrial nation. 'I am here in the centre of the most advanced industry of Europe and of the Universe', said a visiting French textile entrepreneur, a few years earlier. At the time of his visit, by contrast, there were only two steam-engines in Milan, and none in Cairo (the largest city of the African continent) or Tokyo or Peking. By mid-century, Britain was producing two-thirds of the world's coal and over half of its iron and its cotton cloth. Britain had constructed over six thousand miles of railway, a figure far exceeding that of any other country except the United States (which had built nearly nine thousand). Supremely confident of their dominance, the British had abolished practically all tariff protection on their wares. They took for granted that they could outsell every rival. 'Free trade' was beginning to be invested with a sacred significance – the guarantor of universal prosperity and of universal peace.

The Spread of the Machine, 1850–70

In the years 1850–70, Britain appeared to be maintaining its supremacy. To take one index, Britain's production of pig iron in 1850 comfortably exceeded the combined output of the next three producers, France, the United States and the German states. All three greatly expanded production, but Britain too trebled its output between 1850 and 1870, and in 1870 still outmatched the total of the other three economies. The British achievement found its moralist-historian in Samuel Smiles. His *Lives of the Engineers* (five volumes), *Self-Help, Character, Thrift, Duty* and other works urged the reader to better himself, and to model himself upon those heroic individuals, usually of humble birth, who had changed the world from a static to a dynamic place. Reviewing Smiles's *Industrial Biography: Iron-Workers and Tool-Makers*, the London *Times* said that,

Considering what England is, and to what we owe most of our material greatness, the lives of our Engineers are peculiarly worthy of being written. 'The true Epic of our time,' says Mr Carlyle, 'is not Arms and the man, but Tools and the man – an infinitely wider kind Of Epic.' Our machinery has been the making of us; our ironworks have, in spite of the progress of other nations, still kept the balance in our hands. Smith-work in all its branches of engine-making, machine-making, tool-making, cutlery, iron ship-building, and iron-working generally, is our chief glory. England is the mistress of manufactures, and so the queen of the world, because it is the land of Smith; and Mr Smiles's biographies are a history of the great family of Smith.

British cotton spinning and weaving, more concentrated and more heavily mechanized than anywhere else in the world, in fact held its lead until the First World War. The woollen industry,

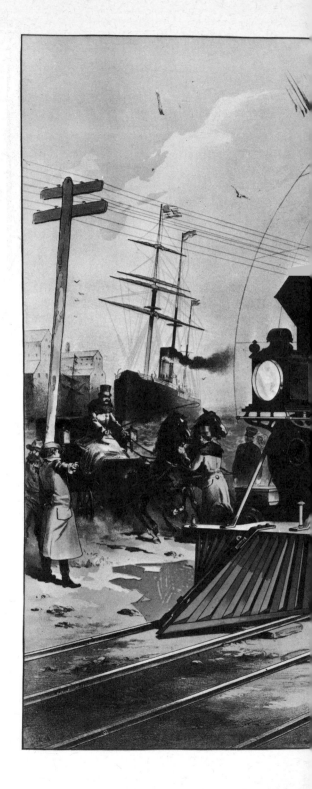

The Railroad Revolution. An American
advertisement of 1882 contrasts the speed and
efficiency of rail with the slowness – and the
perils – of ship, stagecoach and canal.

25

Ruling the Waves. The British Empire was built on maritime supremacy, both naval and commercial. The great Clyde shipyards helped to forge – and profited from – this supremacy.

newer and benefiting from the perfecting of the condenser and machine-comber, was likewise outstripping French and German competition. British shipyards took the transition to steam and iron in their stride. They built a far larger tonnage than any other nation; more ships sailed under British registry; and the name Lloyd's of London was almost synonymous with reliable marine insurance. London was the unquestioned centre of banking and investment. The pattern of these two decades is illustrated in the career of William Wheelwright. He was an American who established a little trading empire in the Chilean port of Valparaiso. Deciding to pioneer a link with Europe, he formed the Pacific Steam Navigation Company and came to England in 1848 to buy some steamships. He became interested in Chilean coal, copper and silver mines and then in railroad building. Through his railroad work, he was drawn into a partnership with Thomas Brassey, whom he met in London, to construct railroads in the Argentine. The capital for their Central Argentine Railway was raised in London; a previous, Spanish promoter had been given the contract but had lacked the necessary backing. Wheel-

26

wright and Brassey, as chief shareholders and contractors, obtained handsome land-grants from the Argentine confederation. Wheelwright wrote jubilantly to Brassey in 1864: 'Our [land] titles are clear and investigationable. We have at least the halo of British protection and that is the only true way of seeing it. . . .'

British dominance in 1850–70 was however not as secure as it might seem. True, there were impressive new advances in technology. Steel – iron with carbon, phosphorus and other impurities removed – had long been prized for its superior qualities but had never been produceable in quantity. Henry Bessemer's steel converter (1856), a British invention, solved the problem. Yet this and other seeming proofs of superiority were beginning to be challenged. British company law, private banking and capital-formation were now paralleled and in some ways surpassed by new practices in continental Europe. Joint-stock discount banks such as the Brussels *Union du Crédit* (1848) and the Berlin *Discontogesellschaft* (1851) led in succession to institutions like the Paris *Crédit Industriel* (1859), which introduced British devices (including the cheque), and then to a spread of central and branch banks like the *Crédit Lyonnais* (1863). These vastly improved the flow and availability of funds. Continental financiers took a vital and novel step with the introduction of joint-stock investment banking. The French *Crédit Mobilier* (1852), by investing depositors' funds in speculative commercial ventures, matched old savings to new industrial opportunities so successfully that this type of institution soon spread to other countries – sometimes keeping its French name. A good deal of this flow of money, especially in France, went into overseas investment. But the broad picture is of a bringing-together of the effective elements – cash, materials, machines, workers, managers – with a briskness and pragmatic boldness such as had characterized the earlier phase in Britain. In 1850 the world capacity in steam-engines amounted to about four million horse-power. Of this total a third was produced in Great Britain. Europe as a whole, including Britain, accounted for something over half. Most of the remaining capacity was supplied by the United States. By 1870 the world total had soared to about $18\frac{1}{2}$ million horse-power. Europe's share had risen to nearly two-thirds. The figures for the leading nations were: United States 5,590,000; Britain 4,040,000; Germany 2,480,000; France 1,850,000; Russia 920,000; Austria 800,000; Belgium 350,000; Italy 330,000.

As these figures show, Continental Europe was moving up

fast. Inside Europe, Germany, finally unified in 1871, was growing fastest. Outside, the United States was growing faster still. Russia too was lumbering forward. The rest of the world outside Europe and North America was technologically insignificant.

The German expansion held all sorts of lessons, though they would become apparent only with time. One stimulant was the *Zollverein* or internal customs union, pioneered by Prussia as early as 1818 and extended until by the early 1850s only Austria and a few patches of the subsequent German Empire were left outside its shelter. It appeared to be a victory for the British idea of free trade; but in retrospect it presented the spectacle of a widening, rationalized home market not unlike that of the United States. Another factor was railroad building. By the early 1850s, the map of Germany, again excluding Austria, was criss-crossed with six major lines that joined the chief clusters of population. The French scheme of universal banking was quickly adopted. A year after the Pereire brothers formed the *Crédit Mobilier*, there came the first German equivalent, the *Bank für Handel und Industrie* of Darmstadt (the Rothschilds launched their *Kreditanstalt* in Vienna in 1855). Enterprises like the Darmstädter Bank went far beyond the traditional functions of lending, holding and transferring. Their capital was used to create new industries; their officers joined the boards of companies, so that finance and production were there, unlike Great Britain, intimately associated from the start. This mixture of traditional, short-term money dealing and of speculative long-term activity seemed bizarre and unsound to orthodox bankers. The element of risk was obviously greater, and the structure of what was to be called 'finance capitalism' – the next stage after 'carboniferous capitalism' – wobbled alarmingly at each of the periodic depressions in world trade that punctuated the second half of the nineteenth century: 1857, 1873, 1893. The original *Crédit Mobilier* lasted only until 1867. But the investment bank proved too valuable to discard. Indeed, it became a part of the very fabric of the newer industrialism, promoting, organizing, consolidating with an energy that admirers (including contented investors, large and small) thought entirely right and proper, even if radical critics saw the institution as sinisterly rapacious: Mammon Incorporated.

Whatever the moral balance-sheet, the material one was plain to read. Sanguine citizens in the dynamic societies of the era could believe that there was no serious disjunction between God and Mammon. Progress was itself a kind of universal bank in which

every account, every branch, played a part in enriching the fabric. Knowledge was power and power was wealth and wealth was both real and an all-embracing metaphor. Even a dedicated, unworldly scientist like the American Willard Gibbs revealed how far he subscribed to the doctrine of industrial expansion. Explaining the importance of mathematics in a lecture of 1886, he employed the typical vocabulary of pragmatic uplift: 'The human mind has never invented a labor-saving machine equal to algebra. It is but natural and proper that an age like our own, characterized by the multiplication of labor-saving machinery, should be distinguished by an unexampled development of this most refined and most beautiful of machines.'

In Germany, the seeds had been sowed early. As with banking, though to a lesser extent, the German states built on French experience. The new universities of Berlin (1810) and Bonn (1817), for example, were much influenced by the *École Polytechnique* of Paris. Unlike the French universities, however, those in Germany stressed research and their professors in the science-inclined faculties had a wonderful opportunity to direct bands of students into promising fields of inquiry. Chemists like Justus

A compound dynamo on display at Frankfurt in 1891. Towards the end of the nineteenth century German industrial expansion offered a challenge to the rest of Europe and to the United States.

29

Liebig at Giessen (where his pupils included Willard Gibbs from America, Lyon Playfair from England and N. I. Zinin from Russia), Friedrich Wöhler at Göttingen, and Robert Wilhelm Bunsen at Marburg and Heidelberg, gave Germany pre-eminence in chemical research. The Bunsen burner (1850), apart from its utility in laboratory work, represents a step in the application of gas to large-scale heating and lighting. A great deal of fundamental work in physics and mathematics, some of it of crucial importance for the development of electricity, was also being carried on by scholars such as Wilhelm Weber and Karl Friedrich Gauss at Göttingen. A number of scientists, Wöhler among them, moved into university research from teaching in technical schools *(Gewerbeschule)* – a type of institution that began to be established around 1820. Another key educational innovation, starting at Karlsruhe in Baden in 1825 and spreading rapidly through the other state capitals, was the *technische Hochschule*. The *technische Hochschulen* evolved into something much more like the twentieth-century university-level institute of technology than the name 'technical high school' might imply; Albert Einstein was later to be a student at the *technische Hochschule* in Zürich, Switzerland, which was founded in 1855 on the German pattern.

The New York Stock Exchange, 1863. Not yet a rival to London as financial centre of the world, American prosperity nevertheless indicated the shape of things to come.

30

By 1870, for pure and applied science, German education was recognized as the best in the world. On its discoveries rested the brilliantly successful German chemical industry, and the great Zeiss optical factory which started in Jena in 1846. Beginning to develop the Ruhr coalfield in the early 1850s, the Irish civil engineer W. T. Mulvany felt that he was dealing with an industrially unawakened society. 'These people', he said, 'do not know their own wealth.' By 1870, the Germans were fully awake. They no longer needed foreigners to tell them what to do. On the contrary, foreigners came to study with them, and to write wistful memoranda about the need to follow the German example in science. When some patriotic Englishmen put up money for a college of chemistry in London, they asked Liebig to pick a director. His nominee, A. W. Hoffman, inspired a generation of British pupils (W. H. Perkin, F. A. Abel and others) who between them created the coal-tar dye industry.

The United States too, in rather different ways, was establishing itself between 1850 and 1870 as a phenomenally productive industrial society. Sophisticated banking or technological education were not among the reasons for this. Tariff protection and assistance from some state governments should be taken into account. More important, though, were the generally high level of literacy and enterprise; the supply of young immigrants from Europe, and on the west coast from China; and the availability of capital, machinery and fundamental knowledge flowing across the Atlantic. Political stability should also be mentioned, despite the apparent collapse of the American polity in the Civil War of 1861–5 (see Chapter 10). Economic historians disagree as to whether the war itself accelerated or retarded industrialization. What seems undeniable is that the American economy was flourishing well before the break between North and South, and that while the fighting laid waste some areas of the mainly agricultural South, the North escaped with no more damage than might have been caused in ordinary circumstances through, say, crop failure or epidemic disease.

In mid-century, the United States was remarkably well-placed for a technological leap forward. Except for Negro slaves, Indian aborigines and some pockets of white poverty, the country as a whole enjoyed a high living-standard; and the extremes of wealth and poverty were as yet less conspicuous than almost anywhere else in the world. The Americans, as was often observed at the time, were a middle-class people – a nation, in the words of the historian Richard Hofstadter, of 'expectant capitalists'. They had broken out of the mercantilist system with the Revolution of 1776. True, they had had a dependent relationship to Europe for several decades afterward, exchanging raw materials (especially cotton) for manufactures, and beholden to European investors. But the relationship in the outcome stimulated instead of repressing enterprise.

The shape of American development was already discernible at the Great Exhibition held at the Crystal Palace in London in 1851, in the shape of the McCormick reaper, the sewing-machine, the Yale lock and the Colt revolver. Similar objects were being made in Europe, and fundamental inventions continued to emanate largely from Europe. The principles of mass-production and interchangeable parts were known in Europe – witness the very construction of the Crystal Palace. American workmanship, then and later, often struck Europeans as gimcrack and 'cheap' – flimsy bridges, poor-quality iron and steel, inelegant dollar watches and loud-ticking alarm-clocks. The point was that they were deliberately 'cheap': price mattered more than quality, and low prices were a result of standardization for a mass-market coupled with a strongly functional design-sense. Higher labour costs than in Europe and a shortage of skilled labour: these put a premium on labour-saving machinery manufactured by labour-saving methods.

In 1870, to repeat, Britain was still the world's greatest industrial and financial power. But other nations, notably Germany and the United States, were swiftly closing the gap. The machine had its own cruel dictates. Yesterday's pioneer was today's veteran and tomorrow's irrelevance. Innovation implied eventual obsolescence. Vigorous optimism could easily harden into arrogance. Dogmas sound enough in an era of British pre-eminence could become commercially dangerous. Free trade as a unilateral idea seemed suddenly dubious when, for instance, a new and booming British export in screws was shattered by rival manufacturers in the United States who managed to have their country's import tariff on screws raised from twenty-five to seventy-five per cent. Free trade seemed an enemy when it facilitated the expansion of American trade in miscellaneous manufactures with Canada and Australia. British patent law, which did not require the patentee to prove his product, seemed to open the door to foreign domination of the British market: dyestuffs, for instance, were rapidly passing under the control of the German chemical industry. New industrial societies could consolidate and ramify with fewer social or geographical constraints. It was proving easier to build entirely new factories, and to assemble new work-forces from scratch, than to shift existing factories and employees.

For all the worldwide popularity of Samuel Smiles's stirring homilies, and the solace of their emphasis on British achievement, a crucial fact remained: they were histories of what had *been* done, rather than accounts of what was *now* being attempted on the brink of the new era of electricity and petroleum. The finest British writing of the next generation, with the exception of the machine-celebrations of Rudyard Kipling, was to be devoted to misgivings over machine-civilization. The new prophets of industrialism emerged in other countries: for example, among German monistic philosophers like Eugen Dühring and Wilhelm Ostwald who held that 'energy' was the key to everything in the universe, including mankind.

World Mechanization, 1870–1900

By the 1870s, even nations remote from Europe were responding willy-nilly to the tides of a world economy. Steamships carried cargoes of manufactures from the centres of industry. They brought back palm-oil and rubber from the tropics, coffee from Brazil, tea from India and China, beef from the Argentine, meat and dairy products from Australasia, gold and diamonds from South Africa, guano from Peru, copper and nitrates from Chile. New refrigerated ships were making possible these long-distance cargoes in perishable goods. More efficient engines – first through compounding or triple-expansion techniques, and then in the 1880s by means of Charles H. Parsons's steam-turbine – were cutting the time required for voyages. Vastly improved docks and harbours, with new cargo-handling methods, were speeding the turn-round of merchant shipping.

The rich nations also had ever-increasing home markets, and were one another's best customers. Their economies grew symbiotically, one sector stimulating another. Thus the apparently infinite world-demand for textiles spurred on the producers of raw cotton, wool and silk; it brought into being more and bigger mills in the United States, Britain and western Europe, and new ones in India and the Far East; and it quickened the pace of production of engines and looms and machine tools. New service industries emerged to distribute and sell this torrent of cloth and other consumer goods. There was the giant department store such as Bon Marché in Paris or Macy's in New York. There was the chain-store with its string of nearly identical establishments in different cities: Woolworth's, which emphasized cheapness, was a famous American example. There were mail-order firms, notably Montgomery Ward and Sears, Roebuck in Chicago, catering to a small-town and rural clientele with their encyclopaedic annual catalogues. There were co-operatives, starting in England in the 1840s with the Rochdale Pioneers, which endeavoured to sell retail goods at less than retail prices.

And in with a rush came advertising, though its full armoury of enticements was not to be deployed until the twentieth century. Weekly and monthly magazines, which also multiplied in these decades, began to profit from pictorial advertisements in the 1880s. Newspapers, hitherto reluctant to allow their news-columns to be over-shadowed by advertisers, overcame their scruples and the technical difficulties. Soon after 1900, full-page advertisements were occasionally appearing in popular news-papers – most of them inserted by frantically competitive tobacco companies. The pioneer in large-scale publicity was Pears' Soap with its endlessly reiterated slogan: 'Good morning! Have you used Pears' Soap?' In 1887 Pears bought a painting by Sir John Millais of a little boy blowing soap bubbles, and persuaded the artist to let them reproduce it as an advertisement. A rival British firm secured a painting by W. P. Frith entitled *The New Frock* and

An advertisement for Britain's best-known soap, the pioneer of large-scale publicity in the late nineteenth century.

GOOD MORNING! *Have you used* PEARS' SOAP?

put it to the same use. Before long a painting by another Royal Academician, Sir Edwin Landseer, was pressed into service to sell dog biscuits. In the United States, George Eastman's Kodak, the first cheap roll-film camera, was popularized at the end of the 1880s with the motto, 'You press the button – we do the rest.' The perfection of colour lithography at this time led to a new boldness and sophistication in street poster-display: an added pleasure for visitors to Paris who could gaze upon the delightful posters of Jules Cheret and Toulouse-Lautrec. In the 1890s, however, outrage was voiced by travellers who found slogans for margarine daubed on Norwegian fjords, for tooth powder on the rocky islands of the St Lawrence and for chocolate in the Alps. There was even an advertisement on one of the Pyramids in Egypt. Billboards sprouted in the fields alongside railroad tracks. An English parodist wrote:

> Ill fares the land, to hastening ills a prey,
> Where posters flourish and where crops won't pay.

The most brazen of such excesses were removed under public protest: on every other front the adman was victorious.

These were mere fringe activities in the hectic realm of the machine. A more fundamental transformation was under way in those grimy industrial regions where mounds of ore were conjured into metal. By 1880 various techniques for large-scale production of steel had been perfected, thanks to Henry Bessemer, Percy Carlisle Gilchrist and Sidney Thomas in England and the brothers William and Werner Siemens in Germany. There were two main processes, the Bessemer converter and the open-hearth. Production of iron continued and was not exceeded by steel until 1890. But steel was the sought-after material, to replace iron railway tracks and iron steamships. In 1914 the world's main steel producers were the United States, Germany and Britain, with Russia, France and other countries some way behind. But during the 1890s Britain, the innovator and industrial champion, yielded place to its two principal rivals. With each year thereafter, their lead in production became more commanding.

Some of the reasons for this displacement have already been suggested. The British were not slow to mechanize, and their output was considerable by world standards, but there was a certain conservatism in British management and there were real social and physical problems in adjusting to a new set of industrial demands. The more youthful US and German economies found

Opposite above: A Trade Union poster proclaims the improvements made in the cotton industry, and also the benefits offered by the Amalgamated Association of Operative Cotton Spinners.

Opposite below: Late to start, but quick to learn, the Japanese had embarked on the road to industrialization by the 1880s. This nineteenth-century illustration of the Tomisika silk works is an early example of the factory system in Japan.

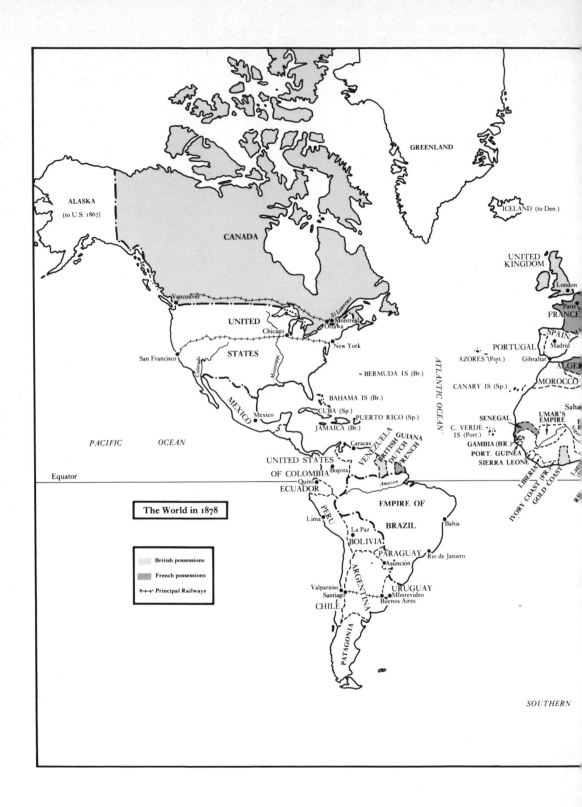

The World in 1878

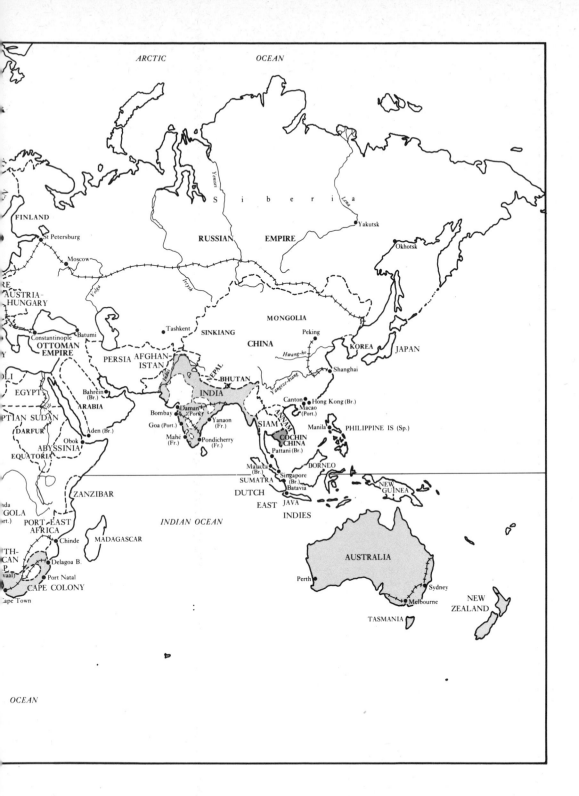

it easier to design their plants on a giant scale. Their national psychologies and their banking systems permitted the grouping of steel and other burgeoning industries into pools, rings, trusts, cartels: combinations designed to tie together the whole production cycle, and to agree with competitors on prices and production quotas. In the United States, at any rate, such devices were hotly condemned as corrupt and monopolistic. The Vanderbilts, Rockefellers, Carnegies and Morgans who made huge fortunes out of their railroad, oil, steel and banking empires were portrayed as 'Robber Barons' holding the public to ransom, in such books as Henry D. Lloyd's *Wealth Against Commonwealth* (1894). Economic historians have tended to put a more favourable construction on their activities.

Each industrial nation, obedient to the imperatives of the machine, fought to dominate its own home market and the maximum share of markets overseas. Smaller successful nations – Sweden and Denmark, Belgium and Holland, Switzerland – remained on the whole fairly modest in their expectations. Moderately dynamic ones – France, Italy, Russia, Austria – were larger in ambition, and by previous standards made considerable strides toward full-scale industrialization. None was content to play second or third fiddle. The Russians, for example, benefiting from German and French investment and from almost frenzied governmental effort, strove to catch up with the other big powers

Steel was one cornerstone of the Industrial Age. The Bessemer converter, pictured here, played its part in feeding the evergrowing demand.

THE WAY TO GROW POOR. ✳ THE WAY TO GROW RICH.

in building railroads. There were nine hundred miles of track in 1860; twelve thousand by 1880; nineteen thousand in 1890. The Trans-Siberian railroad was begun in 1891, reached Port Arthur on the Pacific coast in 1901, and was completed in 1904 – the same year that the United States began to construct the Panama Canal. Russian oil production almost equalled that of the United States in the early years of the twentieth century; and Russia built even bigger industrial plants than those of the USA or Germany. Strenuous efforts were made too to mechanize agriculture, as had been done with astounding success in North America and western Europe. But mere size was not enough. The United States, with half the population of Russia in the late nineteenth century, seemed light-years ahead in industrial appetite. In 1880 Britain and France both possessed more railroad mileage than imperial Russia, while the United States could boast a total seven times as great. Russia's nineteen thousand miles in 1890 was dwarfed by the USA's 125,000. Around 1900, Belgium's little corps of eleven

A summons to the American people in 1875 to return to the traditional virtues of thrift, hard work, and independence.

41

Tsarist Russia, though a
long way behind her more
advanced rivals, did not
neglect industrialization.
A group of Cossacks visits
oil wells at Baku (1905).

thousand iron and steel workers had a greater output than the 140,000 Russians toiling in the iron belt of the Urals. The machine called for a closer dedication on the part of its acolytes if labour was to be more than simply laborious.

So the great powers grew greater: 'To him that hath shall be given.' God might or might not be on the side of the industrial big battalions: Mammon certainly appeared to be. Inventive brilliance was not enough. French science in this era teems with famous names, and the same is true to a lesser extent of the Italians. It was the French who in 1850–70 made the most important early contributions to the internal combustion engine. They were ingenious in experimenting with turbines and with hydraulic and pneumatic mechanisms: Paris was the only capital in the world provided with the express *pneumatique* message service. The British, and to some extent the Americans, counted upon inspired hunches. Bessemer was a sort of handyman-inventor; Gilchrist and Thomas had no theoretical knowledge of steelmaking. In the United States, Thomas Alva Edison, the inventor of the phonograph (1877) and co-inventor (1879) of the incandescent electric light bulb, received almost no formal education. But in general, as the world of machines grew ever more complex, discovery came to depend upon professional training and upon methodical collaboration. The two largest dye factories in the world, Lucius & Bruning of Höchst and the Badische Anilin und Soda-Fabrik (the great monopoly cartel of I. G. Farben in a later incarnation), both founded in the 1860s, almost immediately began to employ university graduates in

42

chemistry in their new research laboratories; and the results were almost immediately evident. The first effective internal combustion engine (1867) was made by Nikolaus Otto and Eugen Langen, in the seminal atmosphere of the Karlsruhe *technische Hochschule*. Gottlieb Daimler, another early automobile inventor, had been trained in a similar establishment at Stuttgart. Rudolf Diesel, the inventor of the compression-ignition engine that bears his name, was a product of the Munich *technische Hochschule*. Alexander Graham Bell, the first to succeed in the electrical transmission of speech (the telephone, 1876), was a Scottish-born immigrant to the United States whose accomplished father had already done much work on acoustics. Remarkable though Edison was, he relied from the start upon the group effort of research assistants.

Tinkerer or professional scientist, the inventor proceeded in step with his society, or rather a little ahead of it – if he went too far ahead the invention would be defective because of inadequate technology or lack of supporting demand. Without a fantastic growth in railroad mileage, the American steel industry's own fantastic growth would have been impossible. The desire for improved communications stimulated a host of inventors. Each advance, though, was conditioned by external factors. The telegraph became feasible in the 1830s: not until 1866 could technology devise and lay a transatlantic cable that would actually function. The automobile – that is, the internal combustion engine on wheels – could not become truly 'mobile' until a liquid form of fuel was available at a reasonable cost. It took the exploitation of oilfields of the right kind in Borneo (1898) and Spindletop, Texas (1901), to convert car-making from a minor diversion to a main industry. The electric power stations that came into operation in the world's great cities during the 1880s rested upon decades of preliminary investigation and a whole series of industrial improvements in seemingly unconnected fields. Machines in all their variety and activity could be seen as analogous to the families of the human race – supporting and breeding one another, contending with and supplanting one another.

The World Picture, 1900–17

Not surprisingly, inventions were sometimes discouraged or indeed suppressed, even in the most dynamic societies. None was as wholeheartedly innovative as it liked to pretend. Businessmen were in a way sensible to recognize that unrestrained innovation, in common with unrestrained competition, was a concept as monstrous as it was – happily – hypothetical. The machine's threat to its master lingered in the subconscious minds of some of its most eager devotees. Mark Twain, technologist-inventor by proxy, gave vent to this secret fear in his fantasy-novel *A Connecticut Yankee in King Arthur's Court* (1889). His burlesque tale lapses into nightmare. The author's plot seems to get out of control and run away with him; its modern mechanic-hero ends by smashing the machine-civilization he has created.

A handful of nervously acute observers were even more apprehensive; and another American, Henry Adams, could be seen as their spokesman. For him the machine was a modern god – a false god – whose power lay in its incomprehensibility. Studying medieval philosophy in Paris, Adams was fascinated by the giant, hooded and cowled machines of the Exposition of 1900. He was only half joking when he told a friend that he went every afternoon and 'prayed to the dynamos':

> The period from 1870 to 1900 is closed. I see that much in the machine-gallery of the Champ de Mars and sit by the hour over the great dynamos, watching them run noiselessly and smoothly as the planets, and asking them with infinite courtesy where in Hell they are going. . . . They are marvellous. The Gods are not in it. Chiefly the Germans [already leaders in the electrical industry]! Steam no longer appears, although still behind the scenes; but one feels no certainty that another ten years may not abolish steam too. The charm of the show, to me, is that no one pretends to understand even in a remote degree, what these weird things are that they call electricity, Roentgen rays, and what not.

Adams, though, was sufficiently a man of his time to cherish the machine for the pleasures it could bring – even if the supreme joy was using it as a time-machine to escape backward from the present: 'My idea of paradise is a perfect automobile going thirty miles an hour on a smooth road to a twelfth-century cathedral.'

Adams was right to worry about the acceleration of social change brought about by accelerated industrialization. (The word 'accelerator', incidentally, as applied to a motor-car, dates from the year 1900.) His forecast of a world at the end of its tether seemed to be borne out when Europe declared war on itself and – so he felt – upon civilization as such in 1914. But that disaster will be discussed later in the book. For the moment our concern is with Adams's more limited insight, that electricity and the auto-

Opposite: One of the great advances of modern communications: Alexander Graham Bell, inventor of the telephone, opens the Chicago-New York line in October 1892.

44

Henry Ford sits proudly in his first car. He was to make others, by the million.

mobile were the symbols of the new era. By 1914 electricity was a vital agent in every factory and city in the world. The machine's transition, one might say, was from railroad-station to power-station. Electricity was at work not only in such obvious shapes as the streetcar and the streetlamp, but in more arcane guises such as the 'wireless' – the word itself drawing attention to the mystery of an invisible means of communication.

It is correct to seize upon the automobile as the climactic innovation of the machine-age, and to single out Henry Ford – as everyone does – as the central figure of that age-long cumulative evolution. In 1906 Woodrow Wilson, then president of Princeton University, made one of those 'conservative' pronouncements that strike us as matched in silliness only by the contrary heralds of complete and instantaneous innnovation. To possess a motor-car, he said, was to display one's wealth so ostentatiously that future development of the industry could only inflame the poor into socialism. Within a few years, Ford had made Wilson's warning sound antediluvian. In the one year 1914, the United States alone manufactured 1,700,000 motor vehicles, and production in England, Germany and France was climbing steeply, though on a

46

lesser scale. In 1909, the year when the Ford assembly-line began to get into its stride, Louis Blériot flew the English channel in an airplane: the internal combustion engine was about to move to another dimension.

Ford, of course, did not invent the automobile. A legion of engineers preceded him. He came out of the late industrial revolution, a research worker from the Edison beehive. Innumerable technologies converged to fabricate Ford's Model T. Vulcanized and pneumatic rubber tyres developed from the thriving bicycle industry (in which Britain was still foremost). Oil-wells and oil-refineries were essential. So were small items such as steel ball-bearings. To us the logic of what Ford did is so elementary as to be commonplace. He merely synthesized the elements of machine-knowledge and machine-myth – what the machine could do and what it ought to do – and brought them together at Fort Dearborn, Detroit, in a controlled chaos of subordinate processes moving step by step toward the central chassis-line. It could be regarded as the orchestration of a vast machine-symphony with Ford holding the baton.

The famous Model T, the 'Tin Lizzie' on its assembly line (1915–17). It was this car which enabled Henry Ford to reach the mass market for the first time.

3 Peoples and Classes

The discovery of the laws of public health, the determination of the conditions of cleanliness, manners, water supply, food, exercise, isolation, medicine, most favourable to life in one city, in one country, is a boon to every city, to every country, for all can profit by the experience.

Registrar-General of England, 1871

The great end of all social arrangements should be to discourage artificial inequalities and to encourage natural ones. It would be a great gain if the former could be abolished altogether, and could this be done, . . . natural inequalities would have no tendency to re-establish them. . . . In the present state of society, even in the most advanced nations . . . , about 80 per cent of the population belong to what we still call the lower classes. These, although they possess natural inequalities [i.e. variations in ability] as clearly marked as those of the upper classes, are practically debarred from their exercise to any useful purpose. . . . The abolition of social classes, could it be accomplished, would therefore increase the efficiency of mankind at least one hundred fold.

Lester F. Ward, presidential address to the American Sociological Society, 1907

People-Productivity

Machine-productivity in the dynamic nations went hand in hand with people-productivity. The industrial revolution was under way before the end of the eighteenth century: so was the demographic revolution. Around 1700, the population of Europe, including European Russia, was somewhere between 100 and 120 million. By 1750 the total had climbed gradually to 120–140 million: the figures are necessarily approximate, since proper statistics were lacking. Between 1750 and 1800, however, there was a marked increase to something between 180 and 190 million. The growth-rate continued to soar. By 1850, the population of

Europe stood at 274 million. By 1900, despite a great deal of emigration, it had shot up to 400 million. Counting in North America, the Euro-American peoples in 1850 represented about 300 million of an estimated world population of 1,100 million. In 1900 Europe and North America accounted for roughly one-third of a world population of 1,500 million. Europe's 400 million in 1900 was about equalled by China's 350 million plus Japan's 45 million. India in the same period had a population around the 300 million mark.

In other words, the dynamic element was largely European. Its population was increasing more rapidly than that of the rest of the world. Toward the end of the period, there were signs of alarm at the supposed 'Yellow Peril' presented by the Orient's teeming millions. But even this minor fear reveals how much thinking about population had changed since Malthus. In his *Essay on Population* (1798), the English economist Thomas Malthus drew a dire picture of future possibilities. He assumed that the amount of food that could be produced was limited. Improvements in agriculture could add to the supply, but only in arithmetical ratio. The numbers of people were increasing far faster, in geometrical ratio. The corollary was that men would starve unless they ceased to breed so prolifically.

The geometrical increase predicted by Malthus occurred. In the second half of the nineteenth century the population of Great Britain (England, Scotland, Wales) doubled in the forty-year period 1850–90, to just over forty millions. The population of the German states and cities rose from thirty-four million in 1850 to sixty-five million in 1910. Russian population more than doubled (seventy-six to 167 million) in the half-century 1860–1910. The growth of the United States was still more spectacular: from twenty-three million people in 1850 to fifty million in 1880, from this fifty million to ninety-two million in 1910. Japan's population nearly doubled between 1850 and 1910 – in which year it stood at fifty-two million. Of the major powers only France seemed to lag, augmenting slowly from thirty-three million in 1850 to forty million in 1910. Only Ireland and Portugal suffered a net loss in population, and this because literally half their inhabitants settled overseas, the great majority in North and South America respectively.

The difference from the era of Malthus was that the nations whose populations quickly increased were those whose wealth and industrial capacity also conspicuously flourished. The

In the Land of Promise by
Charles Ulrich. Castle Garden –
the immigrant landing station in
New York.

50

51

correlation was exactly opposite to what Malthus had supposed. What factors had he left out?

One was emigration. It may be argued that movement from the old into the new countries acted as a safety-valve, reducing the pressure upon food, jobs and space. This would appear true of the Chinese migrations to California or Malaysia, and the Indian exodus to eastern and southern Africa. For the unhappy Irish, and for the Jews who began to flee from Russian *pogroms* in the 1880s, or the Armenians who were driven out of Turkey by persecution, emigration was almost the only salvation. Certainly Europe contributed on a giant scale. From 1871 to 1914, thirty-four million Europeans left for North and South America alone and of these twenty-five million settled permanently. Throughout the period, the United States was the chief absorber of immigrants, though substantial numbers began to flow into Canada, the Argentine and Brazil, South Africa, Australia and New Zealand. About eight million Italians left Europe. More than four million went overseas from Austria-Hungary, and nearly as many from Russia.

The movement outward from Europe was accompanied by

Jews attacked in the streets of Kiev in 1881. The persecution of the Jews in Russia and eastern Europe in the nineteenth century led them to emigrate in large numbers to the West.

migrations inside Europe. About a million French went overseas during our period – mainly to Algeria, North America and Argentina. But by 1914 there were over a million foreigners in France, most of them workers from neighbouring countries. In 1914 there were over half a million Irish in Great Britain and about three hundred thousand other immigrants, many of them Jewish, mostly from the Russian or Austrian empires, where the Jewish population was heavily concentrated in what is today Poland. In the Russian areas, the Jewish population was frequently subjected to vicious attacks and a determined governmental attempt to 'Russify' them. In Austria, the physical dangers were less, but the lack of economic opportunity was a great stimulus to Jewish emigration. On the eve of the 1914 war, there were well over a million foreign workers – Ruthenians, Poles, Italians – in Germany, some of them intending to stay permanently. The Italian emigration to the United States was almost equalled by the numbers of Italians who sought work elsewhere in Europe. In all the dynamic nations there was a marked shift among the native population, from the country into the town. For the very poor, there was often a kind of Malthusian desperation in these wanderings: not joyous adventure but sheer need drove them. Nevertheless, the conclusions to be drawn were non-Malthusian. The growth of cities and of their concomitant industry created employment; industrial wages were sufficient to buy at least as much food as had been available for working-class families in the pre-industrial era; the food no longer produced in the urban-industrial societies could come from the new agricultural zones; there was plenty of room in these new places. In the words of a British settlers' song of the mid-nineteenth century:

> Brave men are we, and be it understood
> We left our country for our country's good,
> And none may doubt our emigration
> Was of great value to the British nation.

Births and Deaths

We still need to consider why Europe should have had a population explosion in the nineteenth century. After all, there were no fundamental changes for the better in the conditions of rural life, while the squalor of the city-slums was unprecedentedly lethal – or so we might gather from eye-witness accounts and from the

53

work of social historians. Friedrich Engels, living in Manchester's equally industrialized neighbour city of Salford in the 1840s, had plenty of material to document his *Condition of the Working Class in England in 1844*. The picture was amplified in *The Bleak Age* (1934), a study of the same scene by J. L. and Barbara Hammond: pallid families dividing their existence between factory-floor and sunless alley with only alcohol for a refuge, and that a fatal one. The Hammonds, in their conclusion, quoted some lines from the third edition (1852) of John Stuart Mill's *Principles of Political Economy*:

It is questionable if all the mechanical inventions yet made have lightened the day's toil of any human being. They have enabled a greater population to live the same life of drudgery and imprisonment, and an increased number of manufacturers and others to make fortunes. They have increased the comforts of the middle classes. But they have not yet begun to effect those great changes in human destiny, which it is in their nature and in their futurity to accomplish.

On a head-count, there were many more poor people than rich manufacturers or comfortable bourgeois. And the nineteenth-century industrial cities were visited by hitherto-unfamiliar scourges. Yellow fever ravaged Philadelphia in 1793, took its toll there and in other American seaports in the next three decades and was brought into Europe from Santo Domingo by French soldiers. As late as 1871, a yellow-fever outbreak killed over thirteen thousand people in Buenos Aires. Asiatic cholera, which had been menacing India since 1817, reached Cairo, St Petersburg, Warsaw and Hamburg in 1831, passed to London in 1832, and thence by ship to Quebec and New Orleans. It returned from America to infect the western Mediterranean. In the 1830s cholera claimed a hundred thousand victims in France and over fifty thousand in Britain. There were further outbreaks, culminating in Europe with a bad epidemic in 1892–3 that caused over eight thousand deaths in Hamburg, and carried off the composer Tchaikovsky in St Petersburg.

Yet population did increase, more rapidly than ever before. It cannot be denied that, as before and since, the poor had far higher mortality rates than the well-to-do, or that until the late nineteenth century these rates were higher in urban than in rural areas. A letter published in the London *Times* in 1849 may have been composed by reformers, imitating what they took to be the style of the near-illiterate: its essential truth was confirmed by *The Times*:

When the Frenchman, Gustave Doré, visited London in the mid nineteenth century he was appalled by the squalor and poverty of London's slums. Scenes such as this were typical of the growing industrial towns and cities of England.

We are ... livin in a Wilderness, so far as the rest of London knows anything of us, or as the rich and great people care about. We live in muck and filth. We aint got no priviz [privies], no dust bins, no water-splies, and no drain or suer [sewer] in the hole place. . . . We all of us suffer, and numbers are ill, and if the Cholera comes Lord help us.

Demographers have also established that the birth-rate began to fall in western Europe after 1880.

The great change came from the decrease in the numbers of

children dying in the first year of life. Here the Scandinavian countries led the way; in 1914 Sweden's infant mortality was the lowest in the world. In England and Wales, during the 1850s, 154 per thousand of babies under one year of age died annually. By the first decade of the twentieth century the rate had dropped to 127·5. The comparable figures for France were 173 and 132. In 1901–10, the rates were appreciably higher in some other countries: 186·5 in Germany, and over 200 in Spain, Austria-Hungary and Russia. But they were improving steadily. Each year made a difference. Infant mortality in the United States stood at 162·4 in 1900; 138·6 in 1907; 107·2 in 1914. There was, of course, still room for improvement, and indeed the infant death-rate was to be halved again during the next few decades. But the gain during our period was evident both at the national level and among individual families. Perhaps demographic statistics help to explain the sentiment that attached to the very idea of the family in nineteenth-century Europe and the United States, and to the related idea of motherhood. To rear a family was to help to make one's nation populous and therefore prosperous. The average married woman was either nursing or bearing a child for about twenty years of her life: a far longer span than is common in the 1970s. The stronger the chance of survival for each newborn child, the more intense the sentiment that attached to childhood as well as to motherhood. The deaths of children in Victorian literature – that of Little Nell in Charles Dickens's *The Old Curiosity Shop* is an example – proved shatteringly effective because parents were beginning to feel that their babies *need not die*. Oscar Wilde's later comment that laughter, not tears, was the appropriate reaction to these set-pieces, is in part to be seen as the attitude of a subsequent generation for whom the likelihood of infant mortality had receded considerably further.

Sanitation and Science

Until about 1870, so far as medicine was concerned, the main factor in reducing mortality was preventive, or what was then sometimes called medical 'police' work. This approach is reflected in the English proverb 'Cleanliness is the elegance of the poor' and in the slogan 'Cleanliness is next to godliness' – coined by the clergyman John Wesley. But important scientific work was also being done before 1870. The hypodermic needle began to be widely used in the 1840s. Anaesthesia made big strides in the same

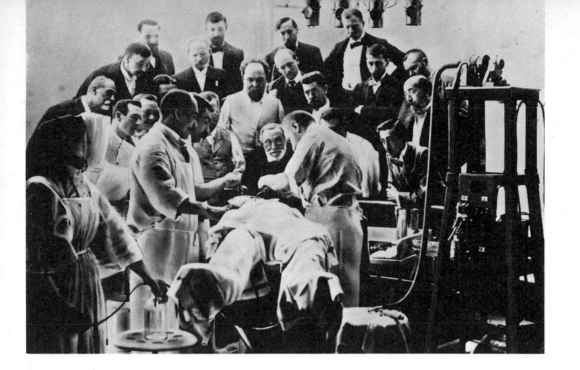

decade. Ether was successfully demonstrated at the Massachusetts General Hospital in Boston. Chloroform, which soon replaced it in surgery, was pioneered by Sir James Simpson in Edinburgh (1847). In 1848 Henry Hancock conducted the first appendix operation in London. Together with ether and chloroform, nitrous oxide ('laughing gas') was being tried out, especially by dentists. In this field the United States soon took the lead. The Baltimore College of Dentistry (1840) was the first such specialist institution in the world. The USA began to export dentists such as Thomas Evans of Philadelphia who looked after the imperial molars of Napoleon III. But in general the most advanced medical practice was in Europe. Paris could boast of the formidable Claude Bernard. The renown of Vienna was sustained by Carl Rokitansky and Josef Skoda, both Bohemians. Research in Germany benefited from being based on university laboratories, though professors unwise enough to express liberal political views were apt to be uprooted. This was temporarily the problem for Rudolf Virchow, 'the Pope of German medicine', who was ousted from Berlin for a few years after 1848 and had to transfer his work in microscopy to Würzburg. Diagnosis became much more sophisticated – helped by the French invention of the stethoscope and the German invention of the ophthalmoscope and otoscope in the 1850s.

In the eyes of the ordinary public, however, medicine remained

Rudolf Virchow – 'the Pope of German medicine' and pioneer in microscopy whose liberal political views led to his expulsion from Berlin after 1848.

an obscure and somewhat suspect art. The average doctor was apt to prescribe from a traditional batch of nostrums, and to reveal all too plainly to his patients that he had no idea how to cure ailments ranging from cholera to the common cold. One of the United States' most intelligent doctors, Oliver Wendell Holmes of Boston, remarked that if the usual medicines were thrown into the sea, it would be so much the better for mankind though so much the worse for the fishes. This was no doubt true, above all of the patent medicines in which the public increasingly put its faith. But the more powerful among them, with their high proportions of alcohol or laudanum (opium), corresponded quite closely to the treatments recommended by general practitioners. The English politician William Ewart Gladstone had a sister whom the family described as an opium addict in the 1840s. Her addiction was probably induced by professional attention, not by nostrums of the kind advertised in the newspapers. Diagnostics would bear fruit later. For the moment, the analytical refinements of Paris and Vienna seemed remote to the point of callousness, and produced an angry reaction from German pathologists: 'We want to heal, not classify.' No wonder that the man in the street sought palliatives in the chemist's shop or turned to herbalists and faith-healers. We should add that this folk-preference persisted long after medicine entered its great post-1870 era, when a great many diseases were genuinely brought under control. Americans and a few Europeans at the end of the century devised a host of mind-cure systems. The American *bon viveur* Horace Fletcher furnishes an amusing minor example. Finding himself dyspeptic and fifty pounds overweight, he hit upon 'Fletcherism' – the idea of eating less, eating more slowly and chewing each mouthful until it 'swallowed itself' – and expounded his doctrine by means of publication (*Happiness as found in Forethought minus Fearthought*, 1897) and the lecture-platform.

In orthodox medicine, preventive theory of course remained fundamental as it always must. Indeed it was reinforced toward the end of the century, not merely by happiness-through-health proponents like Fletcher but by research on nutrition. Scientists confirmed that beri-beri, scurvy, pellagra and rickets were caused by a diet deficiency. Through careful experiment, a Japanese investigator, Kanehiro Takaki, was able to eradicate beri-beri from the Japanese navy. In 1912 Casimir Funk, a young Polish-born American biochemist, introduced the notion of 'vitamines' (later contracted to 'vitamins') to describe a class of nutrients essential to health. In the richer nations, the vogue for walking, camping and cycling in the 1880s and 1890s, the spread of athletic exercise (football was a popular sport in England by 1880, though lawn tennis and golf were more restricted pastimes), the consumption of hitherto exotic fruits such as bananas and grapefruit: all these elements were having a marked effect by the end of the century. Tailors in the United States, for instance, discovered that young men were an inch or two taller than their fathers; producers of mass clothing had to revise their selection of sizes. There was still a great deal of room for improvement. British and German army doctors in 1914-18, and American examiners in 1917, had to reject alarming numbers of recruits as medically unfit; and there was a marked difference in height and build between young people from the richer and the poorer classes. Even so, the gain since the 1840s was substantial.

There were, though, as we have noted, diseases that defied and baffled ordinary treatment. Yellow fever, cholera, typhus, typhoid and malaria spread mysteriously. The more trade developed between continents, the more obviously national frontiers, and their attempts at quarantine, failed to confine the world's cargoes of unseen maladies. Different approaches were needed. They were supplied by scientists, in the most triumphant demonstration of systematic endeavour that the layman had perhaps ever witnessed; and the greatest name of all was that of Louis Pasteur of Paris. But the effort went on in several nations. The words associated with this new microscopic universe – bacterium, bacteriology – were coined in the middle decades of the century. In laboratories, isolated from their parent cultures and magnified into visibility, portrayed for the first time in engravings as weird necklaces and amulets, the hidden infinitesimal immemorial tyrants of mankind were discovered by investigators. The relatively large creatures – hookworm, tapeworm – were detected first. Wounded soldiers and women in labour were at once the subjects and the beneficiaries of experiment. Oliver Wendell Holmes and Ignaz Semmelweis found that antiseptics vastly reduced the incidence of infection – puerperal fever – for the mothers of newly-delivered infants. Joseph Lister in Glasgow, spraying the operating theatre with carbolic acid, helped to make surgery a less lethal ordeal – just as anaesthetics had made it less painful.

Meanwhile Pasteur, the German Robert Koch and others were following subtler trails. By 1870 they had established that bacteria

were associated with contagious diseases, and that particular
bacteria or bacilli caused particular diseases. As the hunt spread
in the next decade, the researches in Paris and Berlin were
paralleled by investigations elsewhere: in Russia, for example, by
Sechenov and Elie Metchnikoff, and in Japan by Kitasato and
Shiga who had been trained in Germany. During the 1880s the
tubercle bacillus was discovered, and soon after, the dipththeria
and typhoid bacilli: the three main killers among the temperate
zones of the world. The effects of immunology in these three
cases can be seen from the medical figures of Massachusetts (an
American state that kept easily the best records of disease before
1900). These are annual death rates per hundred thousand of the
population:

Year	Respiratory tuberculosis	Diphtheria	Typhoid and para-typhoid fever
1870	343·3	46·4	91·5
1880	308·1	134·3	49·5
1890	258·6	72·6	37·3
1900	190·3	52·8	22·1
1910	138·3	21·0	12·5
1916	123·4	16·7	4·6

The introduction of mass vaccination towards the end of the nineteenth century dramatically lowered the death-rate in the cities of Europe and America.

Equally impressive work was done on the contagious diseases that had their chief locale in tropical countries. When cholera broke out in India in 1883, and then moved to Egypt, German and French research teams went to Cairo. One of the French scientists died of the disease. Koch, travelling on to India after he and his associates in Egypt had isolated the 'comma bacillus', was able to confirm its significance and prove that cholera was transmitted through dirty clothes and impure water, as Dr John Snow of London had asserted in the 1850s. The soundness of these observations was shown beyond contradiction in 1892 in Koch's own country. Hamburg was severely smitten by a cholera epidemic; the adjacent city of Altona, which had installed a filtering-system for its water supply, was unaffected. By 1914 sand or mechanical filters were the rule in most municipalities, and typhoid as well as cholera dwindled in consequence. The incidence of tuberculosis and other diseases was sharply reduced, beginning in the 1880s, when Pasteur demonstrated that milk also transmitted deadly bacilli unless treated. His name has deservedly been given to the process of *pasteurization*. In the 1880s too, the tetanus bacillus was discovered and then isolated, by Nicolaier and by Kitasato. As serum became available, tetanus (lock-jaw) lost its terrors.

The effects of malaria had been lessened well before 1850 through the use of quinine. More fundamental advances were achieved in the 1870s and 1880s by a French physician in Algeria who detected the malaria parasite in the blood of affected patients, and by Italian biologists and doctors in Rome. The notion that mosquitoes might be disease-carriers was confirmed in Italy at the end of the century and also by Ronald Ross of the Indian Medical Service. The anopheles mosquito was the key to the mystery. Indeed, to other mysteries. American doctors, together with Dr Carlos Finlay of Cuba, identified the mosquito as the spreader of yellow fever. A British army doctor in South Africa, at the same period, extended the picture of insects as disease-carriers – in this case the tsetse fly, which had been transmitting a disease in cattle and sleeping-sickness among human beings. The role of rats, fleas and lice as carriers was also established. So entomologists and bacteriologists brought to light chains of causation that until now had remained unsuspected or at best unproven. Immunologists – another of the family of 'ologies' – developed serums to protect people by inoculating them with minute doses of the particular disease: a practice first followed though not fully understood in the eighteenth-century expedient of vaccination against smallpox. By 1900, endocrinologists were entering another realm of physiology through their study of the function of the pituitary, thyroid and other ductless glands. Another new word entered the language in 1906: 'hormones' were secretions which, while infinitesimal, could affect the entire efficiency of organs in the body. The great discoveries in this field were to come later. But there were pioneering advances during our period: adrenalin was synthesized as early as 1904.

The Spread of Cities

The movement of people into towns and cities was somewhat exaggerated by contemporaries. In Britain it had undoubtedly gone far; by 1850 the number of city dwellers already equalled the number living in the countryside, and by 1900 more than three–quarters of the population could be defined as 'urban'. Elsewhere, even though the population might be relatively dense, urbanization was less conspicuous. In Germany townsfolk did not outnumber countrymen until about 1890, in Belgium not until 1900, in the United States not until 1920, in Japan not until the 1950s. At the end of our period, only a fifth of the Russian people lived in cities. The majority of mankind were still working in fields or little shops rather than in factories. And by later standards, many of the urban centres of the five continents were still modest in scale – townships with a provincial atmosphere.

Nevertheless, the rise of cities was real, swift and startling, and after 1850 it affected every part of the globe, both directly and indirectly. There had been large old cities well before that time: London, Paris, Naples, Constantinople, Delhi, Peking, Shanghai, Tientsin, Tokyo, Kyoto and so on. In mid-century, Europe counted forty-five cities with a population of over a hundred thousand people, twelve of them in the United Kingdom; North America had 6 and Latin America 2. By 1914 the total had risen to 184 in Europe, fifty-three in North America and eight in Latin America; and the two Australian cities of Sydney and Melbourne had joined the list. At the turn of the century, a dozen cities had passed the million mark. London, the most immense, had over six million inhabitants. There were over three million people in Paris and in New York, and two million in Tokyo. The other cities in this league of giantism were Berlin, Peking, Chicago, Vienna, Philadelphia, St Petersburg, Constantinople (Istanbul in its Turkish name) and Moscow. Others were not far short. Buenos Aires, with 170,000 inhabitants in 1870, was past the million by 1910. Some cities had grown from nothing: Chicago and Melbourne, for instance, were not even villages before the 1830s. It was not uncommon for an already large city to double in population within a decade, as Chicago did in the 1880s. The cost of land and the concentration of business in the middle of each urban web produced crowded slums for the poor, and ever-higher buildings for the office-worker. In the 1870s cast-iron frames permitted office buildings of six or seven storeys. A decade later, steel-frame construction and electric lifts or 'elevators' encouraged aspiring architects to dream of fantastic perpendiculars. A slang dictionary in 1891 was the first to put in print a recently-coined word, 'skyscraper', which it defined as 'a very tall building such as now are being built in Chicago'. The first Chicago skyscraper, of ten storeys, had gone up in 1885; a twenty-

one-storey tower, the Masonic Temple, appeared above the Chicago skyline in 1891.

The enlargement of the great cities appalled many observers. In traditional literature of nearly every culture, the city was the place of vice, crime, corruption. 'God made the country, man made the town.' The bigger the concentration of people, the greater the concentration of wickedness. Hell, in the eyes of the sensitive, was a city much like London. This sort of response was perhaps more common in English and American writing than elsewhere.

A great deal could be, and was, said in defence of the city. One characteristic riposte was the famous English proverb 'Where there's muck there's money.' The mayor of the Yorkshire iron-town of Middlesbrough, speaking at a ceremony to mark the opening of the new town hall in 1887, said that 'If there is one thing more than another that Middlesbrough can be said to be proud of, it is the smoke [*cheers and laughter*]. The smoke is an indication of plenty of work [*applause*] – an indication of prosperous times [*cheers*]. . . .' Another answer was that not every city was mean and grimy. Outside the belts of heavy industry, some were magnificently situated and handsome in layout. This was true both of new cities like Sydney or San Francisco, and of old ones – Paris, Vienna, Brussels, Barcelona – in which at least some of the

A cartoon published in the *New York Herald* in 1896. Many people predicted that the growing weight of Manhattan's skyscrapers would lead to disaster.

Opposite: In 1820 Chicago (*above*) was not even a village. By 1880 (*below*) it was one of the leading industrial cities of America, and its population was to double by 1890.

Overleaf: 'The Black Country' round Birmingham was one of the first parts of Britain to be swallowed up by a new industrial city.

65

people seemed to enjoy 'passing and procession' along the boulevards. Originally, indeed, the word 'boulevard' – a French corruption of the German *Bollwerk* or bulwark – had referred to the flat top of a fortification. In its new meaning, it testified to an ease of access and movement; and a *boulevardier* was a man who relished the pleasures it opened to him.

A further argument was that while the burgeoning cities had their problems, vigorous improvements were in hand. The cities of 1850 had foul-smelling unpaved streets, ill-lit, unpoliced, muddy in winter and dusty in summer. Pigs could be seen scavenging among the refuse – or buzzards in the case of a city such as Rio de Janeiro in Brazil. By 1900, the central districts at least were immeasurably cleaner, safer and more imposing. Old slum-warrens, sanctuaries for thieves and murderers, were torn down. There were regular police patrols, even if they were apt to be brutal as in Paris or venal as in New York. Civic pride had led to the creation of parks, libraries and museums and concert-halls, not only in the capital cities but in the provincial centres anxious to prove themselves metropolitan in outlook. The upper and middle classes could attend the opera (also a popular taste in Latin countries) and the theatre; music halls and café entertainers catered for demotic appetites. There was something for everybody in the big city – brothels, bookshops, clubs, bohemias for the artist and intellectual, cells for the radical, learned societies for the scholar, gullibles for the swindler, shelter for the exile (hence Karl Marx's long years in London, and Emile Zola's flight to the same city from Paris, to escape prosecution for libel after his bold intervention of 1898 in the Dreyfus case), clients for the lawyer, architect and doctor. There were splendid hotels for the rich, boarding-houses for modest customers, doss-houses for the near-destitute, embankments and railway arches for those completely forlorn. People who wished to display themselves and their possessions could do so to marvellous advantage at fashionable occasions – presentations at Court, in the boxes of the 'diamond horseshoe' at the opera, at society weddings and funerals.

At the other extreme, the city gave protective anonymity to those who wished to hide. There was also atrocious loneliness for many; one shudders to think of the isolation of the Japanese man of letters Sōseki Natsume, sent by his government to London in 1900–2 to absorb Western culture and so overwhelmed by alien intricacies that he hardly left his room except to change books at the library.

Opposite: The Last of England by Ford Madox Brown. The economic depression of the 1870s led many Englishmen to seek their fortunes overseas.

68

The multiplicity and the ambiguity of mass-existence were caught in the same year, 1855, by the American Walt Whitman (*Leaves of Grass*) and by the French painter Gustave Courbet. Both men made inventories of living, in an effort to render the endless variety; both claimed artists' privileges of comprehensive comprehension. In Courbet's enormous painting *L'Atelier*, he explained to a friend that his aim was to present his friends and colleagues on one side and on the other the 'world of everyday life; people, misery, poverty, wealth, the exploited and the exploiters'. These included a gaunt Jew he had seen in London, a portly priest, a thin old Frenchman, 'then a hunter, a reaper, a strong man, a clown, a secondhand clothing merchant, a workingman's wife, a workingman, an undertaker's assistant, a skull in a newspaper, an Irish woman nursing a child ...; I met this woman in a London street; she was clothed only in a black straw hat, a ragged green veil, a black fringed shawl under which she carried a naked infant ...'. True, these visions are not confined to the city. Whitman claimed to be the poet of the open road as well as of 'mast-hemm'd Manhattan'. Courbet too included countrymen in his ensemble, and placed himself in the middle, busy with brush and palette on a rural landscape. Yet their message could be taken to mean that the city was the focus of life, or at any rate the best vantage-point from which to survey the entire human scene.

The city, in other words, was both vile and glorious, according to the circumstances of the observer. It was a crueller, uglier, more impersonal environment than ever before in history. The city that grew overnight for industrial purposes, like a mushroom or perhaps like a poisonous toadstool, *was* objectively odious. No wonder some men in the late nineteenth century decided that the city *per se* was a mistake, or – like Ebenezer Howard in England – sought a compromise in the 'garden city' which, as with the actual examples of Letchworth and Welwyn, envisaged a sort of autonomous suburb of a mere thirty-two thousand inhabitants, lying within reach of a 'central city' that was itself to be limited to a modest fifty-eight thousand inhabitants.

Other evidence is equally two-sided. The appearance of humorous and satirical magazines – *Charivari* (1832) in Paris, *Punch* (1841) in London, the *Fliegende Blätter* (1844) in Munich, *Kladderadatsch* (1848) in Berlin, the cartoons of *Harper's Weekly* (1857) in New York – could be taken as a sign of the gaiety and liberalism of city culture; or of frivolity and decadence. The mass-circulation city newspapers, such as London's *Daily Mail*, of the

Opposite above: Work by Ford Madox Brown. This stylized Pre-Raphaelite picture revealed a different conception of realism to that of such painters as Gustave Courbet.

Opposite below: Courbet's painting *L'Atelier* (1855). He explained that his aim was to present his friends and colleagues on one side, and on the other the 'world of everyday life; people, misery, poverty, wealth, the exploited and the exploiters'.

Japanische Tändeleien nach Rappo,

oder

wie die Lasten des Staates gleichmäßig vertheilt sind, um die Krone balanciren zu können.

Der Proletarier vom Bürger gequetscht, der Bürger vom Adel beläſtigt,
So wird die Pyramide des Staats gegipfelt und schlau befeſtigt.
So zeiget ein Jeder auf Höhern Befehl der Kraft und Balance Proben,
Getreu dem alten Naturgeſetz: der Druck kommt ſtets von Oben!

Verantwortlicher Redakteur: E. Dohm — Verlag von A. Hofmann & Comp. in Berlin, Unterwaſſerſtraße 1. — Druck von J. Draeger in Berlin.

late nineteenth century could be seen as triumphs of popular democracy; or as 'cheap' in the bad sense of the word, 'yellow press' rubbish (to use the American term) full of crude scandal and chauvinism. This doubleness can easily be detected among city-dwellers of the period. Perhaps not surprisingly, those whose homes were 'palatial edifices' had a considerable mistrust of the city poor whose homes were 'fearful slums'. From the 1830s onward, first in Europe and later in the United States, the idea developed that cities bred a criminal substratum. By about 1850, a distinction was being drawn between the 'deserving poor', who might occasionally slip into wrongdoing, and the inveterately criminal – between the working classes and the 'dangerous classes'. Some of those who used the term were responsibly concerned. The American Charles Loring Brace, author of *The Dangerous Classes of New York* (1872), helped to establish the Children's Aid Society in that city, an organization that provided cheap boarding-houses, night schools, summer camps and sanitariums. The settlement-house movement of the 1880s, typified by Toynbee Hall in London and Hull-House in Chicago, disclosed a social conscience on the part of at least some people. Paternalistic employers such as Krupp of Essen built towns for their employees that were admirable by the standards of the day. Christian Socialism, beginning in England in the wake of the unsuccessful

Opposite: A caricature of German society in 1849 from *Kladderadatsch,* the satirical German magazine first published in 1848. It shows the proletariat exploited by the bourgeoisie, the bourgeoisie oppressed by the nobility: 'in this way is the pyramid of the state maintained'. King Frederick William IV of Prussia is at the top of the pyramid.

Below: The late nineteenth century saw the foundation of several charitable organizations to alleviate the miseries of the urban poor. But the shelters provided by the Salvation Army offered a grim hospitality: 'the unsightly receptacles for the sleepers are strangely like open coffins'.

73

European revolutions of 1848 and the collapse of the great Chartist movement, perhaps the first truly mass movement in British political history, sought to bring a direct and practical gospel to the poor through institutions like the London Working Men's College.

The Hatch family by Eastman Johnson in 1871. Amid the snobbery of bourgeois America in the late nineteenth century conventional family portraits enjoyed a steady vogue.

Life-styles; Rich, Poor and Middling

In the light of these remarks on cities, it may seem inconsistent to describe the period as one of democratic upsurge. But the two elements, privilege and egalitarianism, ran together. In most of the dynamic nations, every male citizen acquired before 1914 the right to vote in local and national elections; religious and ethnic

disabilities were legally removed; and education became available, indeed obligatory, for all children up to the age of thirteen or fourteen. In France, for example, only half the children of school age were actually being educated in 1850, and two out of every five youths called up for military service were illiterate. By 1914 enrollment in primary schools was over ninety per cent, and illiteracy among conscripts had dropped to under ten per cent. The Second Republic proclaimed universal male suffrage, and Napoleon III's Second Empire sustained this pledge. In several countries, women were by 1914 on the brink of securing the vote; in Australia and in some parts of the United States they had already done so. In a few countries, notably the United States, politics at the local level, and to some extent even at the national level, became genuinely 'popular'. By 1880 or thereabouts, the administration of several American cities had passed into the hands of immigrant groups: Boston was run by the Irish. Social distinctions between class and class, hitherto often drawn with cruel sharpness, appeared to blur. This is not to say that class-consciousness was vanishing. On the contrary, it was, as Karl Marx insisted, a crucial aspect of the era. The novels of the period, and the books of etiquette that it spawned, show an almost obsessive awareness of niceties of rank. Snobbery was a characteristic vice of the period. It seemed to overwhelm Americans of the leisure class toward the end of the century. By 1909, according to one account, five hundred American girls had recently married into titled European families. Jennie Jerome married Lord Randolph Churchill (and became the mother of Winston Churchill); Consuelo Vanderbilt married the Duke of Marlborough; Jay Gould's daughter Anna made a match with Count Boni de Castellane; Ava Astor accepted the hand of Prince Serge Obolensky, Clara Huntington that of Prince von Hatzfeld-Wildenburg. A book entitled *Americans of Royal Descent* ran to seven hundred pages and contained several thousand names.

But such evidence is equivocal. Most of these American girls were heiresses and most of their husbands were impoverished. Multimillionaires felt the novelty of their situation; they were the first of their kind in world history and wanted to consolidate themselves. The aristocracy into which they married was also seeking security, of a more material sort, and showed itself to be quick to seize the main chance. Many an aristocratic family was rescued from comparative poverty by a judicious marriage to an American heiress: Miss May Ogden Goelet, a millionairess,

Cartoon from *Punch*,
1893, contrasting the life
styles of the capitalist
owners of production and
the working classes.

became the Duchess of Roxburgh; the United States also provided
a Countess of Essex, a Duchess of Manchester and a Duchess of
Marlborough. The situation was fluid; the social classes had more
porosity than one might gather from the epoch's habits of black-
balling and cold-shouldering, for in truth these were often
defensive devices, last-ditch ambivalences on the part of the upper
classes when faced with the huge advance of the bourgeoisie.

76

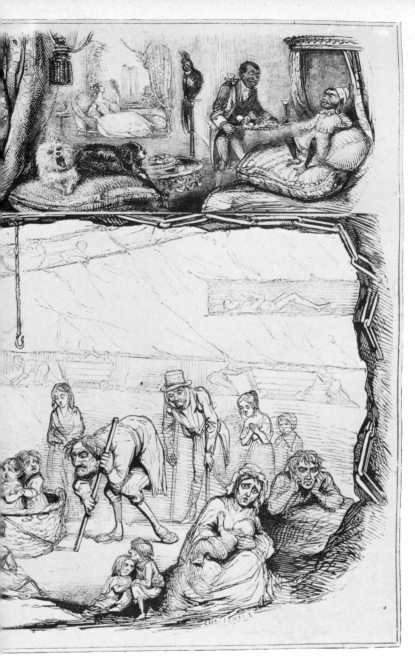

The main reality of the era was the rise of the middle class – *'les
bourgeois conquérants'* in the phrase of a French historian. Perhaps
we should say middle *classes*, and admit that these busy, acquisitive,
aspiring people are too numerous and varied to be defined with
any precision. A banker or a manufacturer might be called
bourgeois: what did he have in common with an employee at the
cash-desk, to whom the term would also be applied? Very little;

and the word may hinder rather than help understanding. The rich bourgeoisie moved toward the aristocracy, seeking to absorb or become absorbed in it. They acquired titles, or patents of nobility. They bought their clothes from Savile Row in London and sent their wives and daughters to be dressed by the great fashion houses of Paris, such as Worth and Poiret. Their sons were despatched to exclusive schools (perhaps Eton in England, Groton in the United States), and then to universities (which were attended in most Western countries by not more than five per cent of the population), or possibly to become subalterns in elegant cavalry regiments. The lesser bourgeoisie on the other hand, far down the social ladder, wore celluloid collars and cuffs, left school at fourteen or fifteen, scrabbled to remain out of debt and learned about high-life from the columns of the *Petit Journal* or the *Daily Mail.* A better division, though still an arbitrary one, might be between those who were obliged to spend whatever they earned, and those who had a surplus available to invest. Income from rents and dividends could be taken as the mark of the middle and upper bourgeoisie. Such people had joined the freemasonry of capitalism; they had been initiated into the century's magic; they had planted money and were learning how to harvest its increase. Their outward lives might or might not reveal how much money they had. What their lives did announce was respectability: the words *property* and *propriety* had after all a common root.

Here, though, we can see how the middle-class value system permeated the dynamic societies, from top to bottom, as thoroughly and as unconsciously as technology or theology spanned the social scale. Critics of bourgeois philistinism, such as Matthew Arnold, tended to blame the middle classes for inventing what they typified. But it was the entire society – omitting those at the very bottom and the very top, who were not allowed or did not care to accept the rules of the game – the entire society that was bourgeois. Everyone except criminals, paupers, lunatics and nobility, that is – groups that were fittingly denied the franchise or immigration privileges in certain countries; except these, and some intellectuals. The rest, the great majority, led highly stratified existences, riddled with prejudice.

4 Nations and Nationalism

Teach us to bear the yoke in youth,
With steadfastness and careful truth;
That, in our time, Thy Grace may give
The truth whereby the nations live.

Rudyard Kipling, 'The Children's Song'

Our need is for men firmly rooted in our soil, in our history, in our national conscience, and adapted to the French necessities of this day and date.

Maurice Barrès, French conservative, 1899

In the struggle between nations, one nation is the hammer and the other the anvil; one is the victor and the other the vanquished. . . . If ever the battle between the higher and lower civilization should cease in the world's history, our belief in the further development of mankind would lose its foundation.

Ex-Chancellor Bernhard von Bülow, German conservative, 1912

Nationalism Defined

So far we have used terms like 'nation', 'society' and 'state' as if they all amounted to much the same thing. During our period, indeed, the dynamic nations tended to assume that such terms were already synonymous – or ought to be made so. Yet this was a nineteenth-century development, emanating from the Western world along with technology and class-consciousness and other key ideas.

In earlier periods, as historians of nationalism point out, loyalties and antipathies operated in a very different context. The first allegiances were to families, clans and tribes – attachments to a limited number of people. There were also attachments to particular places: villages, city-states, counties, provinces. This is the sense of the French word *pays* or countryside, as distinct from the larger entity of the *patrie* or native land. At the other extreme were the transcendent allegiances to religious groupings such as Christendom and Islam that claimed to be universal.

Nationalism was born, in its modern form, from the tumult of the French Revolution. Indeed, nationalism appeared as a kind of religion. Millions of Frenchmen felt themselves converted, reborn into an intoxicating, crusading wholeness. Or it could be compared to a boiling process like that by which sugar is extracted from beet: the rough, raw material disintegrates under heat, the ill-smelling scum and dross are drawn off, leaving the angelically pure, white residue.

Community was communion. 'Society' no longer connoted high society: the upper crust *was* the dross. The 'nation' was no longer the preserve of the privileged but now an entire people, at once militantly patriotic and also infused with the sweet life-giving doctrines of liberty, equality, fraternity.

This faith [in the words of the French historian Jules Michelet], this candour, this immense impulse of concord, . . . was a subject of great astonishment for every nation; it was like a wonderful dream. . . . Several of our confederations had imagined a touching symbol of union, that of celebrating marriages at the altar of the native land [*patrie*]. Confederation itself, a union of France with France, seemed a prophetic symbol of the future alliance of nations, of the general marriage of the world. Another symbol, no less affecting, appeared at these festivals. Occasionally they placed upon the altar a little child whom everybody adopted, and who, endowed with the gifts, the prayers, the tears of the whole assembly, became the relation of everybody.

So nationalism became a sacred cause, a reaching toward a mystical rapport in which the individual expressed the full reach of his personality through the discovery of his affinity with others. National citizenship in effect became one of the crucial rights of man. The duties of citizenship – above all the obligation to military service in the defence of one's country – were according to this creed not burdensome but glorious. Surely there could be no finer opportunity to express one's ultimate quality, as individual and patriot, than in fighting the nation's enemies? The old royal or feudal armies were now popular, national armies; citizens were soldiers and *vice versa*; and the regiments were sustained by the labours of the rest of the nation, old men, women and children in one great irresistible multitude – the nation in arms preached by the Jacobin orator Bertrand Barère in 1793 who envisaged a place for everyone and everyone in his or her place ('The children will

80

make lint out of old linen, and the old men will ... be carried to the public squares to inflame the courage of the young warriors and preach the hatred of kings and the unity of the Republic').

Under Napoleon Bonaparte, French nationalism spread its conquering contagion across Europe. Many states were conquered/liberated. None was unaffected. Even Britain, the arch-enemy of France, repudiating the Gallic revolutionary principles, was compelled to articulate its own counter-creed of national pride. Elsewhere – in Spain, Italy, Germany, Russia – resistance to France often adopted the French ideology. The Italian dramatist Vittorio Alfieri in his savage book *Il Misogallo (Hater of the French*, 1799) insisted that Italy and not France was the true home of culture and liberty. Contemporary Germans like Johann Gottlieb Fichte, Ernst Moritz Arndt and Friedrich Ludwig Jahn ('Father Jahn') similarly urged their fellow German-speakers to throw off the French cultural and political yoke. The Russian historian Nicolai Karamzin, stirred by Napoleon's invasion of his country in 1812, abandoned his own previous admiration for France and urged his countrymen to realize that 'The Orthodox Russian is the most perfect citizen on earth and Holy Russia the first state.'

Implicit within these moves was the idea that the nation was an ancient bond, of the kind expressed in the German word *Volk*, re-emerging in the modern conceptions of the 'race' and the People. In England, France and Russia, the immemorial ties had found fulfilment. In Italy, Germany, Poland and elsewhere, the national destiny had been thwarted. Culturally, this sense of the national heritage antedated the French Revolution, though powerfully reinforced by it. Thomas Percy's collection of old ballads, songs and romances, *Reliques of Ancient English Poetry*, appeared as early as 1765, and James Macpherson's supposed translations from the Scottish bard Ossian in the same decade. Gerolamo Tiraboschi's *Storia della letteratura italiana* beginning with the Etruscans (despite the entire absence of surviving examples) and coming down almost to his own day, was first published in 1781. At the end of the century, German scholars began to issue eloquent appeals for a similar exploration of their own cultural roots. In the words of Friedrich Schlegel (*Lectures on the History of Literature*, 1818), 'There is nothing so necessary to the ... whole intellectual existence of a nation, as the possession of a plentiful store of those national recollections and associations, which are lost in a great measure during the dark ages of infant society, but which it forms the great object of the poetical art to perpetuate and adorn.' Folklore (a word first used in English in 1846) became a passion of European *savants* and imaginative writers. The brothers Jacob and Wilhelm Grimm issued their great collection of German folk-tales, *Kinder- und Mausmärchen*, in the ultra-patriotic years 1812–5. Peter Christen Asbjörnsen and Jörgen Moe performed the same office for Norway (1842–4). Hans Christian Andersen began to bring out his Danish folk-tales in 1835, continuing the prolific sequence for another thirty years and more. In the 1850s and 1860s, Aleksandr Nikolaevich Afanasiev re-introduced the Russian public to such marvellous legends as *Prince Ivan*, the *Firebird*, and the *Gray Wolf*. These tales were usually reworked by their latter-day interpreters. Sometimes, as with Macpherson and various Balkan scribes, the desire to furnish an ancient cultural pedigree led to fabrication. Societies that had no indigenous folk-heritage were obliged to borrow and invent. The American author Washington Irving, for example, adapted his famous *Rip Van Winkle* and several other apparently native stories from European originals; Longfellow based his *Hiawatha* (1855) upon American Indian folklore but narrated it in a metre taken from a Finnish saga. The scholarly or the romantic impulses to establish a traditional past were reinforced by nationalistic fervour; and then nationalism in many lands concentrated upon politics and ideology.

By 1848, the basic tenets of nationalism had taken shape. Nations were historic entities, whether or not they had attained independence. If they had not, then every sentiment of liberalism, brotherhood and race-memory enjoined the people of a submerged nation to fulfil themselves. Self-determination – a term that reached its culminating honorific significance with the peacemaking at the close of the 1914–18 War – was both a right and a duty. Every nation had a destiny, often derived from past moments of glory. Thus Italy, as Giuseppe Mazzini again and again insisted, had not hitherto existed as a sovereign state: 'therefore,' he declared in 1861, 'it must exist in the future'. The reason for his 'therefore' was that although the nineteenth-century country might appear to bear out Metternich's sneer that Italy was a mere 'geographical expression', the peninsula had conferred greatness upon mankind through the Roman Empire and then through the Roman Church. 'The civil primacy twice exercised by Italy – through the arms of the Caesars and by the voice of the Popes – is destined to be held a third time by the people of Italy – the nation.'

To a dedicated, liberal patriot like Mazzini, nationalism was self-evidently a force for good – a generous and ennobling aspiration. To a more detached, conservative scholar like the British historian Lord Acton, it was 'a retrograde step'. In an essay of 1862 which rebuked Mazzini for his mistaken zeal, Acton contended that the states nearest perfection, notably the British and Austrian Empires, were those which 'include various distinct nationalities without oppressing them'. He disliked any system that diminished the liberty of the individual. He thought socialism harmful in this respect. But at least it tried to rescue the downtrodden: 'and if the freedom of the State was sacrificed to the safety of the individual, the more immediate object was, at least in theory, attained'. Nationalism, however, sacrificed both liberty and social welfare to 'the imperative necessity of making the nation the mould and measure of the State'. Its course, he prophesied, 'will be marked with material as well as moral ruin, in order that a new invention may prevail over the works of God and the interests of mankind'.

Not every observer, then or since, would accept Acton's verdicts on the British and Austrian hegemonies, or upon nationalism in general. But was there wisdom in his misgivings? Had nationalism become more of a torment than a sign of progress by the end of our period? The best way to answer is to examine how the phenomenon revealed itself between 1848 and 1916 in different types of society – firstly among the achieved nations; secondly, among those striving for unification and greatness; and thirdly, among those existing states which were likely to fall victims to the new nationalism. In the first group, we can include Britain, France, Russia and the United States, in the second Italy and Germany. Finally, we shall look at two candidates for dissolution, Turkey and Austria-Hungary.

During the nineteenth century, nationalism began to shade off into the wider phenomenon of imperialism, and in the next chapter, imperialism will be analysed in some depth. In the context of the Western world, imperialism was probably the crucial development of the nineteenth century, one which transformed our subject from *European* history to *world* history. The *theory* of nationalism had only a marginal influence in the spread of movements for national self-determination, which mostly developed from deep-seated social and economic motives. In the case of Germany, for example, the propagandists for national union spoke with many contradictory voices, and in most cases simply reflected an existing belief that national union was the recognition of natural tendency. The same may be said for Italy. Indeed, most nationalist movements called for the re-creation of a previous historical entity: the Serbs looked back to the great days of the Serbian empire in the fourteenth century, Czechs campaigned for the re-establishment of the historic Crown of St Wenceslas. For our purposes, we should look for the mechanism by which the new nations were created, and at the political effects which stemmed from the creation of new national units, as well as the particular national motives which lay behind them. By contrast, we shall be more concerned with the theory and ideology of imperialism, and the manner of its spread from one major power to another.

The Achieved Nations

This is a somewhat arbitrary classification, embracing Britain, France, Russia and the United States. Each differed markedly from the others. Indeed, Acton in his 1862 essay took Britain and France to represent diametrically opposite examples. France for him was the absolutist state, Britain the liberal state. In France, 'The theory of unity makes the nation a source of despotism and revolution'; in England, he believed, 'The theory of liberty regards it as the bulwark of self-government, and the foremost limit to the excessive power of the State. . . .' One might present the divergences between the Russia and the United States of 1850 or 1900 in terms almost as stark. It would be silly to pretend that the four nations typified any single brand of nationalism, even though rivalry is no proof of profound ideological difference. On the contrary, the very closeness of outlook and aspiration may make two nations bitter enemies of one another; this happened with Britain and France in the eighteenth century, and sometimes with Britain and the North American ex-colonies in the nineteenth.

The reason for grouping the four nations together is indicated by the sub-head of this section. They were 'achieved' nations, in varying degrees, in that all were nation-states well before 1848. Though they were affected by the new passion for nationalism aroused during the French Revolution, their nationhood preceded it. Britain and France in particular seemed to be organic or ideal nations, in the eyes of men of the Mazzini stamp. Russia and the United States were more problematical. But all four, in one way or another, furnished object-lessons, usually inspirational,

Opposite: The nineteenth century was the age of nationalism. This patriotic poster from America shows that the spirit belonged to the New as well as the Old World.

84

UNITED STATES OF AMERICA.

LONG MAY SHE WAVE!

for other peoples; nationalism, like technology, was imitative and emulative. The lessons read may of course have been incorrect in the light of history. Indeed, some must have been, since some are contradictory.

Thus, now and then, the United States was upheld by its citizens and by outsiders as a nation of nations, according to its early ideal. More commonly, however, the stress was laid upon American unity rather than diversity; and the American population as well as culture were frequently spoken of as 'Anglo-Saxon'. The chief emphasis was on the 'WASP' (White Anglo-Saxon Protestant) component that in fact dominated the United States, numerically and socially, until the end of our period and afterward. Every American president, for example, had been white, Protestant and of British descent. The desirable American immigrant was the person who assimilated himself as rapidly and completely as possible to the WASP norm.

In recent years, the errors in this assumption have been a central concern among American historians. They attack the WASP outlook of their predecessors for its attempt to ignore the sizeable proportion of the American people that was not white or not Anglo-Saxon or not Protestant. They insist that the melting-pot failed to melt. Much of this criticism is salutary; and it is reinforced by the accompanying charge that women and poor people are strangely missing from the story. But it is unhistorical in dodging the point that whether justly or not, the great majority of American movers and shakers during our period were what the national myth asserted: male 'Anglo-Saxons'; and on the whole, those who were not did their best to behave as if they were. The myth, in other words, was so powerful that reality strove to correspond with it.

Seen from outside, the extremes of nationalist feeling are odious or at any rate absurd. Mazzini's claim that Italy was both the shrine and the cradle of inspiration for mankind has already been mentioned. French patriots would have none of this. 'Rome', said Michelet in his book *Le Peuple* (1846), 'held the pontificate of the dark ages. . . . France has been the pontiff of the ages of light. This is not an accident. . . . It is the legitimate result of a particular tradition, connected with a general tradition, for two thousand years. No people has one like it. In this is continued the grand human movement ... from India to Greece and to Rome, and from Rome to us.' The first chapters of the history of Germany and England were 'mutilated' as in a defective manuscript. With

Opposite: William I proclaimed ruler of the German Empire at Versailles, 18 January 1871.

86

Italy, the last chapters were missing. Only France embodied a complete evolution – Roman, Christian, modern; and the culminating principle of this French and yet universal culture was *fraternité*, brotherhood. When we turn to Russian writers, however, the same assertions of priority and superiority confront us. In his book *Russia and Europe* (1869), Nikolai Danilevsky argued that the historical development of the 'Germano-Roman' or western European peoples had been distorted and undermined by their innately violent character. They had fallen into religious, philosophical and socio-political anarchy. Russia and the majority of the Slav peoples, on the other hand, 'became, with the Greeks, the chief guardians of the living tradition of religious truth, Orthodoxy, and in this way they continued the high calling, which was the destiny of Israel and Byzantium: to be the chosen people'.

In Russia, nationalism and imperialism went hand in hand. Visionaries like Danilevsky promoted the idea of a Russia whose influence should stretch from the Atlantic to the Pacific and Mediterranean. General R. A. Fadeyev, who had played a prominent part in the Russian conquest of the Caucasus, declared 'Russia cannot consolidate itself in its present state; political, like natural, history does not lend eternity to undefined, unfinished forms. All depends now on the evolution of the Slavic Question.' Pan-Slavism, the idea of uniting all Slavs under the broad protective umbrella of Russia, of spreading Slav culture even into the empty steppes of Central Asia, became the ideology of Russia's relentless expansion. Germany and Italy had defined national and cultural boundaries that even the most fervent nationalist would be forced to accept: Russia had none. The core of the Russian empire included Poles, Finns, Balts, Ukrainians, Cossacks and a host of smaller social and linguistic groups. It required a process of forced Russification to weld them into a solid and unified nation, and Russia could assimilate any number of other groups by the same process. As the nationalist poet F. I. Tyutchev proclaimed (1844), there was no limit to Russia's growth:

> Seven inland seas and seven mighty rivers
> From the Nile to the Neve
> From the Elbe to China
> From the Volga to the Euphrates
> From the Ganges to the Danube
> Such is our Empire to be.

Because Russia was composed of so many fragments, its nationalism was a largely artifical creation. This is not to say that Pan-Slavism did not have deep roots in Russian patriotism, or in Orthodox religious fervour which identified with co-religionists living under alien rule. But it was promoted deliberately as an aid to Russian expansion. Between 1858 and 1870, Slavonic Benevolent Societies were founded in St Petersburg, Moscow, Kiev and Odessa, with the aim of propagandizing the scheme for the union of all Slavs, and, secretly, of fostering revolts in Austria and Turkey, the two countries with the largest Slav populations outside Russia. Although many army officers and officials belonged to these societies, the government had, officially, no connection with them. In fact, they were deliberately used to whip up support for a policy of expansive nationalism.

Russia expanded south and east more or less simultaneously, although her southward expansion was checked. In 1854, England and France entered the Crimean War to halt Russia's pressure on Turkey, and in 1878, the European powers did the same again, though across the conference table at the Congress of Berlin rather than on the battlefield. The great prize in Russian eyes was Constantinople, the heart of the Eastern Orthodox faith, and in the hands of the Turk. Religion and politics went neatly hand in hand, for possession of Constantinople would have allowed Russia access to the Near East and Africa. In 1878, the Russian armies reached the outskirts of the city and could see the great church of Hagia Sophia in the distance. After 1878, she pursued the same persistent objective by Pan-Slav agitation among the Balkan states, until the Balkan wars were renewed in 1912, although in a manner not entirely to Russia's liking. To the East there were fewer problems. Central Asia was divided up into loosely controlled Islamic states, like the Khanates of Khiva, Tashkent and Bokhara. By 1868, Russia had extended her empire in Asia as far as the city of Samarkand, by 1895 to the southern borders of China. Russia's intentions in the East were symbolized by the building of the new capital, Vladivostok (Ruler of the East), on the Pacific coast in 1860. In 1891, a start was made on the Trans-Siberian railway, to link Russia's eastern empire with the West. The advance in the East was only checked by Russia's disastrous defeat at the hands of the Japanese in 1904–5, and Britain's resistance to Russia's ostensible threat towards India. But Russian expansion was only halted, not ended; nationalism had become transmuted into a voracious imperialism which, as the First World War drew closer, began to look for gains in western Europe from the weakening Austrian empire.

The United States like Russia, claimed to be *the* perfect, universal nation founded on universal principles. It was destined, according to John L. O'Sullivan in 1839, 'to establish on earth the noblest temple ever dedicated to the worship of the Most High, ... owning no man master, but governed by God's ... law of brotherhood'. Nor were the British unduly reticent about their qualities or their value for the rest of mankind. According to the Scottish writer Robert Louis Stevenson, in an essay of 1881, 'magnanimity and virtue' were the forces that had 'famed this island, and raised her head in glory, higher than the great kingdoms of the neighbouring continent'.

If the United States extolled itself as the prime example of democratic pluralism, England pictured itself as the fountainhead of such ideas, and sometimes enrolled North America, indeed all English-speaking or 'Anglo-Saxon' countries, under its own banner. Sir Charles Wentworth Dilke's *Greater Britain* (1868) maintained that 'the grandeur of our race' had enabled peoples of British extraction to rule over an area of the globe four and a half times as large as the Roman Empire at its greatest extent. The 'Saxon' was outstripping the 'Muscovite' in conquest. Nothing could prevent 'the English race itself in 1970 numbering 300 millions ... of one national character and one tongue. Italy, Spain, France, Russia become pigmies by the side of such a people.'

In general, the achieved nations represented the rightness of nationalism. The complex, providential operations of history had, they believed, made their unification inevitable. Historic forces would guarantee each of them its peculiar destiny. For the British and the Americans, economic mastery and empire-building within a context of democratic liberalism. For the Russians, the dream of a vast Eurasian domain, ruled by a people Orthodox in religion and Slav in race. For the French too, prosperity and empire, but also a unique cultural brilliance, partly perhaps as a psychological consolation-prize for their failure to match rival nations in technological and population growth. Other aspiring nations envied them and yearned to match and surpass them. Idealistic patriots such as Mazzini readily adopted their insistence that true nations were leagues of brotherhood, tending somehow toward an eventual mystic union of all mankind – or at any rate of all the white peoples of mankind: none of these nationalists believed that non-white peoples might legitimately strive for similar goals.

Overleaf: 'The Russian Octopus' – this famous Japanese cartoon of the time of the Russo-Japanese War (1904) shows one view of Russian expansionism.

Would-be Nations

The period 1848–1914 saw the addition of two new European states to the tally of 'great powers': the kingdom of Italy and imperial Germany. The process of unification was superficially very similar in both countries: wars to establish national independence, a new ideology of nationality expounded in political speeches, writings, poetry, painting and even music, and the creation of a new nation along largely linguistic frontiers: the kingdom of the *Italians*, the empire of the *Germans* (although in the latter case German-speaking Austria was excluded). But despite the similarities, Italy and Germany represented two different types of successful nationalism.

The siege of Venice (1848–9), painting by V. Giacomelli. To unify Italy the Italians had first to drive the Austrians from their strongholds in Venetia and Lombardy.

The redemption of Italy

Since the sixteenth century, Italy had been the victim of her neighbours' greed, traditionally fought over by the Habsburgs and the French. In three centuries of war and diplomacy, Italy had been a catspaw in others' quarrels, a situation exemplified by its fragmentation into a number of states. In the north, the country was dominated by two large Austrian possessions, the provinces of Lombardy and Venetia, with their capitals at Milan and Venice. In the north-west, Piedmont-Savoy, together with the remote island of Sardinia, was organized as the kingdom of Sardinia, with its capital at Turin. The centre of Italy was dominated by the Papal States, and to a lesser extent, smaller states ruled by the Habsburgs, as in Tuscany with Florence as its chief city. Italy was created by a war of liberation, the *Risorgimento*, which began (disastrously) in 1848, and ended with the triumphal reoccupation of Rome in 1870. The stages of this process of liberation are given later in this section. But Italy had always, in the past, lost from other people's quarrels, and merely exchanged one master for another.

The same danger existed during the Risorgimento, with the threat of French external domination replacing the rule of Austria. The redemption of Italy was compounded of two main factors: a skilful exploitation of the disputes between the powers of Europe, and a revolutionary movement of such charismatic appeal as to frighten, and eventually overwhelm, the traditional rulers of the Italian states. The two aspects of the movement of liberation are exemplified in the characters of Count Cavour and Giuseppe Garibaldi, the former a great statesman and adept at the ploys of international diplomacy, who slowly advanced the claims of Italy to nationhood, and looked for a strong centralized state under the control of his master, the King of Sardinia, and the latter the professional revolutionary, the leader of the Thousand, the red-shirted elite of the Risorgimento, who represented the anarchic, repressed forces in Italian society which had little love, and less respect, for monarchs. The new Italy was a mixture of these two tendencies, a compromise between the desire for a firm monarchical state and the fundamentally republican aspirations of the revolutionaries. Even after the period of unification, the debate as to the nature of the state continued, and became one of the dominant submerged issues in Italian politics and society. Thus the experience and nature of the process of unification, the union of many fundamentally antagonistic elements within one state (north and south Italy, for example, had

Mazzini, the Italian patriot whose ideals helped to inspire the struggle for unification and independence.

little in common save language) produced a new political unit, but a sense of nationhood emerged only gradually.

In Italy before 1848 some people like the Milanese scholar Carlo Cattaneo advocated a republic with federalist, semi-autonomous government for the various parts. Mazzini, as a republican, wanted a centralized government based on Rome. Others, including the Piedmontese philosopher Vincenzo Gioberti, envisaged a federation presided over by the Pope, who was not only a spiritual leader but the temporal head of the sizeable Papal States. Most of Cattaneo's followers in Milan, at least when they first rose against Austrian rule in 1848, thought of the Papacy as a national symbol and the newly elected Pius IX as a liberal pontiff: their proclamations were prefaced with 'Free Italy. Long Live Pius IX'. Others again, Count Cavour among them, looked to unification under the auspices of the Piedmontese House of Savoy. Cavour's periodical *Il Risorgimento*, founded in 1847, urged the necessity of a monarchist nation with the throne occupied by the King of Sardinia. These were fundamental issues; and by a painful irony the impulse toward unity itself tended to intensify disagreement. The return of the uncompromising patriots from exile – Mazzini from Paris, Garibaldi from years of guerrilla warfare in Brazil – heightened the tensions. In the uprisings of 1848, Josef Radetzky's Austrian army was dislodged from Lombardy with dreamlike ease, and the province voted by plebiscite to join Piedmont. But Radetzky came back and routed the Piedmontese at Custozza in 1848. He beat them again, decisively, at Novara in 1849, so that the King of Sardinia was obliged to abdicate in favour of his son Victor Emmanuel. Lombardy and Venetia were brought firmly back under Austrian control; and pessimists noted that the two provinces, the richest part of Italy, were also the most efficiently and mildly governed – at least in normal circumstances. So the Sardinian monarchy was discredited for the time being.

In Rome, the Pope repudiated his initially liberal instincts and retreated from the Vatican to the reactionary atmosphere of Naples. He was now the pig, '*Porco Pio Nono*' ('Pig Pius IX'), to the masses who had lately counted on him to work a miracle. Any detached analysis must have shown that he could not possibly provide the focus for Italian nationalism even if he had been a man of more sanguine temperament. As the Austrians were quick to argue, the Pope was the high priest of an international religion: how could he confine his blessings to his Italian subjects, dis-

96

criminating against the millions of good Catholics in Austria and elsewhere? With the Pope gone from Rome, other countries had a perfect excuse to send their troops into Italy to restore him, as the French did in 1849; and to keep their soldiers on the ground thereafter, as the French did in Rome and Austria in the rest of the Papal States. The shortlived republic of Rome collapsed. Its foremost warrior, Garibaldi, had to escape into exile in New York. Its prime theorist, Mazzini, fled ignominiously to the safety of London. In the north too, after a long and heroic resistance, the republic of Venice was forced to surrender to the besieging Austrians, and its president Daniele Manin disappeared into exile aboard a French warship. The Italian revolutions of 1848 all ended with disaster, and the previous reactionary regimes were established.

But, if unification was an idea whose time had not yet come, the leaders of the various Italian movements clung to the faith that the time was not far off. There was the encouraging example of the achieved nations. Manin confessed during the siege of Venice that his supreme ambition was to behave like George Washington, the architect of American independence. Mazzini was delighted with the celebrated incident of 1852 when Cockney brewery workers attacked an Austrian General Julius Haynau, who was visiting Barclay's Brewery. Haynau, nicknamed the 'Hanging General' first gained his reputation for savage brutality during the repression of the Italians in 1848, followed by even greater viciousness in the repression of Hungary. The British government declined to punish the culprits. Austrian severity supplied a whole crop of new legends to stimulate native patriotism; attempts by the authorities to prohibit the display of the Italian green-white-and-red tricolour only encouraged ingeniously impudent evasion of the rule. French behaviour had been equivocal. Yet Louis Napoleon conveniently believed in national destiny, as well as in power politics. By 1858, Napoleon III, as he had become, was ready to intervene once more.

The agreement he reached was with Sardinia, the only part of Italy to present a clear, realistic programme. Its new king Victor Emmanuel was gradually persuaded by his able ministers Massimo d'Azeglio and Cavour to present himself as a constitutional monarch round whom the rest of the nation should rally. However uneasy republicans like Mazzini might be at this development, they were still more alarmed by the prospect of either extreme socialist or papal domination. 'We thirst for authority', Mazzini

Count Cavour, the
architect of Italian
unification.

told a London audience in 1852. 'But ... where is it? With the
Pope – with the Emperor [of Austria] – with the ferocious or
idiotic princes, now keeping our Italy dismembered ...?' Despotism and anarchy, he said, were the menaces. 'The first destroys
liberty; the second society.' In 1858 Cavour reached a secret
understanding with Napoleon III. The French would join
Piedmont-Sardinia in expelling the Austrians. Italy would be
formed into a federation of four states under the nominal presidency
of the Pope. 'Since Your Majesty would be the ruler of the richest
and strongest half of Italy,' Cavour reported to Victor Emmanuel,
'you would in fact be the ruler of the whole peninsula.' In return
France claimed Savoy and Nice.

In 1859, the deal was consummated, though not as planned.
French and Piedmontese troops defeated the Austrians in the
two battles of Magenta and Solferino; Napoleon III made a
separate truce but the central Italian principalities fell to Piedmont
without fighting; and in 1860 Garibaldi swept through Sicily
and Naples before presenting his conquests – much to the relief
of Cavour – to Victor Emmanuel. In 1861 Victor Emmanuel was
proclaimed King of Italy, except for Venetia and the shrunken

98

papal enclave of Latinum. In 1866, the Italians took advantage of German rivalries to side with Prussia against Austria and received Venetia as a reward. Finally, in 1870, the Franco-Prussian War led to the withdrawal of French troops from Rome and its occupation by Italian columns. The annexation of Latinum completed the Italian jigsaw, although Savoy and Nice were ceded to France. Cavour had died in 1861, having seen the fulfilment of most of his hopes. D'Azeglio lived until 1866, Mazzini until 1872, but neither was exhilarated. Unification had been brought about by force and a certain amount of fraud, largely through foreign auspices. Magenta was a French victory: there were more Italians on the Austrian side than on the 'patriotic' one. In 1866, the Italians were beaten on land at Custozza and at sea at Lissa by the Austrians. Two expeditions to liberate Rome during the 1860s led by Garibaldi were thwarted by the French army of occupation. There was not much glory in the final overthrow of papal authority; and Pius IX, 'the prisoner of the Vatican', never reconciled himself to the new order. The dying Mazzini called Italy a corpse, a structure without a soul pieced together by unscrupulous foreigners.

The battle of Magenta (1859), one of the decisive Austrian defeats which led to a united Italy and the expulsion of the Habsburgs.

The famous meeting between Garibaldi and Victor Emmanuel at Teano outside Naples on 26 October 1860, at which Garibaldi handed over command of his soldiers to the king.

The formation of the German Empire

There were lessons of another kind in the course of German unification, which like that of Italy was more or less sealed in 1871. As with Italy, the 1848 revolutions set loose a storm of reformist and nationalist sentiment, with apparent spectacular successes followed by failure, repression and despair. As with Italy, the centripetal pull of nationalism was countered by the weight of conservative regimes, and by divisions between a more industrially active north and a more traditionally rural south. In the German states, these antagonisms were emphasized by the gulf between Protestants and Catholics. In Germany too, there were rival programmes, centralizers disputing with federalists, monarchists with republicans. Comparable parts were played in both situations by Sardinia and Prussia – northern kingdoms not hitherto renowned for culture and learning. Their respective capitals, Turin and Berlin, were relative parvenus when set against Rome, or Munich, Dresden and Vienna. Sardinia and Prussia both thrust themselves into the lead, obliging the nationalist movements to accept their terms.

But there were vital differences between the Italian and the German circumstances. While Italian developments had been largely dictated by outsiders, German integration was entirely a problem for German-speaking peoples; and the area covered by Germanic administrations was big and variegated. Just how big should it be? The practical meaning of this question was: should the projected new country include or exclude the Austrian provinces? And it derived from another question: who should dominate the new country, Prussia or Austria? Pan-Germanism remained an appealing vision throughout our period. To many, the Great Germany conception sounded self-evidently better than the Little Germany one. Radetzky hoped for a Germanic empire of language, feeling and trade that would reach from the Baltic to the Adriatic. To All-German patriots of his stamp, Venice was a German port.

The grandiosity of such a dream was undeniable: so were the difficulties surrounding it. Prussia and Austria could not both lead, and neither was willing to relinquish the chance. In 1830 the cosmopolitan old poet Johann Wolfgang von Goethe, discussing nationalism with his friend Johann Peter Eckermann, criticized the hatreds it aroused. Nor could he believe there was an authentic nucleus 'of which we could decidedly say – *Here is Germany!* If we inquire in Vienna, the answer is – This is Austria; and if in Berlin, the answer is – This is Prussia!' Goethe had not warmed to the nationalism of Jahn, who in his book *Das deutsche Volkstum* (1810) declared: 'Prussia has always been for me the kernel of a Germany broken into fragments. Austria is a large melting pot composed of people speaking seven languages. Other German states ... are either powerless, lacking outlet to the sea, or dependent on foreign influences. ... The spirit of the old, noble German *Reich* lives in Prussia.'

Goethe's attitudes found some echo among German liberals distrustful of the militarist and autocratic spirit of Prussia's Hohenzollern dynasty. They wanted a republic, not a monarchy. If German unity could only be encompassed through a monarchy, then they wanted a constitutional monarchy. Their suspicions were not allayed by the erratic behaviour of Prussia's Frederick William IV during the hectic months of 1848–9. At first, he announced that he was prepared to merge Prussia with Germany and lead the united nation. A year later, when the federal Diet or parliament of the loose German Confederation had been replaced by a national assembly at Frankfurt-am-Main, Frederick William refused to accept its offer to elect him hereditary emperor of Germany, picking up a crown 'from the gutter' – by mere vote of an elected assembly of nobodies, instead of having it tendered by all the German princes on the principle of divine right. The outcome was the disintegration of the Frankfurt assembly, a return to the old Confederation, and a decade of stalemate managed by Austrian diplomacy.

German unification was eventually carried out in the 1860s under the aegis of William I, the new king of Prussia, and his chief minister Otto von Bismarck. Like Sardinia's, theirs was a programme of force. The Prussian soldiers were sensationally successful in battle. In 1864, a brisk little campaign in alliance with Austria against Denmark secured the duchies of Schleswig and Holstein for a future Germany. In 1866, the rivalry between Prussia and Austria came to a head. Disputes over the administration of Schleswig-Holstein and over the much bigger issue of the shape of the German Confederation were used by Bismarck to bring on a war with Francis Joseph. The Austrian Empire seemed a formidable opponent, especially when supported by the south German states of Baden, Württemberg, Saxony and Bavaria. The war was, however, over in seven weeks; one major battle at Sadowa (or Königgrätz) in Bohemia persuaded the Austrians to cut their losses and sue for peace.

Nothing succeeds like success. The fulfilment of Bismarck's schemes made them appear not a gamble but rather an irresistible prophecy. His previously nervous royal master was convinced; opposition in the Prussian *Landtag* dwindled; by the peace treaty, Prussia annexed Hanover, Hesse-Cassel, Nassau and Frankfurt, as well as Schleswig-Holstein; and William I became president and commander-in-chief of the freshly-created North German Confederation, with Count Bismarck as its chancellor. In 1870 the Confederation, augmented by south German armies, marched against France – once more with shattering effect. Bismarck selected the Hall of Mirrors in Versailles for the setting of the grand finale: the proclamation before the princes and rulers of Germany (excluding Austria) that there was again a German Emperor in the person of William I of Prussia. It could be called a battlefield ceremony. A few miles away lay besieged Paris. Bismarck's policy of 'blood and iron' had broken the various resistances to a Prussianized Second *Reich*. The peace settlement with France added Alsace-Lorraine to the new Germany.

By the usual criteria, German unification was foreordained: the precise methods employed could be deemed immaterial so long as the end was gained. In size, competence and activity – not least technological advancement – the new nation at once became established as a great power.

Despite the appearance to the outside world of an almost

The battle of Sadowa (1866). This German print shows Crown Prince Frederick William in heroic pose as the Prussians defeat Austria in the struggle for the mastery of Germany.

monolithic solidity, Germany was in fact riven by differences in religion (the north was largely Protestant, the south, Catholic), and by a growing spirit of class divisiveness. Many Germans in positions of authority thought Germany's foundations were shaky, agreeing with the *eminence grise* of German diplomacy, Friedrich von Holstein, that Germany was a 'mosaic of tribes', liable at any moment to split asunder. The real cement of the state was the economic unity of the country, which was already well advanced before 1870. As Germany became richer, all groups and classes shared in the economic advance; with growing prosperity, the divisive tendencies, despite the fears of the pessimists, began to disappear. Unlike Italy, where unification became the excuse for the north to exploit the south, building new antagonisms into the state, the creation of a united Germany solved many of the old problems and tensions of German society, by harnessing national resources, human as well as material, to a single goal.

The First *Reich*: Saxony gratefully shelters beneath the German shield as a united Germany becomes a reality in 1871.

Once the nationalist aim of a new German empire had been achieved, German nationalism was transmuted, slowly, into German imperialism.

The Sick Men of Europe

By the outbreak of the First World War in 1914, two states were confidently expected to break up under the pressure of the new demands for national self determination. The fact that they survived until the general collapse of 1918 reveals the strength of even moribund institutions. Austria and Turkey, or more accurately, the Habsburg and the Ottoman Empires, were ostensibly anachronisms in the nineteenth century, and more so in the twentieth. They lacked the linguistic and cultural unity possessed by the other states of Europe (except Russia). As forms of social and political organization, they stemmed directly from the seventeenth-century age of religious warfare: the Habsburg Empire had developed as a response to the Islamic invasions from the East, the Ottoman Empire was a state dedicated to the 'jihad' or holy war. They lacked many of the unifying factors which typified both the 'achieved' nations, and the products of nineteenth-century unification, like Italy and Germany. It was this apparent disunity which seemed to make them natural victims.

The Habsburg Empire

Our period neatly coincides in the Habsburg Empire with the reign of the Emperor Francis Joseph (1848–1916). He came to the throne as a direct result of the revolution of 1848, pushed forward by the reactionary Court circles, as the young forceful ruler able to stand up to the revolutionary forces. The crises which faced him at the beginning of his reign remained, in one form or another, with him throughout his reign. Nationalism had been at the root of the revolutions, coupled with resistance to the central authority of Vienna. The Habsburg Empire was an artificial creation, with a German-speaking core and an assorted collection of territories – Hungary, Bohemia, part of Poland and Italy which had been acquired by wars over the centuries or by fortunate dynastic marriages. As a result it had a strong centrifugal tendency – and it was in the lands on the periphery where the separatist movements grew strongest. After 1848 the government's defensive tendency was to centralize, to hold the state together by drawing all the links of communication, trade and administration towards the centre, to the imperial capital at Vienna. The state was thus in an uneasy state of balance, between inner cohesion and dissolution. Increasingly, what held the Empire together was an administration which was trained to stand aloof from national loyalties, and the army which was the main support of the central imperial authority.

The key event, some might say the bane, of the Empire, was the constitutional settlement of 1867, designed to re-establish the state on a firmer and more secure basis, by the creation of two centres of power, in Vienna and the Hungarian capital of Budapest. What was established was a 'dual monarchy', united only in the person of the joint monarch, Francis Joseph. The Hungarians (Magyars) were admitted to power only because their capacity to

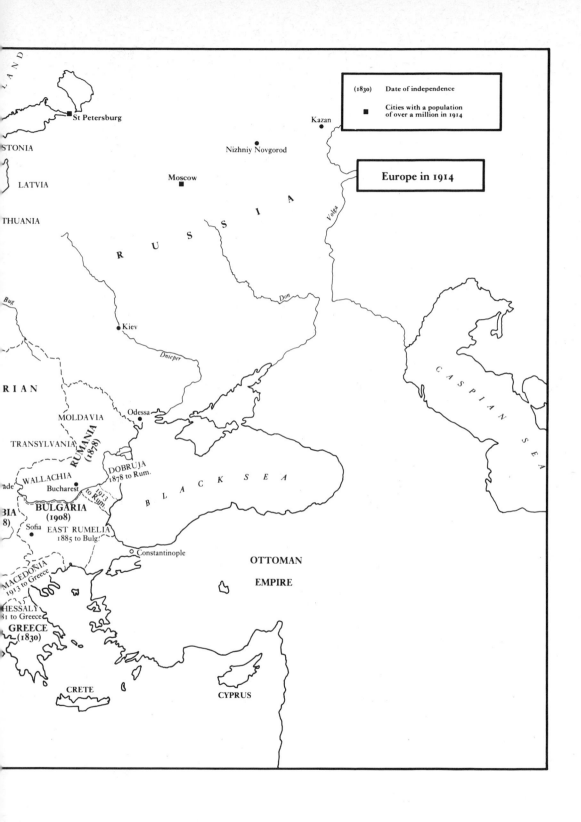

Europe in 1914

LAND

STONIA

LATVIA

THUANIA

■ St Petersburg

Nizhniy Novgorod •

Moscow ■

Kazan •

R U S S I A

Volga

Bug

Don

• Kiev

Dnieper

RIAN

MOLDAVIA

TRANSYLVANIA

RUMANIA (1878)

WALLACHIA

ade

Bucharest •

BULGARIA (1908)

• Sofia

EAST RUMELIA 1885 to Bulg.

BIA 8)

8)

• Odessa

DOBRUJA 1878 to Rum.

1913 to Rum.

B L A C K   S E A

C A S P I A N   S E A

◦ Constantinople

MACEDONIA 1913 to Greece

HESSALY 81 to Greece

GREECE (1830)

OTTOMAN

EMPIRE

CRETE

CYPRUS

resist central authority had made them a danger to the stability of the Empire in the wars of 1859–66: once in power, the Magyars took care to ensure that no other group – the Slavs, Italians, Romanians, which were the most significant minorities in the empire – was able to follow their example. From 1867, the Habsburg Empire was more commonly known as the Dual Monarchy, or the Austro-Hungarian Monarchy, reflecting the new constitutional situation.

The privileged position given to the Hungarians hardened the resistance from the other nationalities. The Slav peoples, the Czechs, Slovaks, Serbs, Croats, Poles, Slovenes and, after 1878, when Austria assumed the government of the Turkish provinces of Bosnia and Herzegovina, the Bosnians, did not form a homogenous group (indeed they were often at each others' throats). But they were susceptible to the seductive lure of Pan-Slavism, and with the exception of the Poles, Russia looked on them as potential protégés. Austria-Hungary and Russia both came to see the Balkans as their natural sphere for expansion, and the constant danger of conflict existed for forty years before the First World War finally broke out as a result of the assassination of the Austrian heir to the throne, Francis Ferdinand, in the Bosnian town of Sarajevo, by a Bosnian nationalist. There was repeated danger of war in 1878 and in 1887 between Austria-Hungary and Russia, until they reached an agreement in the 1890s to defuse the Balkan situation. This balance was once again upset by the Balkan wars of 1912, when the emergent Balkan nations – Serbia, Bulgaria, Romania and Greece – sought to destroy the final vestiges of Turkish power in Europe.

Francis Joseph's reign corresponded to Britain's Victorian heyday, and despite the inherent tensions of the state, the Empire grew richer and more productive. But its inner tensions prevented the development of the dynamism and harnessing of resources which characterized the successful growth of Germany. Austria-Hungary became by 1914 an elegant, amiable backwater, less and less a first rank power. As if to replace the decline of political power, came a great development of cultural life, the result of the meeting of many different cultural influences, particularly in Vienna. The fundamental political aim of the Empire was that expressed by Count Eduard Franz Joseph von Taaffe, to keep the nationalities in a state of 'well modulated discontent', playing one off against another. But it was an endgame, as a British diplomat acutely observed after the great settlement of 1867:

'Only the most perfect harmony and a sincere desire on all sides to labour unremittingly for the general interests of the monarchy can afford the slight chance of duration and success to so novel and unwieldy a system, but such complete harmony will be difficult to establish or maintain for any lengthened period in a nation so heterogenous as Austria.'

By the beginning of the twentieth century, acute observers were predicting the dissolution of the Empire, or at least that it would succeed Turkey as the 'Sick Man of Europe'. Such gloomy prognostications were mistaken, and the powers of Europe had a strong vested interest in maintaining Austria-Hungary. To countenance the destruction of European Turkey, at the periphery of Europe was one thing: but the Habsburg Empire provided the only foreseeable hope for stability in central Europe, the alternative to an unstable power vacuum. Before the First World War, it seemed likely that against the tide of nationalism, Austria-Hungary would survive, perhaps as a federation of racial groups, by an extension of the constitutional arrangements of 1867. Such speculations, which centred on the aims and personality of the heir to the throne, Francis Ferdinand, were brought to an end by the bullets fired by Gavrilo Prinćip in Sarajevo.

The Ottoman Empire

The true victim of emergent nationalism was the Ottoman Empire. The expansive phase of Ottoman imperialism during the sixteenth and seventeenth centuries had given an Islamic state a huge subject Christian population in the European part of the Empire, and it was from this essentially social and religious disharmony between the Christian and the Muslim world that many of Turkey's troubles sprang. The difficulties and dangers suffered by the Christian populations gave an excuse for foreign (especially Russian) intervention, and usually ensured a bad press for the Ottomans throughout Europe. Under the guise of support for Christian co-religionists, baser motives lurked: foreigners saw within the Turkish hegemony innumerable opportunities for profit.

The territorial and economic integrity of Turkey was steadily whittled away. Most of Greece had already been liberated by 1828: the Treaty of Adrianople (1829) established an independent Greek state. Turkey lost Romania (1856) as an outcome of the peace treaty following the Crimean war, then Bulgaria, Bosnia, Herzegovina, effectively by the Berlin settlement of 1878, and

Serbia, during the 1860s. Crete rebelled against Turkish rule in
1866, but without achieving independence. Turkey was at war
with Russia in 1854 and 1877–8, and against the Balkan powers
without Russia in 1912. Yet despite a steady series of adversities,
Turkey still survived in Europe, largely through the wily diplomacy of the Sultan Abdul Hamid II, who came to the throne in
1876 and reigned as undisputed, autocratic ruler of the Ottoman
Empire until the 'Young Turk' revolution in 1908.

The crucial factor both in the development of the Ottoman
Empire and in its nineteenth-century decline was the dual nature
of the Ottoman state. The Sultan had both a temporal and a
religious role, as Caliph of Islam. He was the central figure of the
Islamic world, whose duties still included the responsibility of
declaring a holy war, which all true Muslims were bound to obey.
This religious sanction gave the Sultan a theoretical although
limited authority even beyond the borders of the Empire, and
among his Muslim subjects, made him an object of veneration.
Pan-Islam could be developed to be as powerful an emotive force
as Pan-Slavism, a factor of which the British, with a large Muslim
population in India, were well aware. The impression of the
Ottoman Empire created in the West was of a decadent society
ripe for Westernization and exploitation; in reality, the truth was
less black and white. Turkish administration conformed to

Asian rather than European standards of honesty and efficiency, but it did operate: taxes were gathered, law was enforced and the Sultan's edict ran in the farthest recesses of the Empire. Indeed, his system of information and his network of spies kept him better informed than many European statesmen. To an even greater extent than Austria-Hungary, Turkey was incapable of becoming a dynamic nation within the social and political structure of the Ottoman empire. When a new, remodelled society began to develop after the First World War, under the leadership of Mustafa Kemal, who became better known as Kemal Ataturk, a clean break was made with the past, and Turkish society threw off the conservative restraints of Islamic theocracy.

The beginning of the new era was the revolution instituted by a group of army officers in Macedonia, known as the Committee of Union and Progress, which forced Abdul Hamid to restore parliamentary rule which had existed briefly in 1876; after a few

German cartoon of the Balkan wars in 1912. Bulgaria, Montenegro and Serbia attack Turkey from the rear while the Italians attack from the front.

111

months, he was forced to abdicate. The main aim of the Committee was to force the pace of Westernization, a challenge which the Germans, with grandiose plans for expansion to the east, were happy to accept. By 1914, the Turkish army was German-trained and armed and German influence in the Turkish economy (especially in the railway system) was greatly increased. The pressure behind the revolutionary movement was largely a nationalist one, Turkish nationalism replacing the traditional Ottoman standards and attitudes of the past. It was a task made easier partly by the shrinking of the limit of the Empire to what could be effectively controlled. Turkey's theoretical power in Egypt was lost in 1886, in Tunisia with the French invasion of 1881, in Tripoli in 1911. The Balkan wars of 1912 left Turkey in Europe as a narrow strip, a tiny fraction of the former territories. But these approached much more closely to 'natural, cultural, and in part, linguistic frontiers, and the new Turkish republic which was to be born out of the First World War was an Anatolian national state'.

Part Two

Europe and the World

5 European Settlement and Imperial Impulse

The conquest of the earth, which mostly means the taking it away from those who have a different complexion or slightly flatter noses than ourselves, is not a pretty thing when you look at it too much. What redeems it is the idea only. An idea at the back of it; not a sentimental pretence but an idea; and an unselfish belief in the idea – something you set up, and bow down before, and offer a sacrifice to.

Marlow in Joseph Conrad, The Heart of Darkness, *1902*

From Empire to Imperialism

The established empires of the early nineteenth century were in the process of contraction rather than expansion. The empires of Spain and Portugal lost much of their power and prestige with the liberation of their possessions on the American continent. Turkey, soon to become the 'Sick Man of Europe', was losing control of its possessions both in Europe, with the growth of the independence movements in the Balkans, and in the Middle East, as Egypt became virtually independent. The Dutch pre-eminence as a trading nation in the Far East was challenged, and the French expansion into Algeria, which began in 1830, was largely dictated by the exigencies of internal politics. The empires of Europe, after the settlement at the Congress of Vienna in 1815, were restricted to two: Austria and Russia, and neither then looked much beyond Europe as their sphere of activity. The greatest expansive imperial power lacked the title of empire: yet the British Empire was a prototype of the new imperialism.

Britain appeared to be the great exception. Huge areas of the world, and a quantity of islands and ports of call, were coloured red for British by the map-makers. There were the colonies of settlement: the parts of North America later to be known collectively as Canada, the tip of southern Africa, Australia (including Van Diemen's Land, or Tasmania) and New Zealand.

There were the sugar islands of the West Indies and the mainland holdings of British Guiana and Honduras. Above all, there were India and Ceylon, an immense and growing patchwork of provinces and kingly states directly or indirectly ruled over by Queen Victoria. With the largest navy in the world, Britain's imperial pre-eminence could not be challenged, even though it might make her heartily disliked by every other nation with pretensions to power.

Yet in mid-century, the British conception of empire was peculiarly indefinite. As the doctrine of free trade triumphed, so the ancient mercantilist argument for colonies lost force. Other arguments were less than universally persuasive. The idea that colonies supported the mother-country was false. Colonial exports, excluding India, brought in only £8 million a year, and a full half of that sum had to be expended annually on supplying troops and arms for colonial defence. Colonial wars, such as the Sikh campaigns of the 1840s to strengthen India's north-west frontier, were a heavy additional cost. Even when they went well the British public was only mildly gratified. When they went badly, there was an outcry in Parliament and in the newspapers. Conservatives were apt to regard colonies as complicated nuisances. Radicals, noting that the Colonial Secretary was also at this time the Secretary for War, concluded that overseas garrisons and appointments were part of the apparatus of aristocratic favouritism. The officials themselves appeared indifferent. Only one Colonial Secretary in the first thirty years of Victoria's reign actually visited a colony – and this because he was accompanying the Prince of Wales on a tour of the United States and Canada in 1860.

There was a group of colonizing enthusiasts, for whom Edward Gibbon Wakefield acted as the chief spokesman, who saw the white colonies as good places to absorb British emigration. The government was persuaded to pay the passage-money of citizens wishing to settle in Australia or New Zealand. But the offer was slightly suspect to working men who knew that until the 1850s Van Diemen's Land was still being used as a dumping-ground for convicts. Most of those who did go to the colonies of settlement paid their own way. The United States was easily the most attractive country for British emigrants, and lured many who had made for Canada in the first place. Not government policy but the gold-rush of 1851 and subsequent years brought Australia its first big inflow of settlers. On the eve of the Bathurst gold-strike, the entire white population of Australia, concentrated mainly in

116

the south-east corner of the sub-continent, was only about four hundred thousand. Ten years later it was still only a little over one million.

Relations between the white colonists and the home government were equivocal. Both sides, with some reservations, wanted the colonies to become self-governing as soon as possible. The situation in South Africa was complicated by friction with the Boers, descendants of the original Dutch settlers in the seventeenth century who resented British surveillance and disagreed on how the natives should be treated. The Boers were a predominately farming people, sternly religious and believing in a severe fundamentalist God. They looked upon the British as corrupters of their traditional patterns of behaviour, and resented British attempts to exert political control over them. In 1880, they defeated the British in the First Boer War. Thereafter, the British were more wary in their dealings with the fiercely independent

An artist's impression of the Australian gold rush of the 1850s. Gold proved a powerful incentive to immigration.

117

Boer population. Yet here too British policy implied a gradual withdrawal; by mid-century, London had relinquished its hold over the inland settlements of the Transvaal and Orange Free State. The average colonist was thought of by the average middle-class Englishman as rough, greedy and somewhat disreputable.

The possession of India was another matter. India was huge, populous, complex. The British *raj* had involved generations of merchants, soldiers, administrators. India was a source of profit and employment for a considerable number of white people. Yet here too doctrine was equivocal. Much of the actual running of India in mid-century was left in the private hands of the East India Company. The Company had, for instance, its own large army of native troops with white officers, paid for out of Company revenues. The British regiments also stationed in India – usually for twenty years at a stretch – might add another twenty thousand to the Company's private army of a hundred thousand. British officialdom treated India as a responsibility that was neither permanent nor temporary. It was believed that one day the British would terminate their trusteeship. How, when and to whom they would hand over was not specified because they had no firm idea. The 1857 Mutiny among units of the Company army seemed to be another example of circumstances shaping policy in the British Empire. It led to a tightening of authority. The government took over entirely from the East India Company. Having answered the atrocities of the mutineers with at least equal punitive ferocity, the *raj* was increasingly reluctant to entrust native Indians with positions of responsibility.

We shall come back to India's role in the imperial scheme. For immediate purposes, its ill-defined destiny serves to reinforce the point that if there were empires in 1850, there was as yet little sign of the rhetoric, the jostling, the commercial activity that in sum are usually associated with 'imperialism'. Historians can always find evidence to show that a phenomenon has earlier roots than was supposed. So, with mid-century imperial ventures, we can stress the mutual jealousies of France and England, in the Pacific as well as in North America; or British uneasiness over Russian expansion eastward from the Caspian towards the north-west frontiers of India; or the British bullying of China in the 'Opium War' of 1840, as a result of which Hong Kong became a leasehold property under the Union Jack. The essential fact remains. In 1850 the white nations were not clamouring for colonies; and the British in particular seemed not to know what to do with, say,

the rapidly declining sugar islands of the West Indies, or their fever-ridden outposts in West Africa. Yet, a generation later, the atmosphere was transformed; and by 1914, almost every acquirable corner of the globe was either owned by or dominated by one of the imperial powers. In 1850 the African hinterland was *terra incognita* to the white man. By 1914, every part of Africa except the little black republic of Liberia and the unsubduable fastnesses of Ethiopia was staked out as a colony or protectorate; and even here Liberia was an American creation, for freed slaves, while Italy had made two attempts to seize Ethiopia. The biggest proprietors were France and Britain, but Spain, Portugal, Belgium, Germany and Italy also held substantial areas.

Elsewhere in the world, China, Thailand, Afghanistan and Persia survived more or less intact because the great powers could not agree on a division of the spoils. Other lands, to be had for the taking, had duly been taken. Starting at the end of the 1850s, the French over the next half-century won control of Indo-China – areas recognizable also under the names of Vietnam, Laos and Cambodia. The British formalized their hold over Malaya and northern Borneo, and in 1886 annexed Burma. The Dutch consolidated their colonies in the East Indies. Islands in the Pacific were divided up between France, Germany, Britain and the United States. The great powers nibbled at China, securing treaty ports and spheres of influence along the coast.

What had happened? Why did Disraeli, who in 1852 was supposed to have described colonies as 'millstones' around the British neck, resort in old age to imperial drama, and metamorphose Queen Victoria into Empress of India? How did Germany, entirely without empire in 1870, end up with Togoland, the

A German cartoon of 1900 shows the Western powers queueing up for their slice of China.

Cameroons, South-West Africa, East Africa (Tanganyika), a naval base at Kiao-Chow, part of Samoa? What impelled Italy to join the rush in Africa and lay claim to Eritrea, part of Somaliland, the whole of Libya? By what processes did the United States annex Hawaii (1893), and replace Spain as overlord of the Philippines, Guam, Puerto Rico? Some would date the change, at least for England, from the early 1870s. Others see the early 1880s as the turning-point. There is general agreement that a profound alteration in attitudes did take place, even if we choose to argue that it entailed a swift acceleration in the tempo of imperialist activity rather than an unprecedented development. The great-power pretensions of France or Britain might not be new: how to account, though, for the fever that seized King Leopold II of

♥JOHN BULL
LE PROTECTEVR
DES OPPRIMÉS

EGYPTE INDES   IRLAND   BELGIQUE   TRANSVAAL

JOHN BULL DER FREUND UND BESCHÜTZER DER KLEINEN.

modest little Belgium, leading him to create an immense semi-private exploitative colony in the Congo? Several different interpretations have been offered – depending in part on how one defines 'imperialism'. None is ultimately provable; none has gained universal acceptance. It is therefore necessary to review the main rival theories, since the beginning of this century.

What was Imperialism?

The first full-scale critique, *Imperialism* (1902), was by the prolific English writer J. A. Hobson, who had recently visited South Africa as a correspondent for the *Manchester Guardian*. Hobson supplied figures for the acquisitive energy of the major powers in the period 1870–1900. The United Kingdom, for example, with an area of 121,000 square miles and a population of 41 million, ruled an empire of well over 11 million square miles and a colonial population of 345 million. France, with an area of 204,000 square miles, asserted her authority over 3,741,000 square miles. Germany, with about the same area, controlled colonies totalling more than a million square miles. Nearly all the new colonies were in tropical regions, unsuitable for white settlement and thickly inhabited by 'lower races', whose voice in their own government was virtually non-existent and likely to remain so. These new colonies brought no benefit to the natives, and very little to the mass of people in the white overlord-countries. Why then had they been seized?

Hobson's explanation was that dominant economic interests *were* profiting from imperialism, and were able to direct national policy. In Britain these 'pushful Imperialists' included manu-facturers and contractors associated with ship-construction and armaments; exporters of textiles, machinery and hardware centred in cities like Manchester, Sheffield and Birmingham; the ship-building industry, which had managed to secure state subsidies 'for purposes of imperial safety and defence' (so that the British government underwrote the construction costs of the Cunard Line's ill-fated S.S. *Lusitania*); the army and navy, professionally concerned with the advancement of belligerence wherever feasible; and the other professions, 'diplomacy, the church, the bar, teaching and engineering', for whom 'Greater Britain serves for an overflow, relieving the congestion of the home market and offering chances to more reckless or adventurous

Opposite: A German wartime cartoon (1915) showing Great Britain posing as the champion of freedom while oppressing those nations under her sway.

123

A German view of Britain's involvement in the Boer War. Indifferent to European disapproval 'John Bulldog' is guarding the Kimberley Mines. 'Bark as much as you like, none of you is biting.'

members, while it furnishes a convenient limbo for damaged characters and careers.' Businessmen, the upper classes and the educated classes thus all had a bias toward imperialism.

The central economic factor was, however, investment, and the most active agents were bankers and financiers. Spare capital from the advanced nations was being placed abroad, with ruthless and irresponsible manipulative skill. Low wages in these countries kept down domestic consumption, so that home markets appeared to be glutted through overproduction. Manufactures as well as markets were being forced into colonial outlets, needlessly and ominously.

Lenin, drawing also upon the work of the Austrian economist Rudolph Hilferding, took further the arguments of Hobson in his book *Imperialism: The Highest Stage of Capitalism*, written in exile in Switzerland in 1916. According to Lenin, capitalism had passed from free competition to monopoly: 'cartels, syndicates and trusts, and merging with them, the capital of a dozen or so banks manipulating thousands of millions'. Imperialism was therefore, in the simplest terms, the monopoly stage of capitalism. Hobson had admitted that there might be several complementary explanations for imperialism. To the extent that it was irrational – that is, not in the true interests of the majority of people – he felt that it might indicate an upsurge of atavistic violence. So he ended his study by describing the movement as 'a depraved choice of national life, imposed by self-seeking interests which appeal to the lusts of quantitative acquisitiveness and of forceful domination surviving in a nation from early centuries of animal struggle for existence'. To the extent that he gave primacy of place to economic factors, he stopped short of indicting the whole structure of capitalist industry. As a good liberal reformer, Hobson deplored the 'under-consumption' forced upon the English workman. He was willing to think that a more equitable distribution of wealth in Britain and the other industrial nations might have made imperialist appetites unnecessary, or at any rate much milder.

Lenin's Marxist analysis focused upon the presumed inevitability of imperialism. Cartels and trusts had multiplied since the publication of Hobson's book. In response to what Lenin saw as an inexorable necessity, finance capitalism had persisted with its division of the spoils until none were left. Nor had activity been confined to straightforward acquisition. There were colonies, there were protectorates, there were spheres of influence and there were 'economic colonies' which might outwardly appear fully sovereign, or even, as in the case of Portugal, actually themselves possess colonies, yet be exploited by richer nations. For Lenin, something must give way when the imperialist carve-up was complete. Intolerable tensions had built up and must find release. The release, he thought, must entail a resort to force, in other words to war; and so the outbreak of war in 1914 was to Lenin essentially an imperialist conflict that helped to confirm the correctness of his diagnosis.

In face of a volume of supporting testimony, critics of the economic interpretation of imperialism have sometimes sounded either niggling or imprecise. It has been said, for instance, that Lenin and such writers as Leonard Woolf (*Empire and Commerce in Africa: A Study in Economic Imperialism*, 1919) are wrong because in fact little profit was derived from the new colonies as a whole. Though the Niger Company prospered, Rhodes's South Africa Company paid no dividend for several years. The East Africa Company never got going, and could not raise the money to build the projected Uganda railway that might have rescued it. Investment went mainly elsewhere, to more established societies. Two-thirds of the British capital invested abroad between 1870 and 1914 – a total of over £3,500 million – was laid out in the United States, Canada, Argentina, Australia and South Africa.

The entire German financial stake in Africa, up to 1914, amounted to less than their investment in Austria. But answers can be found to these contentions. Thus, it could be pointed out that one-fifth of Britain's overseas investments were in India, which also absorbed one-fifth of Britain's exports. Or we might note Lenin's insistence that a 'colony' need not be a recently acquired patch of jungle or desert. It could be any part of the world – a cattle-ranch in South America, a banana-plantation in the Caribbean, or even a subordinate *industrialized* area – where the finance capital of the 'usurer states' could parasitically attach itself. Another answer could be drawn from Hobson's admission that imperialism entailed a good deal of delusive folly. The important thing, he could have argued, was not whether new colonies were really profitable, but whether men and governments convinced themselves that there was a *potential* for profit – or that they could not afford to let competitors get in ahead of them, even if no immediate commercial advantage was discernible. Lenin too insisted on the insensate greed of monopoly capitalism: it strove to control the future as well as the present.

As for imprecision, this charge could be levelled against *Towards a Sociology of Imperialism* (1919), a famous essay by the Austrian economist Joseph Schumpeter. Picking up Hobson's suggestion that imperialism was in one context an atavistic survival, Schumpeter maintained that this was its central significance. Imperialism was not an economic instrument but a blind, tribal impulse: as he put it, 'the objectless disposition on the part of a state to unlimited forcible expansion', carried out by an anachronistic warrior-class which demanded 'war for the sake of fighting, victory for the sake of winning, dominion for the sake of ruling'. Schumpeter's ingenious thesis involved a denial that imperialism was a modern phenomenon. Capitalism was relatively modern, on his broad time-scale. But being modern, it was not anachronistic, not irrational, not belligerent; in fact capitalism, as illustrated by British nineteenth-century experience, was most successful where least distorted by protectionism and monopoly. And capitalism was unaggressive, in promoting democracy, individualism, Quakerishly peaceable instincts.

The weakness of Schumpeter's theory consists perhaps in his having portrayed capitalism as sensible, constructive and in a sense uncompetitive, and so in divorcing it altogether from 'kilometritis', 'milomania', *Torschlusspanik* – acquisitive greed, or – more negatively – fear of the closing door as a result of the activities of one's rivals. To say that these were ancient appetites was not to demonstrate that economic fevers did not affect them. Schumpeter's vision of nineteenth-century capitalism, with Britain the free-trader as the ideal example, is hard to square with the actual pace of imperial annexation, or with the way in which imperial spokesmen brought economic issues into their speeches. He overlooks the trend toward protectionism, which left the British in uneasy isolation, no longer able to dictate the patterns of world trade – and faced with protective tariffs in their own colony of Canada.

Nevertheless, we may conclude that if Schumpeter erred in one direction, by minimizing the tendencies of capitalism, Lenin erred at the opposite extreme by exaggerating them. His notion that any area economically weaker than some other area might serve as a 'colony' for finance capitalism – Belgian industry, for example, in relation to Germany, or the cotton-fields of Turkestan in relation to Tsarist Russia – is so broad as to be almost meaningless. By 1900, the American economy was the strongest in the world, yet a great deal of European capital was invested there. Did this render the United States a European colony? As we shall see in Chapter 6, Europeans were beginning to complain that the boot was on the other foot: they were subservient to American exports. It is true that in the 1890s American radicals, represented by the leaders of the Populist party, voiced intense economic grievances. In their view, the United States was being exploited by European international bankers, especially in tying them to the British gold-standard. Hobson too dwelt upon the machinations of the bankers (and with the same hint of anti-Semitism, as when he referred to the supposed international network of the Rothschilds). The Populists likewise asserted that the agrarian West and South of the United States were under the thumb of the industrial North-East. Such claims were not entirely unfounded. They could have been made for Ireland and Scotland within the British Isles, or for the relatively impoverished peasants of southern Italy as compared to the flourishing business communities of Turin and Milan. Lenin would no doubt have retorted that imperialism was merely the latest, most conspicuous manifestation of finance capitalism: the basic division in the world was not between one race and another, or one nation or empire and another, but between exploiters and exploited. Placed on this level of generalization, the Marxist analysis cannot be finally refuted. Nor however is it susceptible of proof. But certain of the

stages in Lenin's thesis appear dubious, as with all interpretations that seek to give primacy to economic motives.

Thus, can finance capitalism be said to be all-powerful if its chief agents were not themselves omnipotent? The international bankers, whatever their alleged intentions, clearly did not prevent the United States from becoming the leading economic nation in the world. If they, and industrial monopolists, were in collusion, why did they not collude more harmoniously? Theories of economic conspiracy are ultimately vague on this question of whether the conspirators succeeded in their aims, or failed. If

Livingstone in Africa. 'The Village of Manyema' from a sketch by H. M. Stanley. Missionary zeal such as Livingstone's paved the way for white settlement in many parts of the under-developed world.

128

they can be deemed successful, it is difficult to see why they countenanced a war in 1914 – a war that was to destroy empires, to ruin some of their societies, to kill some of their sons. To call the 1914–18 war 'imperialist' is to stretch the meaning of that term beyond manageable definition.

Other historians, moving further away from economic issues, have put more weight upon alternative factors. One element in the story is the apparent reluctance of governments to take on responsibilities overseas. Congress, which grumbled at the purchase-price of Alaska ('Seward's Folly' – in reference to Secretary of State William H. Seward), a mere $7,200,000 – could not be persuaded at all in the same year, 1867, to buy the Virgin Islands from Denmark, and did not complete the deal until 1916. British government spokesmen, Liberal and Conservative, were apt to talk of colonial problems in oddly funereal accents. The reason why the British found themselves in sole military occupation of Egypt in 1882 was that the French Chamber of Deputies refused to vote the expenses of a projected French expedition. This, note, was several years after the international slump of 1873, which has been cited as a reason for European capital to look elsewhere for more generous returns.

One theory, as expounded by the American historian Carlton J. H. Hayes, is that governments and businessmen needed to be primed to act, and that the stimulus came initially from explorers, romantics, professors, intellectuals. Some of the pioneers had served in the army or navy, which might have encouraged them to think of conquest. But they could also be seen as pure men of action – intrepid wanderers like the Frenchmen René Caillié and Pierre Brazza in equatorial Africa, the German surgeon Gustav Nachtigal in the Sudan, the Englishmen Harry Johnston and Frederick Lugard in East Africa, the Russian Skobelev in Turkestan. Or there were missionaries such as the German Friedrich Fabri, and the Scottish David Livingstone. The lectures and the writings of this breed of men, it is argued, caught the popular imagination to an extraordinary degree. Through Caillié, for instance, the public learned about the habits of gorillas, and enjoyed debating whether this animal was the 'missing link' between ape and man. Through Henry Morton Stanley, correspondent for the New York *Herald*, they re-lived the moment when he 'found' a supposedly missing hero and uttered the immortal words: 'Dr Livingstone, I presume?' Livingstone, having died in Africa, was borne home for a stately burial in England's national shrine, Westminster Abbey, in 1874.

After the tale, the moral. These gallant men were forerunners, blazing the trail for their countrymen to follow. Hence the publication of books like Sir Charles Dilke's *Greater Britain* (1868), the result of a world-tour, and *De la Colonisation chez les peuples modernes* (1874) by the French economist Paul Leroy-Beaulieu – incidentally an advocate of free-trade. Hence the sober eloquence of the historian Heinrich von Treitschke, firing his student audiences at the University of Berlin with the message that 'Every virile people has established colonial power'. Hence J. R. Seeley's contemporary lectures at Cambridge which, published in book-form as *The Expansion of England* (1883) sold eighty thousand copies in two years and brought him a knighthood. Missionaries such as Fabri imparted the same idea. Academics collaborated with public figures in founding 'colonial societies'. Leroy-Beaulieu, bringing out a new edition of his book in 1882, added the dictum that 'Colonization is for France a question of life and death: either France will become a great African power, or in a century or two she will be no more than a secondary European power; she will count for about as much in the world as Greece and Romania in Europe.'

In short, imperialism in this interpretation was not wholly, and perhaps not mainly, a matter of economics. It was a manifestation of the varied, miscellaneous yet impelling emotion of nationalism, an aspect examined in the previous chapter. One might expect it to mean different things to different nations, as a reflection of the blend of hopes, fears, interests, heritage peculiar to each. Once the competitive tempo had heightened, no nation dreaming of greatness dare stand aside. This would account for an apparent unanimity of behaviour despite the considerable variations in economic situation that bedevil strictly economic interpretations. The essential point would not be whether a nation possessed surplus capital or not, but how it visualized itself.

For some historians, imperialism is a mere by-product of European statecraft, especially as a makeweight in the manœuvres between Germany, France and Britain. A. J. P. Taylor is one of the scholars who has assigned the principal or at least the most dynamic role to Germany, more particularly to Bismarck as German Chancellor during the key decade of the 1880s. Taylor's argument, not accepted by all specialists, is that Germany acquired colonies as the accidental consequence of Bismarck's temporary preoccupation, around 1884, with a scheme for a Franco-German pact. The details of such theories need not concern us. Their broad assumption is that colonial expansion was an outcome – sometimes incidental, sometimes accidental – of diplomatic sparring.

Diplomatic history, moulded by the material it investigates, is apt to turn into a minute investigation of personal encounters and hypothetical calculations. If we broaden the inquiry a little, to take in domestic politics, this does seem to reinforce the theory that Bismarck used colonies as pawns. Indeed he may have intensified his consideration of colonial problems so as to preempt a line of attack by his opponents in the Reichstag. Bismarck is said to have remarked to a subordinate in 1884: 'All this colonial business is a sham but we need it for the elections.' Probably, in his few remaining years of power, he did come to share the increasing German conviction that colonies were essential, if only because other countries were swallowing them up.

A further interpretation suggests that Britain acquired colonies because she was already powerful, at any rate in naval and commercial respects. Interpretation has been given an intriguing twist by R. Robinson and J. Gallagher, most fully in their book *Africa and the Victorians* (1961). The Robinson-Gallagher theory dismisses economic interpretations as confusing cause and effect. They assume that British policy-makers had one overriding concern: the protection of India. This was consistent and logically applied. But the applications were as far-reaching as they were unforeseen. In order to make the Suez Canal secure, although they had not built it and not wished it to be built, the British, through the medium of Disraeli, were propelled into purchasing the Khedive's Canal shares. A few years afterward, though Gladstone in opposition had criticized the share-transaction, he was, as prime minister, obliged to send troops to occupy Egypt. This embroiled Britain also in the Sudan, leading to twenty years of strained relations with France and a number of crises – including the death of General Gordon at Khartum in 1885 and a sharp Franco-British clash at Fashoda in 1898.

Meanwhile, the Robinson-Gallagher theory claims, the whole partition of Africa followed as a chain-reaction. Jealousies between Britain and France set off a scramble in west Africa; and so on. The theory also emphasizes the early emergence of African (or rather, Islamic) nationalism. A rising of this type against the Bey of Tunis had prompted French intervention in

Overleaf: Port Said and the entrance to the Suez Canal, pictured at the end of the nineteenth century. Suez greatly extended the markets of the Far East and the Pacific to European trade.

131

Tunisia, as it was to bring the British into Egypt, to shore up the Khedive Tewfik against Arabi Pasha, and as it was to foment trouble for the British in the Sudan. The sequence of events does not seem to fit the Robinson-Gallagher argument at all points; nor perhaps have they accounted satisfactorily for the activities of other nations. What this and other interpretations do agree upon is the extent to which expansionism was produced by non-imperial factors, and, second, the extent to which the imperial nations were in fact trapped – just as opposition spokesmen were always warning governments. Once committed, they could not extricate themselves. Many Europeans no doubt sincerely believed in the expansionist rhetoric. For some political leaders, challenged to justify obscure deals or palpable setbacks, such rhetoric must have offered a welcome smokescreen.

Imperialism in the Balance

The auditors will probably never strike a final balance-sheet for the agglomerate loosely styled 'imperialism'. No single interpretation seems adequate to encompass all that was entailed. Some explanations cancel one another out. Thus imperialism can be faulted as a reckless, short-sighted activity, a matter of grabbing possessions because they were there and because someone else might grab them. Hence the absence of any coherent, systematic forecast of the future development of the colonies. 'Informal' economic imperialism did not require actual annexation, perhaps not even spheres of influence. But if that is an indictment of imperialism, it can also be cited in vindication, or at least in mitigation. Several of the new colonies had been colonies of older empires, and were only exchanging one overlord for another. Several were in turmoil before the white man arrived. If the Boers and Cape British were interlopers, so were the Bantu pushing down from the north. It is hard to believe that Egypt would have remained stable if the Suez Canal had never been built and the whites had stayed away. White ideological importations may have been as disruptive of native society as white technology. Yet surely these ideas of national and individual rights supplied the rationale of counter-imperialism? If mastery was one European precept, freedom and rebellion were the other side of a single coin. The new imperialism, which endured only a few decades, carried the seeds of its own destruction – if we view it as a formal apparatus.

134

Imperialism does not however seem to have been more than a minor factor in the destruction of Europe – the old Europe, that is – occasioned by the 1914–18 war. There were a number of apparently acute crises resulting from imperial rivalry. One came in 1884–5, when a Russian column occupied Pendjeh, close to the border of Afghanistan, and the British feared an invasion. There was the provocation of the 'Kruger telegram' in 1896, when the Kaiser cabled the president of the Transvaal to congratulate him on the failure of a foolish and unauthorized raid led by a British expansionist, Dr Leander Starr Jameson. There was the tension of 1898 when a British force led by Herbert Kitchener confronted a French detachment under Jean Baptiste Marchand at Fashoda in the Sudan. There were two patches of alarm, in 1905 and 1909, over German displays of involvement in Morocco. But none of these brought on a war. Britain's main rival in colonization, France, was her ally in 1914. Of her two chief rivals in trade, Germany and the United States, she went to war with one but was aided by the other.

In their own terms, the leading nations did face a dilemma. This was succinctly put by President McKinley in telling a delegation of clergymen how he had wrestled with the question of what to do about the Philippines, once the United States had defeated their Spanish occupiers:

It came to me this way ...: (1) That we could not give them back to Spain – that would be cowardly and dishonourable; (2) that we could not turn them over to France or Germany – our commercial rivals in the Orient – that would be bad business and discreditable; (3) that we could not leave them to themselves – they were unfit for self-government – and they would soon have anarchy and misrule ... worse than Spain's was; and (4) that there was nothing left for us to do but to take them all, and to educate the Filipinos, and uplift and civilize and Christianize them, and by God's grace do the very best we could by them, as our fellow men, for whom Christ also died.

McKinley, of course, reveals his ignorance; France was not a serious rival, and the Filipinos had been exposed to Christianity for centuries. Otherwise, his diagnosis was fairly sound, given the universal white conviction of superiority. Imperialists simply did not believe they could stand aside. We may feel they were hyperactive, and that they did far more harm than good.

That is a matter for debate. What does seem undeniable is that no part of the world could hope to remain unaffected for long by white magic, for good or for ill. It penetrated everywhere sooner or later, and was irresistibly fascinating. Once a hunter had seen a rifle, he was no longer content with arrow or spear. An iron pot was incontestably better than a clay pot for cooking on an open fire. Steampower was stronger than manpower. Was it the opening of Pandora's box? Perhaps. But the opening, once done, was irrevocable. The white nations would still have been immensely richer, more resourceful, more variously competent, if they had never possessed a colony. They came to depend upon tea, rubber, coffee, palm-oil and so on. But they could have acquired these to a modest extent by trade, or found substitutes. But why should they? The new imperialism was new in intensity. Otherwise it was the outcome of millennia of strife, experiment, motion, inquisitiveness, in which some societies had advanced so far ahead of the others in material accomplishment that any encounter between them was bound to be grossly unequal.

6 The American Continent

In the beginning was Action. With these famous words of Faust the future historian of the great Republic may begin. . . . Their genius may be defined as the universe of the *Dynamists*: force in movement. Above all, it has the capacity, the enthusiasm, the fortunate vocation, for doing things. . . . Their history is above all a very paroxysm of virile activity. Their typical figure should be entitled not Superman, but He Who Wants. . . . Today they openly aspire to the primacy of the world's civilization, . . . and think themselves the forerunners of all culture that is to prevail. . . . It were useless to seek to convince them that the fires lit upon European altars, . . . a work still being carried on and in whose traditions and teachings we South Americans live, makes a sum which cannot be equalled by any equation of Washington plus Edison. Would they even revise the Book of Genesis, to put themselves upon the front page? . . .

José Enrique Rodó, Ariel, *1900*

The oft-repeated contrast between a dynamic young continent and a tired elderly one had a particular appeal for Americans. The nineteenth-century Europeans who accepted it as accurate tended to regard North American life as a horrible warning to Europe. They saw the United States as an example of lawless, mercenary individualism: Europe's future fate unless 'Americanization' were resisted. Or, as men of culture, they were disturbed by what they took to be American philistinism. The obvious American response was either to retort that Europe was already in decay, or else that America's triumph was simply a matter of time. 'Other nations boast of what they are or have been,' said the British observer Alexander Mackay in his book *The Western World* (1849): 'the true citizen of the United States exalts his head to the skies in the contemplation of what the grandeur of his country is *going* to be. . . . If an English traveller complains of their inns and hints his dislike to sleeping four in a bed, he is first denounced as a calumniator and then told to wait a hundred years and see the superiority of American inns to British.'

Can we accommodate 'western' Europe and the transatlantic 'West' in the same scheme of things? A possible explanation is that the United States was even more grandiloquently sure of its greatness than were Britain, France or Germany. All flourishing nations in the epoch, we have seen, maintained that they were the standard-bearers of civilization, the repository of mankind's accumulated wisdom. 'Just cross the frontier', in the jocular boast of Alfred D'Almbert (*Flânerie Parisienne aux Etats Unis*, 1856), 'and it at once begins to dawn upon us how unrivalled we stand in all the tests of moral and spiritual refinement. . . . We must travel, travel, especially to the United States, only to see how wisely the good God has given the finest country to the best of nations – France.' The Americans had plenty of competition when they announced that the United States was in the van, the predestined champion of might and right. So we may discount some of the New World's zestful patriotism as the product of youthful exuberance, and remember that other nations were not renowned for modesty about themselves. American pretensions would then be recognized as fitting within the general pattern of braggart rivalry common to several dynamic nations.

What of the word 'America' or of the idea of Pan-Americanism? Did the independent nations of the American continent perceive common interests that bound them together and differentiated them from Europe? If so, did the United States function as their spokesman, or typify their reactions to the Old World? Writing in the early nineteenth century, Simón Bolívar the Liberator praised as a noble idea the attempt 'to form one single nation out of the whole new world with a single bond joining the parts to each other and to the whole'. In 1823, through the mouth of President James Monroe, the United States put forward a hemispheric doctrine that seemed to align all the nations of America into one emphatically non-European group. The Monroe Doctrine, as this policy-declaration came to be called, maintained that no part of the American continent should be subject to future European colonization; that the Americas had a political system essentially different from that of Europe; and that while the United States would oppose any European interference in the affairs of the New World, the US would respect the position of existing colonies and would keep clear of involvements in European internal affairs. A year later, Bolívar addressed a letter to the new govern-

Opposite above: The wagon trail moves West. Throughout the nineteenth century the westward movement of settlement was a constant theme of American development.

Opposite below: Cotton plantation on the Mississippi (1884). 'King Cotton' dominated the agricultural output of much of America's South.

138

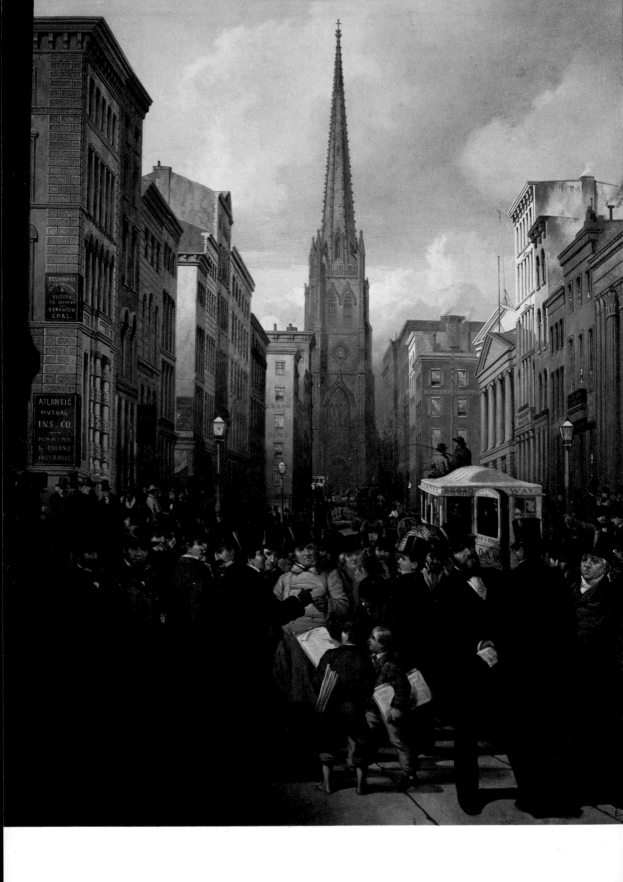

ments of Colombia, Rio de la Plata, Chile, Guatemala and Mexico that sounded equally ambitious in scope. He called for a meeting of the American republics, with the eventual aim of fusing them into 'one great body politic'. Such a meeting was held at Panama in 1826; in addition to the Latin American nations, the United States, Britain and the Netherlands were also invited.

On the surface, North and South America acknowledged a common heritage and a common purpose, at least in the realm of international politics. British participation could be accepted because Britain had sympathized with the Hispanic colonies and made clear its intention to resist any effort by the Holy Alliance of continental Europe to aid Spain in suppressing colonial revolt. Some historians portray Bolívar as an American 'continentalist'. In the view of the Mexican scholar Cuevas Cancino, 'Pan-Americanism originates in the Spanish-American countries; from them, it extends to include the Portuguese [in Brazil], then the free Anglo-Saxons [the United States], and finally, according to Bolívar's concept, the whole continent' – which would presumably embrace British Canada, Russian Alaska and other European mainland and Caribbean possessions such as Spanish Cuba and Puerto Rico. But this interpretation is disputed. Bolívar, it is said, spoke of his projected union as composed of nations with 'the same origin, language, customs, and religion': a definition that would exclude non-Spanish, non-Catholic countries. In his summons of 1824, he referred to 'the interests and relations linking the American republics, previously Spanish colonies'. The invitation to the United States to attend the Panama congress did not come from Bolívar but from his colleague Francisco de Paula Santander. On the other hand, he did think British protection essential for the planned union of Latin American states. 'Believe me, my dear General,' he wrote to Santander in 1825, 'we shall save the New World if we come to an agreement with England in *political and military matters*.'

If the Hispanic American attitude to hemispheric unity was ambivalent in these early stages, so was that of the United States. Ex-President Thomas Jefferson, discussing with Alexander von Humboldt the movement toward independence in the Spanish colonies, said in 1811 that whatever forms of government resulted, 'they will be *American* governments, no longer to be involved in the never-ceasing broils of Europe. The European nations constitute a separate division of the globe; ... they have a set of interests of their own in which it is our business never to engage

Opposite: Wall Street, Half Past Two in the Afternoon, by H. Cafferty. By the end of the nineteenth century Wall Street had an importance second only to London's Stock Exchange in the world of high finance.

141

ourselves. America has a hemisphere to itself.' Like his predecessor George Washington, Jefferson emphasized a recurrent anxiety of statesmen in both North and South America. They feared embroilment in wars brought on by Europe. Collective security was thus one aim of American nations; and in the early years of the century they were much more afraid of complications with Europe than, as later, of quarrels between themselves. But Jefferson had a further, almost mystically broad notion of America

An allegorical illustration of American progress (1873). The Indian retreats before the advance of the white man's pursuit of happiness.

142

that transcended politics and geography. Something in the hemispheric atmosphere, he seemed to think, would produce 'American' governments. Arthur P. Whitaker, in his analysis of *The Western Hemisphere Idea* (1954), notes that Jefferson claimed not that America *was* a separate hemisphere but that America *had* a separate hemisphere: he 'endowed this personified continent with supernatural powers'. Those who followed him in making American policy during the next few decades appear never to have quite jettisoned the belief in a hemispheric environmental magic: a magic also implied in the Spanish-American word *Americanidad* ('Americanity'). But on the whole, they tended to differentiate between the United States and its neighbours to the south. In 1820 Senator Henry Clay suggested an all-American solidarity to establish a 'rallying-point of human wisdom against the despotism of the Old World'. Next year, though developing the same theme, he perhaps significantly proposed an ideological counterforce to Europe's Holy Alliance 'in the two Americas'. Monroe's 1823 declaration also spoke in the plural of 'the American continents', as if geographically at any rate they were separated. In 1821, Monroe's secretary of state John Adams announced flatly that 'There is no community of interests between North and South America.' If there was any such thing as an American system, he had previously maintained, 'we [the United States] have it – we constitute the whole of it'. As a principal architect of the Monroe Doctrine, Adams seems to have incorporated these convictions in the new statement of continental oneness. The United States was to be the arbiter of hemispheric destiny, so far as the outside world was concerned.

Here a semantic confusion began to typify the equation of United States with hemispheric responsibility. Adams's nation referred to itself as 'American' because there was no other convenient adjective. The European usage 'Yankee' or the Latin American 'Yanqui' were pejorative in tone. That might not have mattered to citizens of the United States. The main trouble may have been that in their country a Yankee was a man from a particular area, New England. The term could not be applied to a Southerner or a Westerner, or even a New Yorker. Whatever the reason, citizens of the United States were content to call themselves 'Americans', with the effect that they seemed to annex the entire continent, claiming the part for the whole. To their neighbours it was one more example of Yanqui expansionism. Nor would any other term quite do. If US citizens were labelled

143

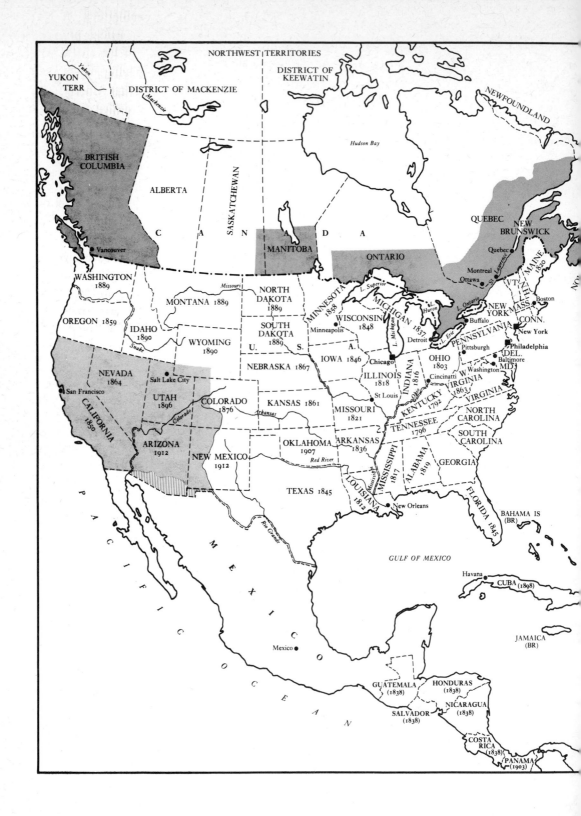

NORTHWEST TERRITORIES

DISTRICT OF KEEWATIN

YUKON TERR

DISTRICT OF MACKENZIE

Yukon

Mackenzie

NEWFOUNDLAND

BRITISH COLUMBIA

ALBERTA

SASKATCHEWAN

C   A   N   A   D   A

MANITOBA

Hudson Bay

ONTARIO

QUEBEC

NEW BRUNSWICK

Vancouver

Quebec

Montreal

Ottawa

St. Lawrence

MAINE 1820

WASHINGTON 1889

Missouri

MONTANA 1889

NORTH DAKOTA 1889

MINNESOTA 1858

L. Superior

MICHIGAN 1837

L. Huron

L. Ontario

NEW YORK

VT. N.H.

MASS.

Boston

OREGON 1859

IDAHO 1890

Snake

SOUTH DAKOTA 1889

WISCONSIN 1848

L. Michigan

Detroit

L. Erie

Buffalo

CONN.

WYOMING 1890

U.   S.   A.

IOWA 1846

Minneapolis

Chicago

OHIO 1803

PENNSYLVANIA

Pittsburgh

Philadelphia

New York

NEVADA 1864

Salt Lake City

NEBRASKA 1867

ILLINOIS 1818

INDIANA 1816

Ohio

W Washington

DEL. MD.

Baltimore

San Francisco

UTAH 1896

COLORADO 1876

KANSAS 1861

MISSOURI 1821

St Louis

KENTUCKY 1792

VIRGINIA

W VIRGINIA 1863

CALIFORNIA 1850

Colorado

Arkansas

TENNESSEE 1796

NORTH CAROLINA

ARIZONA 1912

NEW MEXICO 1912

OKLAHOMA 1907

ARKANSAS 1836

Red River

MISSISSIPPI 1817

ALABAMA 1819

GEORGIA

SOUTH CAROLINA

TEXAS 1845

LOUISIANA 1812

Mississippi

New Orleans

FLORIDA 1845

BAHAMA IS (BR)

Rio Grande

M   E   X   I   C   O

GULF OF MEXICO

Havana

CUBA (1898)

P   A   C   I   F   I   C

Mexico

JAMAICA (BR)

O   C   E   A   N

GUATEMALA (1838)

HONDURAS (1838)

SALVADOR (1838)

NICARAGUA (1838)

COSTA RICA (1838)

PANAMA (1903)

norteamericanos, North Americans, that obliterated the Canadians. 'Anglo-Saxon' was fair enough, considering that South America was dubbed 'Latin', but a vague designation, laying more stress on the European WASP background of the United States than some of its inhabitants found palatable.

The Newness of the New World

During the nineteenth century, various European liberals, reformers and technologists continued to treat America, by which they had come to mean the United States, as a special place enjoying freedoms that were absent elsewhere. Across the Atlantic, according to Englishmen like Richard Cobden and John Bright, democracy and minimal government were twin achievements.

The American was not taxed to pay for monarchical courts and hangers-on, or for armies and fleets; on the eve of its civil war, the United States had fewer than twenty thousand professional soldiers. This handful was raised without conscription, and enlisted for much shorter periods than among the armies of Europe. All male American citizens were entitled to vote well before the 1840s; there was no longer a property qualification. Class distinctions were far less sharp than in the Old World. Until the 1890s, the United States declined to appoint diplomatic officials to the top rank of ambassador; none held a higher post than that of minister.

Whether immigrant or native-born, most Americans were quick to accept that there was a profound difference between the New World and the Old, and to believe that the advantage lay with the New. This was probably true also of Latin America. The northern part of the continent cherished its tales of British brutality and snobbery, as these were supposed to have been revealed during the Revolutionary era. Anglophobia was kept alive in the nineteenth century by Irish-Americans in particular, but also through a general mood of exasperated rivalry; and a more diffused xenophobia led Americans to treat mainland Europe as quaint, backward, corrupt, unhygienic, incompetent, priestridden and so on. North Americans were apt to dismiss Europe as a superannuated irrelevance, at least in their more exuberant moments. Spanish Americans, on the other hand, complained that they were still being clutched by the dead hand of the past. In both cases, though, the patriotic impulse stirred them to look for indigenous models.

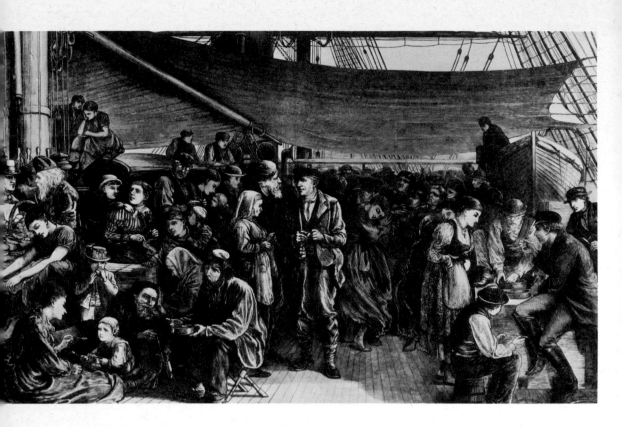

The American population expanded throughout the nineteenth century, largely as a result of immigration from Europe. Here an engraving of a German steamship (1872) shows steerage class passengers on the way to the New World.

In both halves of the hemisphere, novelties of environment could be perceived. All the new nations had been largely peopled from overseas, though they had also had to reckon with the aboriginal population and had been affected by this contact in various ways. In the family history of every settler was the gigantic experience – some writers have called it a trauma – of the ocean crossing. The great majority meant to transplant themselves permanently and did so. Even toward the end of the period, when steamship travel was safe, quick and fairly cheap, emigration was a momentous decision for the ordinary person. The Atlantic Ocean distanced those who traversed it from their old countries, metaphorically no less than literally. To the sea-gulf was added the new sense of distance absorbed by settlers who might once have measured their lives on the parish scale but who were now, however vicariously, the masters of a seemingly limitless domain.

The mingling of peoples was another unique feature of the New World, according to its interpreters. They poured in and then were poured together. The process is lyrically celebrated in *Redburn* (1849), a semi-autobiographical novel by Herman

146

Melville, who had watched German emigrants preparing to leave Europe *via* Liverpool for New York. He praised the sobriety and sturdiness of these pilgrim bands:

Our blood is as the flood of the Amazon, made up of a thousand noble currents all pouring into one. . . . We are the heirs of all time, and with all nations we divide our inheritance. On this Western Hemisphere all tribes and people are forming into one federated whole; and there is a future which shall see the estranged children of Adam restored as to the old hearth-stone in Eden.

Such rhetoric would not have appealed to the American Indian or to the involuntary immigrant carried from black Africa into New World slavery. For good or ill, though, Negro slavery was yet another feature common to North and South America and distinguishing them from Europe. Hardly an Adamic experience, it was nevertheless a special and profound one; and for whatever reasons Americans might deplore the presence of Negroes on their continent, they could lay the initial blame at the feet of Europe for having introduced the trade to the hapless New World colonies. Slavery, plantations, racial mixture, schemes for emancipation, social and economic consequences: these were to a peculiar degree preoccupations of the New World – ironic, tragic perhaps, in the light of the visionary assertion that it was the earthly paradise, yet something to be lived with in the American context. Indeed, for Latin America it was in sheer numbers almost a paramount factor. During the 1820s, the 'era of independence', only one in five of a total population of twenty-three million were white. No less than forty-five per cent were Negro or part-Negro (mulatto), and the remainder Indian.

Patriots preferred to dwell on more attractive aspects of Americanness: on freedoms, that is, rather than subjugation. The ideal America of the nineteenth century, extolled by political orators and given mythical resonance in imaginative literature, was republican, democratic, individualistic, informal, agrarian or pastoral.

The Leatherstocking novels of James Fenimore Cooper sprinkled the wilderness landscape with figures, and provided readers on both sides of the Atlantic with living symbols of New World heroism. Cooper's central white hero is given the inelegant name of Natty Bumppo, as if the author wished to indicate that he is no well-bred character of conventional fiction; Leatherstocking, the Indian name for him, referring to the clothes he wears, is equally remote from the world of the salon. Natty is, in the words of the French writer Honoré de Balzac, a 'magnificent hermaphrodite, born between the savage and the civilized'. He is a noble savage who also possesses the white man's gifts – at least the more admirable ones. He can live in the forest or prairie wilderness as successfully as his Indian friends and enemies; he is a native who has not 'gone native'. Modest, humane, intuitive, stoical, chivalrous, reticent, resourceful, Natty is thus a new American creation. He is nature's gentleman, in answer to the European conception of a gentleman as the product and ornament of high society. Natty's code of conduct is personal, not social. As the United States declared its independence of Britain, so Natty has severed himself from the complexities of settled existence. In this enduring New World myth, the individual hero re-enacts in his own person the larger hemispheric dramas of repudiation and mobility. There were other versions of the basic myth. Cooper presented memorable Indian heroes, notably the Mohican chief Chingachgook; and the popularity of novels about Red Indians by the Anglo-Irishman Mayne Reid, the Frenchman Gustave Aimard and the prolific German author Karl May, showed that the appetite for American wilderness themes was universal.

In the public sphere, the United States produced actual heroes whose qualities could be thought characteristic of a New World environment. President Andrew Jackson, who died in 1845, symbolized opportunity, achievement and courage. Almost without formal education, he had yet been successful as lawyer, planter, soldier and politician; and, being from Tennessee, counted as a Westerner. Abraham Lincoln of Illinois was likewise self-made, a 'log-cabin-to-White-House' statesman. The novelist Nathaniel Hawthorne, after meeting him in 1862, said that

Western man though he be, and Kentuckian by birth, President Lincoln is the essential representative of all Yankees, and the veritable specimen, physically, of what the world seems determined to regard as our characteristic qualities.... There is no describing his lengthy awkwardness ...; and yet it seemed as if I had been in the habit of seeing him daily, and had shaken hands with him a thousand times in some village street; so true was he to the aspect of the pattern American....

When Lincoln's assassination made him a martyr, in 1865, at the moment of victory in the Civil War, his place in history was

THE
LAST OF THE MOHICANS.

BY

JAMES FENIMORE COOPER.

NEW YORK:
D. APPLETON AND COMPANY, PUBLISHERS.

Above: The assassination
of Abraham Lincoln,
President of the United
States during the crisis of
Civil War, on 14 April
1865.

Right: Roping Wild Horse,
a painting by James
Walker (1877).

150

assured. Much derided, at home and abroad, he was now to be depicted as the apotheosis of the common man. On Lincoln's death, the editor of London's *Punch*, hitherto highly critical, belatedly but contritely found 'this rail-splitter a true-born king of men'. To the Boston *littérateur* James Russell Lowell, Lincoln was: 'new birth of our new soil, the first American'. The epitome of the West, he was also the supreme exemplar of the Union, the entire nation.

In American symbolism, this was only natural. It was frequently said that the West was the most American part of the continent: the least settled, the furthest away from European influences. The wide open spaces were the realm of the horseman, the cattle-ranch, the cowboy. In Latin America, indeed, the *gaucho*, the *llanero*, the *charro* preceded the North American cowboy, and passed earlier into legend, imparting to the popular literature of the United States several words – *coyote, desperado, sombrero, vamoose, bronco, hombre, lasso, calaboose* and the like – that the ordinary Anglo-Saxon reader soon took to be part and parcel of the Wild West's 'traditions'. The actual life-span of the open-range cattle kingdom in the United States was extremely

short. It was confined within the decades of 1870–90 and was already acquiring a tinge of folklorish nostalgia when Theodore Roosevelt, who had lost most of his investment as a young rancher in Dakota during the 1880s, captured the newspaper headlines by raising a volunteer regiment of 'Roughriders' for service in the Spanish-American War of 1898.

> Across the plains where once there roamed
>   The Indian and the scout
> The Swede with alcoholic breath
>   Sets rows of cabbage out.

This doggerel of the 1890s recorded the supersession of the cowboy by the humdrum farmer. But in the realm of myth, the cowboy was only beginning to assume his role in the American dream, as a latter-day Leatherstocking, a mounted knight without ancestry, owning little more than a saddle, a blanket and a Colt revolver. The *gaucho* was celebrated in some near-epic poetry such as the Argentine *Martín Fierro* (1872).

A hundred years after Jefferson, America still 'signified' something, to Europeans as well as its own inhabitants. Its geography, including the very term 'America', was hard to pin down. America was a place but also a state of mind – and this conditioned the place. Certain observers had always suspected that its real quality was not innocence but vulgarity, greed, violence, especially where the United States was concerned. By about 1890, foreign travellers were more intrigued by such symbols of Americanness as factories, hotels, skyscrapers and city bosses than by forest and prairie. They went to the Rocky Mountains not for Alpine scenery but to look at gold-rush towns of the sort made famous in the stories of Bret Harte. As with the folklore of the Wild West, there was something anachronistic, or at any rate difficult to locate precisely in time or space, in the celebrated 'frontier thesis' propounded by the historian Frederick Jackson Turner in 1893. He took as his starting-point the disclosure of the recent national census that the United States no longer had a frontier of open land awaiting white settlement. The first transcontinental railroad had been completed as far back as 1869; the great herds of buffalo, slaughtered by the million, were almost vanished; the Mormons' desert territory of Utah had at last joined the Union. At this poignant stage in American development, Turner offered a culminating theory of what had made the New World a different place. America, he reiterated,

Opposite: From the Atlantic to the Pacific. A poster of 1869 heralds the railroad link from ocean to ocean.

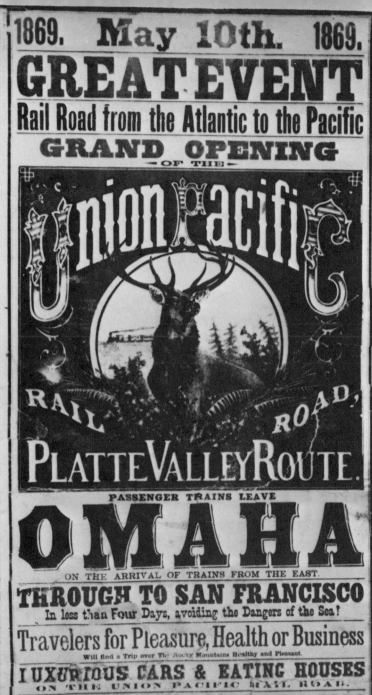

1869. May 10th. 1869.
GREAT EVENT
Rail Road from the Atlantic to the Pacific
GRAND OPENING
— OF THE —

Union Pacific
RAIL ROAD,
PLATTE VALLEY ROUTE.

PASSENGER TRAINS LEAVE
OMAHA
ON THE ARRIVAL OF TRAINS FROM THE EAST.

THROUGH TO SAN FRANCISCO
In less than Four Days, avoiding the Dangers of the Sea!

Travelers for Pleasure, Health or Business
Will find a Trip over The Rocky Mountains Healthy and Pleasant.

LUXURIOUS CARS & EATING HOUSES
ON THE UNION PACIFIC RAIL ROAD.

PULLMAN'S PALACE SLEEPING CARS
RUN WITH ALL THROUGH PASSENGER TRAINS.

GOLD, SILVER AND OTHER MINERS!
Now is the time to seek your Fortunes in Nebraska, Wyoming, Arizona, Washington, Dakotah Colorado, Utah, Oregon, Montana, New Mexico, Idaho, Nevada or California.

CONNECTIONS MADE AT
CHEYENNE for DENVER, CENTRAL CITY & SANTA FE
AT OGDEN AND CORINNE FOR HELENA, BOISE CITY, VIRGINIA CITY, SALT LAKE CITY AND ARIZONA.

THROUGH TICKETS FOR SALE AT ALL PRINCIPAL RAILROAD OFFICES!
Be Sure they Read via Platte Valley or Omaha

Company's Office 72 La Salle St., opposite City Hall and Court House Square, Chicago,
CHARLES E. NICHOLS, Ticket Agent.

G. P. GILMAN,	JOHN P. HART,	J. BUDD,	W. SNYDER,
South-eastern Traveling Agent,	Gen'l Pass. Agt., 72 La Salle St., Chicago.	Gen'l Ticket Act., Omaha, Neb.	Gen'l Superintendent, Omaha, Neb.

ROUNDS & LEONARD RAILROAD PRINTERS, CHICAGO.

was a westering pioneer civilization, formed by the necessity of discarding its baggage of Europeanness and confronting the edge of the wilderness. The settlers had had to start all over again and to keep on doing this. Not European heredity but the frontier environment had shaped the American character: restless, democratic, Jacksonian and Lincolnian, impatient of authority, inclined to pugnacity, sanguine, pragmatic.

Turner summarized and articulated what had long been felt. He consoled himself and his countrymen, at the moment when they seemed about to lose a distinguishing aspect of identity, with the assertion that the New World environment had in fact supplied a heritage if not a heredity. True, there were logical difficulties in the frontier thesis. If environment were so powerful, what would happen to the American character when the scene became predominantly urban and industrial? There were frontiers of the Turnerian sort all over the world. Each according to his thesis ought to produce the same kind of freedom-loving temperament. If each did, then what of the Turnerian implication that the United States had evolved a unique character? If, on the other hand, these frontier societies displayed varying characteristics, might this not indicate the persistence of Old World traits? For the next generation of confident Americans, Theodore Roosevelt and Woodrow Wilson among them, such queries seemed unimportant. America they felt was a palimpsest in which every decipherable layer referred to indigenous sources. The remoter ones in time were European, in the sense that the Atlantic seaboard settlements had once been Europe's frontier, but had been Americanized. America was a successive chronology of frontier Wests.

Transatlantic Links

Turner was himself a Middle Westerner, from Wisconsin. His first research was on the Indian fur trade. He was reacting against the 'germ theory' of historical evolution which sought to trace latter-day institutions back to earliest origins. In the case of legal and governmental institutions, this usually led scholars back to Anglo-Saxon England, and further beyond into tribal Germany. To some extent, then, Turner's ideas were conditioned by boyhood days in Portage, Wisconsin, and the germ theory – frontier theory dispute was a scholastic one, since all historical interpretations boil down to an argument over continuity versus discontinuity. Turner was too professional a historian to be unaware of what he was doing. As a young scholar, casting about for a worthwhile task, he noted that there were two major themes in modern history, each concerned with shifts of population. One was the settlement of new lands; the other was the growth of cities. Both were prominent in American experience. But urbanization had also been a European phenomenon; so, in his eagerness to stress 'Americanity', he decided to fasten upon the frontier.

Such dilemmas were not restricted to the academic community. They were faced by every thoughtful inhabitant of the New World – as well as by other settler countries. In *The Founding of New Societies* (1964), Louis Hartz and some colleagues attempt to compare the United States, Latin America, French Canada, South Africa and Australia. Hartz, who dismisses Turner in a paragraph, believes that they should all be regarded as parts of a European whole. More exactly, the parts are fragments. Each fragment society is dominated by one element from the richly diverse parent culture. It is therefore incomplete, and it is ideologically static no matter how bustling in other ways. The fragment society lacks a full dialectic, so its controversies are sterile and repetitious. Thus the United States is stuck with a set of eighteenth-century Enlightenment ideas, Latin America with still more ancient philosophical conceptions.

The fragment theory departs fundamentally from the Turnerian emphasis on geography. Far from being ignored, European origins are given pride of place. Hartz's formulation is a welcome relief from preoccupation with Americanness; his comparative approach represents an effort to deal with several continents, not simply with the components of a hypothetical Atlantic Civilization. By focusing on intellectual-cum-sociological history, it intriguingly reverses the notion that if Europe was dynamic, the United States was still more so. In the Hartzian view, the fragment cultures contributed little or nothing to ideological kinesis: Europe still headed the field.

One defect of the fragment idea may be that it limits influences upon America to Europe. Recent writers, also trying to broaden the scope of history, maintain that African and Asian elements in American development should be given fuller recognition. A more serious objection, hinted at in the story of Turner's memorandum to himself, is that for Hartz, as for Turner, Europe is not much more than a bygone factor, a mere backdrop. Americans and Europeans of our period remained much more aware of one another and had much more effect upon one another than could be gathered from *The Founding of New Societies.* The book does usefully draw attention to the existence of a Europe-America dialectic, but not to the continuance of this. Even the most intransigent expressions of 'Americanity' invoked a European antithesis. America had to be defined in terms of what it was *not*; and Europeans likewise tended to call upon an idea of America – not necessarily a well-informed idea – in order to establish what they would wish their own societies to be.

Examined in this light, many assertions of American difference make no sense unless Europe is brought in to provide an imagined contrast. Different from *what*? Different from Europe. Any other comparison would give very little purchase. A contrast, that is, entails being able to draw up a schedule of items that can meaningfully be put into parallel columns. One cannot compare a sewing-machine with a camel, or an oyster with a prayer-mat. There must be a congruity; and this existed abundantly in both Americas, so far as Europe was involved. It is easy to think of the kinds of differences that have already been enumerated, and important to understand the New World's psychological need to feel it represented a fresh start. But the contrary can be stated with equal validity: continuity can be seen as more impressive than discontinuity. North America continued to speak English; throughout our period, English literature and thought prevailed over native products – a fact often deplored by Americans but not overcome. Americanisms and some American books did have an impact across the Atlantic, yet this interplay was remarkably smooth. Institutions were mutually involved in the same way. The two continents learned from one another, though it should be said that the United States drew increasingly upon the experience of continental Europe, especially Germany, for innovations in such fields as education.

Almost every North American writer of consequence – Whitman is a lonely exception – travelled in Europe; some, including Cooper, Hawthorne and Twain, stayed for several years; others, including Henry James and T. S. Eliot, came for good. The majority of well-known British authors visited and wrote about the United States: Charles Dickens, Anthony Trollope, Matthew Arnold, Rudyard Kipling, Robert Louis Stevenson and H. G. Wells are examples. 'The longer I lived in the States,' the Englishman Edward Dicey said of a journey made in 1862, 'the more I became convinced that America was, to use a mathematical metaphor, the complement of England. The national failings, as well as the national virtues of the New World, are very much those of the mother country, developed on a different and a broader scale' – in this case, referring to racial prejudice in the two nations. An American contributor to the *Atlantic Monthly*, just a few months earlier, insisted that 'The features of society in Great Britain and in all our Northern regions are almost identically the same, or run in parallelisms, by which we might match every phenomenon, incident, prejudice, and folly, every good and every bad trait ... in the one place with something exactly like it in the other.' A minor case relates to transatlantic borrowings in sensational literature. Eugène Sue's *Mysteries of Paris* (1842), a work of titillation and melodrama, stimulated an English journalist to produce *The Mysteries of London* (1845–8), and an American followed with *The Mysteries and Miseries of New York* (1848). What was true at a trivial level – transatlantic enthusiams, say, for the light operas of Offenbach and Gilbert and Sullivan, or for recreations like tennis, cycling and golf – was also true of high and middlebrow culture. Charles Darwin, Herbert Spencer, John Ruskin, Robert Browning were revered names among the reading public of the United States. Henry Wadsworth Longfellow, Oliver Wendell Holmes and Mark Twain were almost equally admired in Europe. Cosmopolitan Americans made themselves thoroughly at home in the Old World. The historian John L. Motley knew Bismarck from his days as a student in Germany, wrote the universally praised *Rise of the Dutch Republic* (1856), served as United States minister in Vienna and London and was given a memorial sermon in Westminster Abbey in which Dean Stanley said that Holland would be 'indissolubly connected with the name of Motley in that union of the ancient culture of Europe with the aspirations of America'. Twentieth-century interpreters of the United States have preferred to fasten upon more singularly native cultural representatives such as Whitman and Herman Melville, or the sculptor Horatio Greenough who proclaimed that beauty of design derived not from decoration but from functional rightness – as with the clipper ship. But in the nineteenth century Whitman and Melville were secondary figures, whose reputations stood somewhat higher in Europe than in their own country; and Greenough's doctrines failed to impress his contemporaries.

In Latin America too, *Americanidad* ('Americanness') proved to be an elusive notion. Not one state ratified a treaty of alliance drawn up at the Lima Congress of 1864–5. The Argentinian foreign minister Elizalde maintained that 'The American republics have more ties of common interest and sympathy with several of the European states than with one another.' Though Latin American men of letters of the era – the Venezuelan Andrés Bello, the Chilean Francisco Bilbao, the Cuban José Martí – postulated a New World spirit, they leaned heavily upon European literary modes. In the second half of the nineteenth century, the positivism of Auguste Comte enjoyed an extraordinary vogue. Hispanic American intellectuals, in tune with leading politicians, laboured to introduce into their societies everything they took to be progressive in European thought and technology. Sometimes, as with the Argentinians Domingo Sarmiento and Alberdi, this appeared to take the form of a repudiation of Europe and an attachment to the New World model of prosperous liberty associated with the United States. But theirs was only a temporary recommendation; nor were they resurrecting a truly hemispheric dream. What they were exasperated by was the backwardness of Latin civilization, the heritage of Iberian and Mediterranean Europe; Anglo-Saxon energy, whether displayed in northern Europe or in the United States, was what they envied. The intelligentsia craved modernity wherever it came from.

By 1900 Europeans were complaining with almost hysterical vehemence that their continent was being Americanized, or joked resignedly about the flood of American food and manufactures. One British account, *The Invaders*, pictured a Londoner eating an American breakfast and reading a newspaper printed on American woodpulp by American machines. 'At his office, of course, everything is American. He sits on a Nebraskan swivel chair, before a Michigan roll-top desk, writes his letters on a Syracuse typewriter, signing them with a New York fountain pen, and drying them with a blotting-sheet from New England. The letter copies are put away in files manufactured in Grand Rapids.' This passage is cited in another British book, W. T. Stead's *The Americanization of the World* (1901), but, to be fair, German economic imperialism was similarly attacked, in a campaign against goods 'Made in Germany', from the mid-1890s. Some Europeans spoke of 'the American Peril', but they were exaggerating, for comic or polemic effect. And they were really talking about modernization rather than about specific American influences. The dynamic nations were getting more like one another; the triumph of the United States consisted in having outclassed

Opposite: An American view, 1901. New World prosperity seemed set fair on a course of unending growth at the expense of the Old World.

Journal.]   [New York.

What it may come to.

Uncle Sam: "I'll let you keep your little stand in front of my place
John, as long as you behave yourself."

The Fathers of Confederation, a painting by Robert Harris. As a result of their deliberations Canada was formed, in 1867, from the provinces of Upper and Lower Canada, New Brunswick and Nova Scotia.

the parent societies, in having more successfully applied the European gospel of work, thrift, acquisition. Certain previous expectations had turned out to be wrong, though this was not always realized. In the mid-nineteenth century, for example, there was a fairly widespread assumption in the United States that British North America must inevitably come under the Stars and Stripes. In a sense it did. The self-governing Dominion of Canada (1867) threatened to become a poor relation of the United States, vulnerable to economic penetration and losing population. During the 1880s, over a million people emigrated across the border: more than a fifth of the entire population of Canada. Then, however, Canada began to boom. By 1914, the flow of settlement had been reversed, bringing over a million Americans into the Canadian prairie provinces; and Canadian national pride, a factor that had been overlooked in American prognostications, was actually heightened rather than undermined by proximity to Uncle Sam.

160

The Two Americas

One of Motley's main beliefs, shared by various British and German historians and with his American *confrères* George Bancroft, William H. Prescott and Francis Parkman, was that Northern races were innately superior. History proved as much. Democracy, energy, stability were the hallmark of the predominantly Protestant Anglo-Saxon or Teutonic nations: aristocracy, sloth and instability characterized the Latin or Celt of Roman Catholic lands. This notion was not incompatible with a conviction that the United States led the leaders. England was regarded as an unduly complacent, deferential society, and Germany as dangerously militarist. Nevertheless, there was a strong feeling of ancestral affinity with Britain and Germany, a certain racial pride in their imperial prowess and a readiness to agree in distinguishing between what the British parliamentarian Dilke called the 'dear' and the 'cheap' races.

Racial dogmas provided a convenient shorthand explanation for North America of what had gone wrong in the rest of the hemisphere. The Anglo-Saxons had a 'manifest destiny' to overspread the continent. Might was a proof of right. Indeed, superiority was not a matter of numbers but of vigour and courage. So, in the common United States view, Mexico's larger army was bound to be defeated in the war of 1846–8, and in the logic of history foreordained to relinquish California and New Mexico to a race better equipped to develop these regions. Including Texas, which was annexed to the Union in 1845, the United States took possession of nearly a million square miles of territory formerly under the Mexican flag. North Americans could discern no geographical inevitability in the shifting boundaries and demarcation conflicts of the Latin republics. While the United States was from the outset a 'continental' nation in aim, the former Spanish colonies seemed to risk becoming fragments of a fragment – emerging like Uruguay (1828) as a bone of contention between Argentina and Brazil; or disintegrating as the Central American Federation did (1838) into a jigsaw of small states (Guatemala, Honduras, El Salvador, Nicaragua, Costa Rica);

Paraguayan gunboats sink a Brazilian warship in the war of the Triple Alliance (1864–70). As a result of this war, however, Paraguay suffered considerable territorial losses to her neighbours.

or re-forming out of hopeful early visions (Bolívar's large northern nation split into New Granada – later Colombia – and Venezuela and Ecuador). In mid-century, only Chile and the ex-Portuguese colony of Brazil, an 'empire' under a Portuguese dynasty until 1889, seemed stable; Argentina was in the grip of a ruthless dictator, Juan Manuel de Rosas, 'the boss of Buenos Aires', who was finally overthrown in 1852. Frontiers were not sacrosanct in Latin America: witness the War of the Triple Alliance (1864–70), in which Paraguay lost a considerable amount of territory to Argentina, Brazil and Uruguay, or the grandly named War of the Pacific (1879–83), which enabled Chile to seize rich nitrate deposits from Bolivia and Peru. To the outside world, Latin America was a chaos of strife between nation and nation, and inside each nation between centralizers and federalists, reactionaries and revolutionaries, the leader of the moment and others seeking to topple his régime. In some countries, such as Argentina and Chile, power was held firmly in the hands of a small clique; in other countries, such as Mexico, the political establishment was under much pressure from below. In Mexico, the opposition to the dictator Porfirio Díaz embraced constitutionalists, like Francisco Madero, the military, in the person of General Huerta, and, a peculiarly Mexican phenomenon, the people, in the form of the almost messianic peasant leader, Emiliano Zapata. But in most countries of Hispanic America, there was a group which succeeded the Spanish as the holders of power who were often as divorced from the people as the Spanish had been. 'Anglo Saxon' onlookers tended to class *all* Latin Americans as 'dagoes', ripe for exploitation.

So they had few scruples in treating Latin America as a lucrative but risky field for investment, with the rider that it might be necessary to intervene in order to safeguard foreign capital. Britain and France blockaded the Plate river in 1845. They co-operated with Spain in establishing a Mexican monarchy under Maximilian, the brother of the Austrian emperor, in 1864–7, though the main initiative was French. In 1895, Britain occupied a Nicaraguan port to enforce payment of debts. In 1902–3 British, German and Italian warships blockaded Venezuela for the same purpose. Spain refused to recognize the independence of ex-colonies. Mexico had to wait until 1839 for this formal acknowledgment. Honduras, the last to receive it, was ignored by Madrid until 1895.

The reactions of the United States could be seen as equivocal.

On the one hand there was the clamour of publicists like the Reverend Josiah Strong, who in his book *Our Country* (1885) argued that the Anglo-Saxon was 'divinely commissioned' to be his brother's keeper. 'If I read not amiss, this powerful race will move down upon Mexico, down upon Central and South America, out upon the islands of the sea, over Africa and beyond. And can anyone doubt that the result of this competition of the races will be the "survival of the fittest"?' On the other hand, as soon as the crisis of its civil war was over, the United States put pressure on Napoleon III to withdraw the troops that were supporting Maximilian in Mexico. In the 1880s, the American secretary of state, James G. Blaine, was the chief architect of a new design for a Pan-American economic and defensive alliance. In 1895, another secretary of state, Richard Olney, with President Cleveland's blessing, delivered a sharp warning to Britain, then involved in a boundary dispute with Venezuela, not to infringe the Monroe Doctrine's principle that 'No European power or combination of European powers shall forcibly deprive an American state of the right and power of self-government and of shaping for itself its own political forces and destinies.' In 1898, the United States again ostensibly championed Latin American interests by going to war to compel Spain to give up Cuba, where a vicious war of rebellion had been dragging on for years.

There was, of course, no real discrepancy. The United States was flexing its muscles, greatly to the annoyance of most of the European powers, and was benefiting from European weaknesses to strengthen its own hemisphere. Olney and Cleveland well knew that 'twisting the lion's tail' by challenging Britain would be popular with the electorate; this was a standard gambit in American domestic politics. If they could steal a march on Britain, the other principal foreign investor in Latin America, so much the better; Blaine, trying to persuade Congress of the advantages of his brand of Pan-Americanism, held out the prospect of 'a large increase in the export trade of the United States, by supplying fabrics in which we are abundantly able to compete with the manufacturing nations of Europe'. But in essence the United States was not taking sides with America against Europe. Olney was sincere when he privately remarked to a British diplomat that 'If only you had agreed [earlier] to our arbitration the President and I would have favoured you in every way we could as against the Spanish-Americans – all our predilections were English.' He added: 'Venezuela has got to do exactly as we tell

164

Caracas

VENEZUELA

PANAMA

Orinoco

BRITISH

DUTCH

FRENCH

G U I A N A

Bogota

COLOMBIA
Rep. from 1886

Negro

Quito

ECUADOR

Manáus

Amazon

UNITED STATES

Ucayali

OF BRAZIL

Tocantins

Until 1889 Empire of Brazil

PERU

Lima

La Paz

São Francisco

BOLIVIA

PACIFIC
OCEAN

Paraguay

Paraná

PARAGUAY

Rio de Janeiro

São Paulo

Asunción

CHILE

Valparaiso

Santiago

URUGUAY

ATLANTIC
OCEAN

Buenos Aires

Montevideo

Concepción

ARGENTINA
Rep. from 1853

Salada

P A T A G O N I A

1881 to Arg.

South America in 1914

A small tug-boat tests the locks on the Panama Canal, prior to its opening as one of the great shipping routes of the world.

her.' This was accurate; the arbitration award was imposed on Venezuela, and conceded much less than had been hoped for in Caracas.

The significance of these activities was that the United States now felt itself to be a world power, strong enough to oblige other nations to accept its predominance throughout the American hemisphere. The Monroe Doctrine, lying dormant for decades, was now resurrected as a self-evident proposition. Pan-Americanism in the United States version was not fraternal but paternal; the 'Colossus of the North' announced that all the republics to the south were henceforward under the benevolent supervision of Washington, DC. In the 'Roosevelt corollary' to the Monroe Doctrine, President Theodore Roosevelt declared in 1904:

Chronic wrongdoing, or an impotence which results in a general loosening of the ties of civilized society, may in America, as elsewhere, ultimately require intervention by some civilized nation, and in the Western Hemisphere, the adherence of the United States to the Monroe Doctrine may force the United States, however reluctantly, in flagrant cases . . . , to the exercise of an international police power.

By then, the United States had taken Puerto Rico from Spain (as well as the Philippines and Guam in the Pacific), established a protectorate in nominally independent Cuba, decided to construct a canal across the isthmus of Panama and, when the Colombian senate protested at the terms negotiated, encouraged the province of Panama to secede from Colombia as an independent state. In the next ten years, while the Panama Canal was being built, the United States landed troops and administered revenues in Cuba, the Dominican Republic, Haiti and Nicaragua, and extended 'dollar diplomacy', or what is sometimes called informal imperialism, throughout Central America and the Caribbean. By the end of our period, President Woodrow Wilson had become embroiled in Mexican internal politics in a way that foreshadowed the unhappy fate of subsequent White House interventions. The more the United States had an economic and strategic stake in Hispanic America, the more difficult its task became. The republics to the south *were* for the most part in sore need of capital, firm government and social reform. But the modernization of agriculture and industry, for example under Porfirio Díaz in Mexico, mainly enriched foreigners or natives already rich at the expense of the poor. This was one of the prime complaints of the Zapatistas during the Mexican Revolution (1910–16); their main demand was for a redistribution of land, and a holding to every peasant. Discontent was if anything increased. Shareholders and those who operated the mines and oilfields and railroads on behalf of foreign companies expected their interests to be protected. They favoured dictators' rule like that of Díaz, because it was tough, to the régimes of men like Díaz's successor Francisco Madero who were high-minded constitutionalists. So, while contemptuous of Latin American politics – Roosevelt spoke of the Colombian legislature as 'those miserable jack-rabbits' – the North Americans tended to oscillate between wishing for republics as wholesomely prosperous as their own, and measures that strengthened dictatorship rather than democracy.

Latin American reactions to the United States, understandably, altered from admiration to resentment. In 1858 the Argentinian Alberdi could write: 'South America is full of copiers of United States doctrines, laws, and books. What South Americans forget to imitate … is her economic practicality, her habits of work, thrift, and sobriety in social life – without which her liberties would be mere myths and abstractions.' Such men could rejoice in the outcome of the American Civil War, seeing in it the vindication of democratic Unionism and the beginning of a new era of racial tolerance. In the next generation, Latin Americans began to regard the United States as a sinister influence. The Civil War in the USA, in this interpretation, resembled the struggle between Prussia and Austria for the leadership of Germany; the industrial North beat the traditional South. As for the end of slavery, it had only turned the Negroes into *peons* – the Spanish word for a pawn in the game of chess, a piece to be sacrificed to the more imperious gambits of knight and bishop, king and queen.

Efforts to imitate the United States seemed hopeless. Liberalism and positivism in economics or government merely ended in Anglo-Saxon overlordship. The United States had escaped its own colonial status only to impose the same subjection on its neighbours. So South American writers vented their anger on the *norteamericanos*; and, somewhat like the 'unreconstructed' patriots of the defeated slave states of the northern Confederacy, *vis-à-vis* the Yankees, they reaffirmed their own identity as something entirely opposite. Francisco Bilbao, writing in the 1850s, could still envy the accomplishments of the United States; but his people, he claimed, 'prefer the individual to the social, beauty to riches, . . . poetry to industry, . . . the pure spirit to calculation. . . . It is this that the citizens of South America dare to place on the scales next to the pride, the riches, and the power of North America.' Half a century afterward, the Peruvian poet José Santos Chocano, referring to the Panama Canal, urged Latin America to

> distrust the blue-eyed man
> When he attempts to steal from us

and loftily asserted:

> Our jungles will not acknowledge a master race.
> Our Andes disdain the whiteness of the White.
> Our rivers will laugh at the greed of the Saxon.

There was a similar invocation of

> The America of the great Montezuma, of the Inca,
> Fragrant America of Christopher Columbus

in an *Ode to Roosevelt* by the Nicaraguan writer Rubén Darío. Theodore Roosevelt was for him a barbarian invader, and the United States a worshipper of 'Hercules and Mammon' – biceps and moneybags. And the same themes were underlined in *Ariel* (1900) by José Rodó of Uruguay, the best-known of all the Latin American ripostes. The northern half of the double-continent, according to Rodó, was prodigiously energetic, a 'Holy Empire of Utilitarianism'. It had wrought miracles through following out the logic of democracy. But they were not true miracles, only immensities of material objects. The Anglo-Saxons lacked a soul; North America was spiritually a brute, like Caliban in Shakespeare's *The Tempest*. Latin America must, on the contrary, be like Ariel, a creature of light and grace, the symbol of genuine individualism instead of the flat uniformity of the North. Latin America, all these writers contended, was an amalgam of ancient, deathless civilizations: Aztec and Inca mingled with the Hispanic and Mediterranean glories. The great past of southern Europe 'in whose ... teachings we South Americans live', said Rodó, 'makes a sum which cannot be equalled by any equation of Washington plus Edison'.

It is easy to point out the flaws in such efforts to define a Latin American identity. Like the Southern agrarians in the United States, who criticized the dominant 'Yankee' mentality in comparable ways, Latin American writers tended to find their homelands more attractive to write about than to live in. Darío preferred Paris to Managua. They were oddly eclectic, at one moment yearning for the old Indian traditions, the next moment taking pride in Spanish ancestors who had obliterated the native cultures. They borrowed their ideas from European, especially French, authors who also affected to despise Yankee materialism. Like these authors, they made the United States a scapegoat for things they distrusted in their own societies. But, in their understandable alarm at Anglo-Saxon commercial aggressiveness and Hispanic American sluggishness, they needed to be able to believe that the one had failed in its very success, while the other's apparent failings carried the seed of ultimate success.

In a sense they were thus still carrying on the hemispheric dream of pristine promise. In other respects, they were conveying a different idea: that America was and always had been not one but two continents, profoundly separate in heritage and temperament. They were answering those exponents of Anglo-Saxonism, in northern Europe and the United States, with a plea for the southern, multi-racial cultures – Moorish, Iberian, Amerindian, Negro. Perhaps also they were implying the existence of two Europes, divided by latitude, the industrious and the easygoing, the bleak and the sunny. If so, all this was of course an oversimplification. Some of Latin America's problems – for instance, the cleavage between city and country, immigrant and native – resembled those of North America. Yet there is an important truth in the concept of a dynamic Euro-American North, and of a Euro-American South struggling to hold its own in a harsh world.

7 Africa and Asia

As early as October, shortly after the first news of the rising in Egypt and Northern Africa had penetrated to Europe, a similar movement was noticeable in European Turkey. . . . There was no doubt that the Sultan had taken up a friendly attitude toward the insurgent movement in Africa. . . . The first successes in Northern Africa immediately set the whole continent aflame. . . . The Arab uprising – with which the heathen negro population, which did not belong to Islam, instinctively associated itself – broke out so suddenly everywhere that in the English, French, and Portuguese possessions, and in the Congo State, such of the garrisons as had not immediately been swept away by the first furious assaults defended themselves only with great difficulty against the onslaught of the enraged savages.

Armageddon, 190–: *English translation (1907) of* 1906 – Der Zusammenbruch der alten Welt, *imaginary German war novel by* '*Seestern*' *(F. H. Grauthoff)*

What will happen when China really wakes up?

Rudyard Kipling, From Sea to Sea, *1900 (describing a visit to the Far East in 1887–8)*

The Problem of Viewpoint

The territories bordering Europe to south and east were ancient melting-pots. Europe's civilization had drawn from the Arab conquerors in Mediterranean Africa and Spain as well as from Judaeo-Hellenic sources. The old Muslim empires, indeed, had spread deep into Africa and into Asia, bringing their religion to large parts of India and as far as Yunnan in western China. Turkey, the heartland of the crumbling Ottoman Empire, was both a European and an Asian country; indeed some of the mosques in Istanbul had once been churches of the Greek (Christian) Orthodox faith. Russia likewise was pulled between

Opposite: A Punch cartoon of 1902 depicts the Russian bear in Manchuria. At the end of the nineteenth century Russia rapidly expanded her Asiatic frontiers.

A MAN OF HIS WORD.

Europe and Asia, somewhat as the United States and other American countries were unsure whether they were 'European' or belonged in some deep sense to their own continent. Fyodor Dostoevsky was among the Russians who dreamed of a Slavic empire, replacing the Ottoman hegemony and reaching out much further into the fastnesses of central Asia. After the Russian capture of the Turcoman stronghold of Geok-Tepe in 1880, Dostoevsky insisted that his countrymen must recognize that their future lay in Asia.

This mistaken view of ours solely as Europeans, and not Asiatics [he said], ... this shame and this faulty opinion have cost us a good deal in the course of the last two centuries, and the price we have had to pay has consisted of the loss of our spiritual independence, of our unsuccessful policies in Europe, and finally of money – God only knows how much money – which we spent in order to prove to Europe that we were Europeans and not Asiatics.

The Europeans never believed them, because they were imitators, remote provincials, incapable of rivalling the true cultural glories of European civilization. 'Europe despises us ... she considers us an inferior race.'

From the inside of the Orient, however, such nuances of cultural identity were unimportant. In fact, to non-white peoples everywhere, Europeans and Americans and Russians were virtually indistinguishable. According to David Livingstone, some African tribesmen believed that the white man had arrived not across the surface of the sea but from the depths of the water. Both in Africa and in Asia, there was a persistent popular belief that Westerners were cannibals. In China this opinion was supported by reference to Christian worship. In the communion service, the 'foreign devils' simulated the consuming of the body and blood of Christ: surely this was an encouragement to them to go and consume the helpless Chinese?

Every society tended to think of itself as the centre of the universe and the summit of civilization. Other societies were not merely alien but 'uncivilized'. One could compile an amusing cross-cultural anthology to illustrate this pattern of self-congratulation coupled with denigration of outsiders. Westerners, for example, invariably criticized non-Western peoples as dirty, cruel, immoral and superstitious; non-Westerners said exactly the same thing of Westerners. The more elaborate and venerable the culture, the more convinced were its devotees that they embodied the ultimate wisdoms. Turkey and Persia (Iran), for instance, sought comfort in their possession of the Sacred Law of Islam.

The most self-absorbed of all the major societies were China and Japan. In the mid-nineteenth century, they were ending two centuries of deliberate loss of contact with Europe, and a far longer period of general indifference to the rest of mankind. Neither country had diplomatic dealings with the world at large. Neither permitted foreigners to visit their land; nor were Chinese or Japanese allowed to travel abroad. China's commerce with the outside world was limited to the single southern port of Canton, where foreign merchants were confined to one small district, and to a few other, traditional concessions such as the annual camel-train of trading goods admitted each year from Russia. Japanese external trade was confined to the port of Nagasaki, where selected Chinese and Dutch were licensed to operate, but no others. Both countries had decided in the seventeenth century to exclude 'barbarians', especially Christian missionaries. When Western ships came to Nagasaki, within the Dutch concession, all books and firearms were required to be sealed in casks and sent ashore to be held by Japanese officials until the vessel was ready to sail.

Some Western ideas and techniques did filter in (and there was in any case a high standard of native craftsmanship, particularly in Japan). Neither society was entirely static, entirely unaffected by foreign ways. China, after all, was an amalgam of former invading cultures and indeed during our period, the state was under the control of the 'foreign' Ch'ing or Manchu dynasty, which had come from Manchuria and seized power in the seventeenth century. The Japanese rejection of the West, partly a result of unpleasant experiences with foreign traders and Christian proselytizers, was also in part a struggle to achieve a separate national identity in relation to China. China was the parent-culture, as was Europe for the United States; and so Japanese self-definition, a complicated matter, depended upon an ambivalence toward China before the ambivalences toward the West arose.

Even so, these societies were, in the early nineteenth century, as closed-off as official policy could make them: which is to say immeasurably more than Russia or coastal Africa or the Middle East. If the Occidental world of that time was dynamic, the Oriental one was hermetic. According to Chinese dogma, the 'Middle Kingdom' of China was in every respect the centre of

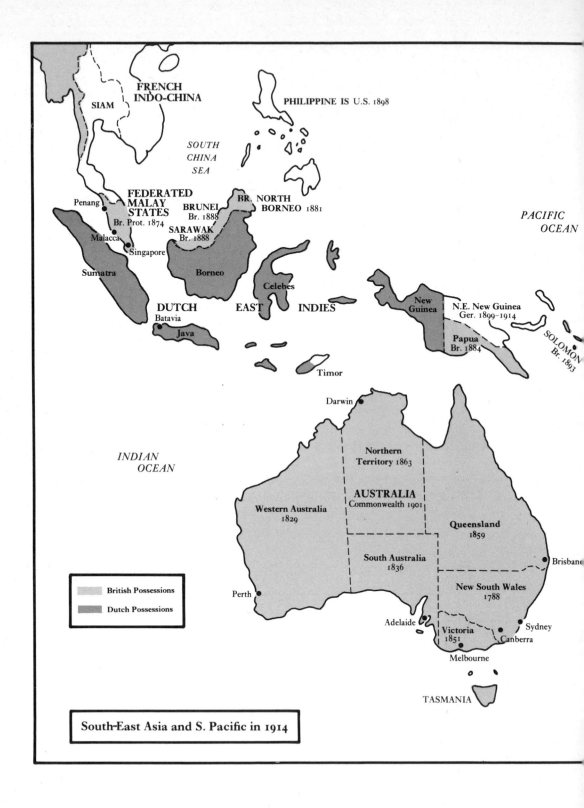

FRENCH
INDO-CHINA

SIAM

PHILIPPINE IS U.S. 1898

*SOUTH
CHINA
SEA*

FEDERATED
MALAY
STATES

Penang

BRUNEI
Br. 1888

BR. NORTH
BORNEO 1881

Br. Prot. 1874

SARAWAK
Br. 1888

Malacca

Singapore

Sumatra

Borneo

Celebes

*PACIFIC
OCEAN*

DUTCH

EAST   INDIES

Batavia

Java

Timor

New
Guinea

N.E. New Guinea
Ger. 1899–1914

Papua
Br. 1884

SOLOMON
Br. 1893

Darwin

*INDIAN
OCEAN*

Northern
Territory 1863

AUSTRALIA
Commonwealth 1901

Western Australia
1829

Queensland
1859

South Australia
1836

Brisbane

British Possessions

Dutch Possessions

Perth

New South Wales
1788

Adelaide

Victoria
1851

Sydney

Canberra

Melbourne

TASMANIA

South-East Asia and S. Pacific in 1914

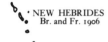

ELLICE IS
Br. 1892

· NEW HEBRIDES
Br. and Fr. 1906

W
LEDONIA Fr. 1853

W ZEALAND
Dominion 1907

Auckland

Wellington

Christchurch

civilization. Surrounding countries – Tibet, Nepal, Indo-China, Korea – were treated as subordinate domains, owing formal tribute to China. It was assumed that countries lying beyond the periphery must be still more inferior. China had no need to take such barbarian states into account. Those that sent diplomatic expeditions to China, as Britain did in 1793, were received with courtesy yet with fundamental condescension, as tribute-bringers whose insistence was a mark of their uncouthness. China had no wish to trade with them, nor to learn more about them. The few descriptions of the West written by Chinese scholars up to 1800 were magnificently ethnocentric. One work described Britain as a province of Holland, and declared that there was practically no difference between northern Europeans on the one hand and Italians or Portuguese or French on the other. Half a century later, an American missionary found that maps in Chinese schools still sometimes showed his country, together with those of Europe, as a group of small islands scattered to the west of the Middle Kingdom. The average Chinese peasant still might be told by the elders that 'foreign devils' had only one eye, or that some of them had a hole in the middle so that they could be strung together in batches like Chinese coins. Even in 1899, a Chinese nationalist newspaper could begin an article analyzing the troubles of the mother-country with the announcement that the world was divided into 'four continents – Asia, Europe, Africa and Australia'. The omission of America was no doubt a slip, but perhaps revealing of the ingrained Chinese reluctance to surrender the old China-centred cosmology to the harsh realities of modern times.

In mid-century, few societies could permit themselves such luxuries of indifference. The impact of the West was far too evident to be overlooked; and this impact was to affect them all. The range of experiences was immense. At one extreme the white man came as conqueror and exploiter, imposing his own rule with scant regard for native ways. This was the fate of most of Africa. At the other extreme lay the situation of Japan, able to avoid military occupation, to combine Westernization with a fierce affirmation of the national heritage and to emerge as a non-Western society that was also industrialized and expansionist. In between were the situations of other once-proud civilizations such as those in the subcontinent of India, obliged to submit to foreign dominance.

Extended though the spectrum is, we can thus survey in broad

terms the problem that faced non-Western societies – whether
or not they wished to face it. From their viewpoint, there was no
basic difference between one Western nation and another; and
they were essentially correct in suspecting that when the white
missionary arrived, the white trader would also come, and sooner
or later the warships, the troops and the government mission.
The missionary might be from Scandinavia or the United States,
in some region that their governments made no attempt to
penetrate. No matter: they were emissaries from the same
thrusting, disturbing, dynamic realm. None of the Western
nations was content to leave things be. Individuals among them
might become profoundly interested in non-Western ways, and
be highly critical of their own societies. But they were a minority.
Even Dostoevsky, proclaiming that Russia was part-Asiatic,
was principally concerned to argue that Russia had an imperial
destiny there. 'In Europe,' he said, 'we were hangers-on and
slaves, whereas we shall go to Asia as masters. In Europe we were
Asiatics, whereas in Asia we, too, are Europeans. Our civilizing
mission in Asia will … drive us thither. It is only necessary that
the movement should start. Build only two railroads: begin with
the one to Siberia, and then – to central Asia – and at once you
will see the consequences.' Forty years earlier, or longer, Russia
had been the most intrusive Western power for the Japanese to
worry about. So for non-Westerners the port of origin of the
West's 'black ships', pouring out smoke from their boilers, was
irrelevant. The outcome would be the same symbolic Western
trinity: Bible, money, rifle. In Africa, particularly in those areas
where Islam had not already established a firm hold, the situation
was starker still. In the awkwardly eloquent words of Charles

Domingo, a Nyasaland nationalist of 1911:

The three combined bodies – Missionaries, Government and Companies or gainers of money – do form the same rule to look upon the native with mockery eyes. It sometimes startles us to see that the three combined bodies are from Europe, and along with them there is a title Christendom. . . . If we had power enough to communicate ourselves to Europe, we would advise them not to call themselves Christendom, but Europeandom. . . . The life of the three combined bodies is altogether too cheaty, too thefty, too mockery.

Whether the Western invasion took the form of outright occupation or was confined to a more limited penetration, it came as a psychological shock. It presented non-Western peoples

Below: A painting by Dauzat of Government Square in Algiers in 1849. Throughout the nineteenth century the European powers sought to establish control over the vital strategic ports of the Mediterranean.

with a new order of technology and ideology that could not be ignored. This Western style might be full of contradictions, as Charles Domingo contended. It was often accompanied by bitter rivalry between competing nations; the intruders spoke with many tongues, figuratively and literally, which added to the bewilderment and perhaps the disdain of those intruded upon. But the shock was heightened because few of the non-Western peoples could remain confident that their own ways of life were altogether superior. The steamboat and the railroad, the telegraph and the printing-press, were achievements that could not be gainsaid. Western ideas on religion, democracy and social reform reached some non-Western societies at the moment when they were far from content with their own social frameworks. The Western impact in this respect merely accelerated the emergence of domestic disputes.

As the European powers opened up the African continent they ruthlessly plundered her natural resources. This picture shows natives and white settlers in German East Africa grouped round a valuable haul of elephant tusks.

178

Africa

The dominant post-colonial and anti-colonial view of the last 150 years of African history is of destructive exploitation by Europeans, and of valiant but unavailing African resistance. According to this interpretation, for which there is plenty of corroboratory evidence, the white man was fundamentally out of sympathy with African ways. Even where he was well-intentioned, his activites were disruptive. The missionary, it is said, imposed an essentially alien, white man's God; and mission schools sought to convert African children into 'trousered blacks' – or more particularly into black Englishmen or Frenchmen or Germans, each instructed in national history and national culture of the 'mother country'. They might, for instance, be taught poems such as Wordsworth's *Daffodils* when none of them had ever seen a daffodil. The colonial administrator, however upright he might be in his paternalistic fashion, introduced European systems of control, taxation and land-tenure which were often incomprehensible to the African, and oppressive in their operation. The boundaries drawn between colony and colony in the European share-out may have looked tidy in European atlases yet paid little heed to the actual tribal and kinship systems of the Africans themselves. If this was true of the missionary and the administrator, the most humane of the European occupiers, other Europeans were not even well-intentioned. Traders thought only of profit, from the early days of the thriving traffic in human lives carried out along the Slave Coast of West Africa to the later times when they exchanged fire-arms, beads and cheap cotton cloth for ivory. Wherever white men established large-scale enterprises – say, in Leopold's Congo or in the diamond and gold mines of South Africa – they reduced Africans almost to the condition of convict-labour, paying low wages for what was virtually forced work. White settlers, notably the Boers, treated the natives as if they were half-tamed animals. Significantly, 'native' or 'aborigine', meaning the original inhabitant of a country, became equated with savagery, bestiality, inferiority.

Some African peoples, hounded and dispossessed, yielded to a suicidal despair. The Xhosa and Tembu, squeezed by the Europeans on the eastern fringe of the Cape Colony, went so far in 1856–7 as to destroy their cattle and grain, in obedience to a prophecy that in return for this sacrifice their ancestors would reappear and drive the Europeans into the sea. Instead, thousands of them died of starvation and thousands more had to abandon their lands and look for employment in the Cape. Several African societies fought back against European pressure. Those that were most stubborn and uncompromising received a rough handling from punitive expeditions. This was the unlucky experience of the Bunyoro of Uganda, the Mashona in Southern Rhodesia, the Ashanti of Ghana, the old Dahomey empire in French West Africa, the kingdom of Benin in Nigeria. They lost men heavily in the one-sided fighting; spears and obsolescent rifles were no match for machine-gun and fieldpiece. They lost independence. They frequently lost lands they had long tilled or grazed. Perhaps the worst fate was that of the Herero, who went to war in 1904 against the white settlers who were beginning to occupy their land in German South-West Africa. German reprisals brought about the death of two-thirds of the Herero people, and all their tribal territory was confiscated. The landless survivors were obliged to become a servant-class for white masters.

That is one element in the familiar story: the undermining, sometimes the annihilation, of African cultural integrity by the Europeans. A second element is the emphasis on the pride, the vigour and the sophistication of many parts of Africa. There were ancient kingdoms. Africa was criss-crossed with trade routes long before the white man penetrated the interior. When he did he was sometimes astonished by what he found. An English doctor in the pay of the Congo Free State army accompanied the troops on their invasion of the eastern Congo in 1893. At Kasongo, a town on the Lualaba river in the heart of Africa:

Our whole force found new outfits, and even the common soldiers slept on silk and satin mattresses, in carved beds with silk mosquito curtains. The room I took possession of was eighty feet long and fifteen feet wide, with a door leading into an orange garden ...; candles, sugar, matches, silver and glass goblets and decanters were in profusion. The granaries throughout the town were stocked with enormous quantities of rice, coffee, maize ...; the gardens were luxurious and well-planted. . . . The herd of cattle we found in Kasongo was composed of three distinct breeds.

So much for what we have called the dominant view of African history between the middle of the nineteenth century and the 1914–18 war. But it would be wrong to attribute every trouble or every change to the Europeans. Chroniclers of imperialism no

180

doubt greatly exaggerated the altruism of the whites and the barbarism of the Africans – though with honourable exceptions in the case of witnesses like Mary Kingsley, a high-spirited English-woman who travelled in West Africa during the 1890s continu-ously commenting on the innate logic of African customs. Perhaps though, there is now a tendency to exaggerate the stability and wholesomeness of African societies. We may draw too sharp a contrast between white depravity and black innocence. The African continent was far from static before 1850. For some of its restlessness then and later, Europeans were not responsible, or not primarily responsible. Slave-hunting and the slave trade were ancient practices, fully developed before the export trade in human beings began to flourish in response to white demand. The external trade was brought to a halt by about 1860; the internal trade, particularly to areas of East Africa, persisted for a good few more years. David Livingstone was horrified by the callousness of warrior groups that specialized in slave raids. Tribal law was often both ingenious and sensible. It was less draconian than European law in punishing manslaughter; but a European might feel this was because killing – for example of babies that happened to be twins – was more readily sanctioned. Alcohol was not new either. Mary Kingsley contended that 'traders' gin' in West Africa did no harm to Africans already habituated to their own brew of palm-wine; the 'palm-wine drunkard' was a common enough phenom-enon in African society.

Tribal warfare and migration was as old as Africa. Empires rose and fell with the emergence of new leaders or – as in the case of the Zulus trained by Shaka in the early nineteenth century – new methods of fighting. Egyptian expansion south through the Sudan clashed with the revival of the hitherto-decaying Ethiopian empire. The Somali herds of camels and goats ate up the available grazing in their own region and so forced their owners to move on. There was a great southward drift of Bantu peoples, also in search of grazing for their herds of cattle. They had already pushed deep into the territory of the less aggressive Bushmen and Hottentots when they began to collide with parties of Boers trekking north. The fierce Masai in Kenya were a terror to their peaceful neigh-bours. So were the warlike, elephant-hunting Chokwe to the west. Pre-colonial Africa was an enormous mixture of stay-at-home farmers and nomadic pastoral peoples, of the gentle and the truculent, the indolent and the industrious. The types varied as much as the landscape.

Until about 1880, except in North Africa and along some of the coastlines, the white man had not yet transformed the situation. He was, after all, only one more civilization of many that had flowed through the continent. Before the Europeans and overlapping with them were the Arab colonizers, who in their fashion were also agents of quite profound change. The Arabs brought Islam to much of the northern half of Africa, and in the mid-nineteenth century were penetrating fairly deep into East Central Africa. Arab trading posts had existed for centuries along the East African coast. Early in the nineteenth century, the Imam of Muscat, the remarkably enterprising Seyyid Said, began to exploit his hereditary claims to the Zanzibar area. He extended his sway for several hundred miles of coastal strip, with Zanzibar as his flourishing capital. He introduced the clove-tree from the East Indies (as previous voyagers, probably Arabs, had brought back the banana-plant from Malaysia). His plantations were worked by slaves brought from the interior. At his death in 1856, his son Majid took Said's place as Sultan of Zanzibar. Arab influence continued to spread. Many Africans were converted to Islam. Swahili, the common language of East Africa, exemplified the process, since it superimposed Arabic words and phrases on a Bantu base. The Swahili-Arabs, spreading their network of settlement and trade with high skill, and often at the expense of the Portuguese, established links with other energetic peoples such as the Nyamwezi. From the early 1850s until he was shot by a Belgian soldier in 1891, a Nyamwezi merchant known as Msiri ('the mosquito') was unchallenged lord of a vast trading domain in Katanga. North of the Msiri imperium was the Swahili-Arab sultanate of Tippu Tib, an even more powerful figure whose period of authority lasted about as long as Msiri's. He too depended on a large force – as many as fifty thousand at the height of his power – of warriors armed with guns. His was the capital city Kasongo that astonished the invading Europeans in 1893. Arab civilization, in short, anticipated European styles in that it operated through trade, religion, organization, technology, and conquest. Quick-witted, often ruthless dealers in ivory, slaves and other profitable merchandize, the Arabs could hardly be deemed uncommercial. Anxious to remedy their own lack of certain financial skills, they were quick to bring in *Banyans* – Indians accustomed to banking and loans – to East Africa.

What then is there to choose, morally and by the test of results, between the Europeans and the Arabs, or between the whites and

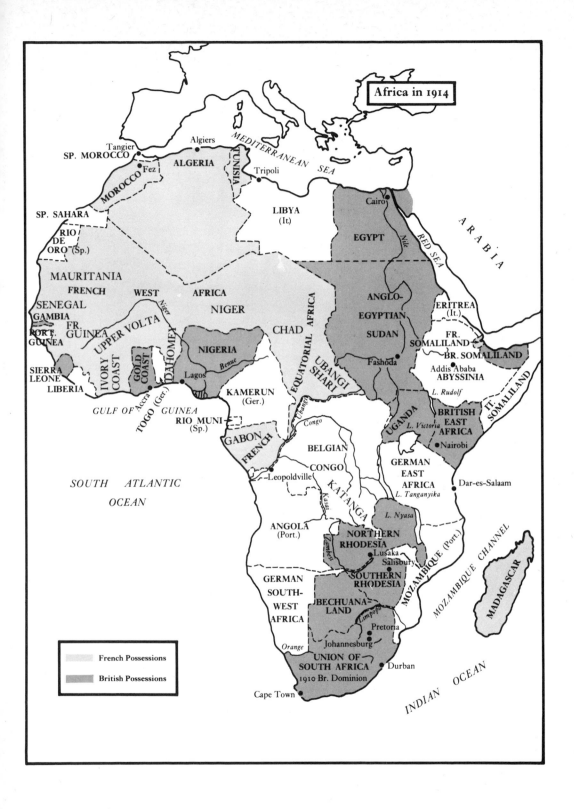

Africa in 1914

SP. MOROCCO
Tangier
Algiers
ALGERIA
TUNISIA
Tripoli
MEDITERRANEAN SEA
Cairo
MOROCCO
Fez
LIBYA
(It)
EGYPT
ARABIA
SP. SAHARA
RIO
DE
ORO (Sp.)
Nile
RED SEA
MAURITANIA
FRENCH
WEST
AFRICA
NIGER
ANGLO-
EGYPTIAN
SUDAN
ERITREA
(It.)
SENEGAL
GAMBIA
FR.
GUINEA
PORT.
GUINEA
Niger
UPPER VOLTA
DAHOMEY
CHAD
EQUATORIAL AFRICA
FR.
SOMALILAND
BR. SOMALILAND
SIERRA
LEONE
LIBERIA
IVORY COAST
GOLD COAST
NIGERIA
Benue
UBANGI
SHARI
Fashoda
Addis Ababa
ABYSSINIA
Lagos
KAMERUN
(Ger.)
L. Rudolf
IT.
SOMALILAND
GULF OF GUINEA
Accra
TOGO (Ger.)
RIO MUNI
(Sp.)
Ubangi
UGANDA
L. Victoria
BRITISH
EAST
AFRICA
GABON
FRENCH
Congo
BELGIAN
CONGO
Nairobi
SOUTH ATLANTIC
OCEAN
Leopoldville
Kasai
KATANGA
GERMAN
EAST
AFRICA
L. Tanganyika
Dar-es-Salaam
L. Nyasa
ANGOLA
(Port.)
Zambezi
NORTHERN
RHODESIA
Lusaka
Salisbury
MOZAMBIQUE (Port.)
MOZAMBIQUE CHANNEL
MADAGASCAR
GERMAN
SOUTH-
WEST
AFRICA
SOUTHERN
RHODESIA
BECHUANA-
LAND
Limpopo
Pretoria
Orange
Johannesburg
UNION OF
SOUTH AFRICA
1910 Br. Dominion
Durban
INDIAN OCEAN
Cape Town

French Possessions
British Possessions

the numerous African peoples who asserted their suzerainty over adjacent tribes by brute force? Why should Christianity appear any more alien than Islam? Both were universal and monotheistic, supplanting forms of worship that were local and usually polytheistic. It is possible to visualize African history as basically a convergence of the outer fringe upon the inner centre – the one active and cosmopolitan, the other passive and parochial. The fringe peoples, the coastmen – Algerians, Tunisians, Egyptians, Swahilis, Yorubas – or those like the Ibos affiliated with the outside world through river-ports, were more adaptable, more eclectic than the peoples of the interior. Repatriated Africans in the ex-slave settlements of Liberia and Sierra Leone were sometimes accused of behaving more like white men than blacks. In Liberia, this meant lording it over the back-country. In Sierra Leone, it meant advocating Westernization in order to raise Africa above its present state. True, the accommodators of Sierra Leone, as typified by the medical officer James Africanus Horton or the gifted lawyer John Mensah Sarbah, dreamed of eventual independence. 'Liberated', that is, educated, Africans of this stamp aimed at another sort of liberation. Through his Aborigines' Rights Protection Society (1897), Mensah Sarbah used his London law training to insist upon the validity of African land-titles. Nevertheless, he could be seen as only the latest in a long line of fringe-innovators, seeking to mediate between outside and inside.

There is something in this contention. Even so, the European impact upon Africa was greater and probably more harmful than that of Islam, or of any combination of internal aggressions by warrior tribes against peaceable ones. Islam was certainly more effective at assimilating Africans within its structures than Christianity, as evidenced by the many Islamic kingdoms of West and Central Africa. Where Christianity spread, it usually brought foreign control in its wake, and a destruction of the native political system. Where existing systems of rule survived in areas dominated by Europeans, it was usually as puppet governments. The racial factor was much more conspicuous and the cultural differences were greater. Race-prejudice is immemorial. But white assumptions of superiority were more disdainful and more unmistakable than any previous ones in African history. The European intervention was more complete, and after 1880 more overwhelmingly sudden. African slave-traders were not notably humanitarian, nor were elephant-hunters concerned with ecology. But in both instances the size and intensity of white demand had disastrous consequences. The American market for slaves was immensely greater than the internal African market; so was the worldwide craving for ivory. Warfare in Africa was age-old, but the muskets and rifles supplied by Europeans stimulated conflict and made it more deadly. In addition, where Islam was a fairly unified culture with Arabic the master-language, the white men had little unity among themselves. Even Christianity appeared in various guises. The Europeans had put their culture into compartments, each with its own methods of trading and governing and its own language – English, French, German, Portuguese, Afrikaans. Any thoughtful African could perceive that the Europeans were at odds with one another. Any educated African discovered not only that the imperial powers were mutually hostile but that some Europeans felt their civilization to be vicious and unsound. The European impact was bewildering in more senses than one. Little could be done to repudiate white rule in the years before 1917; but the seeds were already sown.

India

As in Africa, the white men who entered India found a sub-continent with a history of ancient conquests and upheavals, polyglot, exhibiting great variations in wealth and cultivation, and lacking in national awareness. In the sixteenth and seventeenth centuries, India had been subject to the alien, Islamic rule of the Mughal dynasty, which fell apart in the eighteenth century. From their intervention came the Urdu language, blending Hindi and Persian, and the lingering use of Persian as the medium of conversation in polite circles. After the collapse of the Mughals, the Marathas, a sturdy Indian people, made a bid for supremacy. But by the early nineteenth century the British were the dominant force. In the next fifty years, they took province after province, from Ceylon (Sri Lanka) in the south to the foothills of the Himalayas in the north, from Assam in the east to Sind in the west. Apart from directly-administered British India, there were the princely states, self-governing in most respects though under British surveillance. British India contained about three-quarters of a total population of about 150 million in 1850. Of this figure roughly seventy per cent belonged to one or other of the castes and branches of the Hindu faith and about twenty per cent were Muslim. There were concentrations of Muslims in the north and in east Bengal. Otherwise, having won conversions among Hindus and Buddhists here and there over a long period of time, they were to be found in almost every Indian community.

Mohandas Gandhi was later to remark that no Indian language possessed an equivalent to the word 'independence'. India was accustomed to dependency. There were some old cities, such as Delhi and Lahore, and some relatively new ones such as Bombay, Madras and Calcutta (which served as the headquarters of the British *raj*). But the country was overwhelmingly rural. The standard unit was a village. In one way, therefore, the great majority of Indians appeared to be little affected by the remote hierarchy, Mughal or British, that might claim to be their overlords. Their societies were deeply traditional; their units of consciousness were the family, the immediate district, the particular religious sect, the dialect they happened to speak. Throughout our period most Indians could not read or write even in their own local dialect; only a tiny minority were 'English-knowing'. As late as the 1890s, when the population had risen to nearly three hundred million, the senior British officials of the ICS (Indian Civil Service) numbered less than a thousand plus another four thousand assorted whites of less exalted position, as against five hundred thousand subordinate Indian administrators. The Indian Army of that period contained about sixty-five thousand whites and twice as many Indians. Although the Indians had their own system of officers, usually drawn from the traditionally 'martial races' of the subcontinent, the élite was and continued to be British. But numerically it was so small as to seem insignificant.

Some historians have implied that the British did very little to India or for it: perhaps confusing the 'for' and the 'to'. At almost any point from 1850 to World War I, the British of course would not have accepted that their effect was unimportant. By the 1840s, they had established a system of government and were bringing in a uniform code of law of which they were particularly proud. They also claimed to have brought order to India by suppressing strife and banditry and by protecting the frontiers. In the next half-century, they constructed a network of railways and telegraphs and some highways, notably the Grand Trunk Road from Calcutta to Lahore. They introduced irrigation works, in some cases based upon old Mughal canals and reservoirs, and began to plan methods of controlling famine. The British 'guardians' did, however, agree that the Indian masses appeared indifferent to the upper echelons of government. Insofar as India

Opposite: The British in India carefully preserved the pattern of social life back home. This lithograph was one of a set of forty published by an Indian Army officer showing the entertainments an Indian station could offer.

CURRY & RICE

(ON FORTY PLATES)

OR

THE INGREDIENTS OF SOCIAL LIFE

AT

"OUR" STATION IN INDIA

BY CAPT^N GEO. F. ATKINSON.

LONDON, LITHOGRAPHED, PRINTED & PUBLISHED BY

DAY & SON, LITHOGRAPHERS TO THE QUEEN.

Amir Yahub Khan's
Highlanders in the
Second Afghan War
which was felt by British
to be essential for the
protection of India against
Russian encroachment
from the north.

had a voice, they believed it was theirs. In consequence, they were
as a rule witheringly disdainful of those Indians who began to
press for a greater share in the running of things. The protesters,
in the famous phrase of a British viceroy (governor-general),
were 'a microscopic minority'. They were not aristocrats with an
inbred habit of authority, nor men of military inclination – two
groups whom the British found it natural to admire. Figures such
as the Nizam of Hyderabad and the Nawab of Pataudi, or the
Gurkhas and Sikhs who comprised some of the best regiments in
the Indian Army, were regarded as the 'true' Indians. The British,
on the other hand, despised most of the middle-class, college-
educated, semi-Westernized figures who (in the eyes of officialdom)
were attempting to trespass into spheres beyond their capacity.

The situation was full of ironies. In fact, both the British
administrators and their 'brown-English' critics were extremely
few in numbers. The debate over India's future was conducted by

188

diminutive teams. Both figuratively and literally, they often spoke the same language. India's first native spokesmen, predominantly Hindu, had usually been educated at one of the colleges founded under government or missionary auspices, or perhaps at the universities of Calcutta, Bombay and Madras which had been opened in 1857. Initially many of them subscribed to the pioneering ideas of the great Brahmin scholar Ram Mohan Roy, who died in England in 1833 as ambassador to the pensioned-off Mughal emperor. Ram Mohan Roy, having explored European as well as several branches of Indian philosophy, concluded that the two cultures were compatible, perhaps even complementary. Both rested upon notions of reason and individual rights. Christian scripture and the Hindu *Upanishads* conveyed the same fundamental message. The study of English language and literature, and of Western sciences, would help Indians to recover the bases of their own culture, and to purify it of its abuses – idolatry, caste, sex-discrimination.

The Hindu professional classes responded eagerly to new opportunities, producing a cadre of lawyers, doctors, teachers, merchants, civil servants, journalists. Under the stimulus of education, literacy increased to such a degree that by 1880 there were twenty English-language newspapers in India, and two hundred printed in the languages of the country. Some middle-class Indians remained outside the movement, suspicious of Westernism and preferring traditional concepts of law or medicine. As a whole, Muslims were more conservative than Hindus; in proportion, markedly fewer attended 'European' colleges. Other Indians, likewise made uneasy by the eclecticism of Ram Mohan Roy and his kind, reacted by re-examining the tenets of their religion. One fundamentalist sect, active in the Punjab, was the *Arya Samaj*, founded in 1875 by the Gujarati Brahmin Swami Dayananda, whose followers tended to be hostile to both Muslims and Christians. The *Arya Samaj* went behind the *Upanishads* to the *Vedas*, the primordial testaments of Hinduism. So did the Swami Vivekananda and his saffron-robed monks, and sundry saintly instructors and hermits. In general, however, Western attitudes were not resisted by the Indian professional class. Their speeches and writings were peppered with references to English poetry and political theory. Until late in the century, their petitions to the authorities in London and Calcutta were almost deferentially moderate. All that they sought was a wider involvement in the responsibilities of government. They rested their case not upon extreme radical doctrine but simply upon British liberal precepts and British declarations of intent. In 1858, the East India Company, once the principal agent of authority, ceased to operate. Queen Victoria's proclamation of that year reaffirmed a promise already given as early as 1833: 'that, as far as may be, our subjects, of whatever race or creed, be freely and impartially admitted to office in our service'. But 'Indianization' of the ICS seemed to be deliberately withheld. From the 1850s, entry was by examination; yet the examination was conducted in England, and in 1878 the age of entry was lowered from twenty-one to nineteen, as if to debar any Indian applicant except the privileged few who were being schooled in England. The age was raised again in 1892. But progress was painfully, insultingly slow. Only twenty-one of the 939 members of the ICS in 1892 were Indian; and in 1913 less than ten per cent of the senior level in the public service were Indians.

The grand irony was that Britain supposedly stood for innovative reform, while India represented sheer inertia; but in fact the roles were reversed. British officials were preoccupied with law and order, which in practice meant keeping things as they were, while their Indian counterparts appealed to the dynamic aspects of Western liberalism. The viceroy and the ICS were evidently proud of their British nationalism, and as symbol of this the Queen-Empress undoubtedly evoked patriotic emotions among some Indians. But the rhetoric and the outward signs of British nationalism also inevitably prompted Indians to conceive of their sub-continent in kindred terms – as an entity, as 'Mother India', as a nation in the making.

The evolution of Indian nationalism is a classic instance of small complaints brushed aside because they were small, of protest and officialdom both becoming more intrangsigent, of concessions granted too late to satisfy the dissidents. The first stage was set by the Mutiny of 1857. Though some Indian writers portray it as a consciously nationalistic rising, the British designation seems accurate. It was a mutiny, mainly within the East India Company's Bengal army – by possible implication, a mutiny against the whole British *raj*, but in 1857 a mutiny against conditions of service imposed by the military upon the *sepoy* (Indian native infantry) rank-and-file. It was a large-scale rising, with much slaughter on both sides. The upshot was a thorough reorganization of British control, including the end of 'John Company'. The new régime was more efficient but more wary of

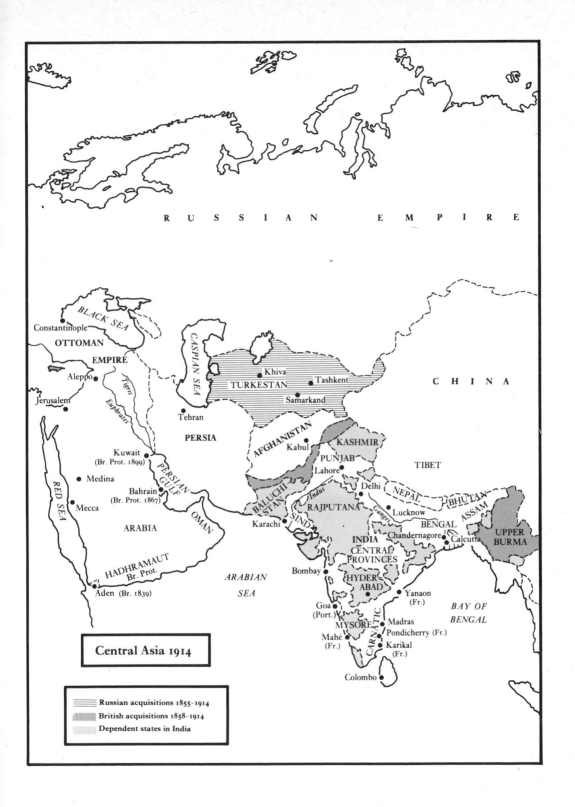

RUSSIAN EMPIRE

BLACK SEA

Constantinople

OTTOMAN

EMPIRE

Aleppo

Jerusalem

Tigris

Euphrates

CASPIAN SEA

Khiva

TURKESTAN

Tashkent

Samarkand

CHINA

Tehran

PERSIA

AFGHANISTAN

Kabul

KASHMIR

PUNJAB

Lahore

TIBET

RED SEA

Kuwait
(Br. Prot. 1899)

Medina

Bahrain
(Br. Prot. 1867)

Mecca

PERSIAN GULF

OMAN

ARABIA

BALUCHISTAN

Indus

Delhi

NEPAL

BHUTAN

ASSAM

Karachi

SIND

RAJPUTANA

Ganges

Lucknow

BENGAL

Chandernagore

Calcutta

UPPER
BURMA

HADHRAMAUT
Br. Prot.

Aden (Br. 1839)

*ARABIAN
SEA*

Bombay

INDIA
CENTRAL
PROVINCES

HYDER-
ABAD

Yanaon
(Fr.)

*BAY OF
BENGAL*

Goa
(Port.)

Mahé
(Fr.)

MYSORE

CARNATIC

Madras

Pondicherry (Fr.)

Karikal
(Fr.)

Colombo

Central Asia 1914

Russian acquisitions 1855–1914

British acquisitions 1858–1914

Dependent states in India

risking unrest. One of the lessons drawn was that the previous policy of moving toward Indian participation in government was premature; so too with the previous active encouragement of Westernism. The new policy was to modernize by means of public works, with an eye to military needs where roads and railways were concerned, but in other respects to leave Indian institutions alone. Whether or not this was right in the abstract, it was done for the wrong reasons and carried out in the wrong way. Thenceforward, administrators tended to harden into supercilious paternalism. In the words of Sir John Strachey, a senior bureaucrat (1894): 'Let there be no hypocrisy about our intention to keep in the hands of our own people those executive posts ... on which, and on our political and military power, our actual hold on the country depends.'

The British government was not altogether obdurate. Viceroys appointed by Liberal administrations – Lord Ripon (1880–4) and Lord Minto (1907–10) – took cautious steps toward self-government, mostly on the local and provincial level. But the British retained ultimate sovereignty and the ICS hugged the important administrative problems close to its bosom. Efficiency and honesty were all very well; but aloofness of the kind displayed by Lord Curzon (Viceroy from 1899 to 1905) was no longer acceptable.

Minto was much preferred to Curzon, and the Morley-Minto

Two Indian mutineers are hanged after the British reasserted their control over India. The mutiny led to a thorough reorganization of British rule and the end of the East India Company.

reforms showed a disposition to place India on the same footing as Canada and the other self-governing white Dominions. The outbreak of war in 1914, which the Germans hoped would be the signal for a general rising in India, revealed instead an astonishing spirit of goodwill. The princely states vied with one another in contributions of men and money. British India, though admittedly prodded by the authorities, was no less forthcoming. A million Indians were enlisted in the army. At the outset, morale was high. The British were honouring their pledges to India, belatedly yet persuasively. They had, for instance, shifted the capital from Calcutta to the old Mughal capital of Delhi, a popular transfer, and Indian advisers were now seated in the Viceroy's legislative council. The British would soon finish the war victoriously and India would reap the reward for her unstinted loyalty.

Alas for fine sentiments: the war went badly, and slowly. Indian troops despatched to the Western Front and other theatres suffered heavy losses; rumours of horror and stalemate came back from them. Muslims, hitherto angered by the apparent Hindu pre-emption of Indian nationalism, were themselves nationalistically as well as religiously provoked because Britain was at war with Turkey. Turkey was an Islamic nation and the Sultan was the Caliph – the protector of the holy places. The surrender of a British army to Turkish troops at Kut-el-Amara, Iraq, in 1916 brought ambivalent satisfactions for Hindu and Muslim nationalists alike.

China and Japan

Stories of revival and resistance in non-European countries were exciting news for Indian nationalists. Muslims were particularly stirred to hear of protests against British rule in Egypt, from the Mahdi's Islamic crusade in the Sudan in the 1840s, or gains for constitutionalism in Persia (Iran), to the Young Turk ferment in Turkey in 1908 – even if in this last situation they might also have observed with disquiet the plight of non-Turkish minorities. Nevertheless, the challenge to the established order in several countries was heartening for Indians. All of those committed to change and aggrieved by European dominance could rejoice in the battles won by another Asian race during the Russo-Japanese War of 1904–5; and a good many were pleased to learn of the overthrow of the Manchu dynasty in China in 1911. Islam and Asia were on the march.

But China was to undergo many travails before 1911 – and indeed after. Curiously enough, India (though not the Indians) was responsible for some of her humiliation. The forcible opening-up of China, beginning with the British in the early 1840s, was a result of the opium trade. Chinese exports were much in demand in the West but China showed almost no interest in importing Western products. The British found an answer in Indian-grown opium, a substance forbidden in China but easy to sell at a handsome profit with the connivance of Chinese officials. The Emperor became alarmed at the spread of opium-smoking in the Middle Kingdom, and instructed his commissioners to destroy all stocks of the narcotic held by foreign merchants at Canton and to take other steps to wipe out the traffic. An expeditionary force was sent from India to uphold British honour. After some sharp but one-sided encounters, the Chinese were forced to accept the Treaty of Nanking (1842). By its terms, the British were to have access to five treaty ports: Amoy, Foochow, Ningpo and Shanghai in addition to Canton. They were to annex Hong Kong and to be paid an indemnity. Other nations quickly followed; within a few years France, the United States, Russia and some smaller countries had all obliged the Emperor to give them similar trade concessions. 'Most-favoured nation' clauses, first insisted upon by the British, were secured by their rivals, so that whatever bargain was extorted by one country, the others likewise claimed parity of treatment. Chinese exports of tea and silk did rapidly increase through the trade treaties. But the advantages gained were offset by a reciprocally booming import-market, still centred on Canton, in opium. More and more fields in corners of India were given over to the opium poppy, under British supervision. Consummate hypocrisy enabled them to argue that they were merely satisfying an insatiable Chinese appetite for the drug. The Western world convinced itself, as we may see from popular fiction of the period, that the opium-den was a central feature of Chinese life. True, the Protestant and Catholic missionaries who were now given access to China under treaty-protection objected to the trade. Yet they too often saw it as an example of Chinese rather than of Western depravity.

For the next sixty years, relations between the two cultures tended to freeze into mutually hostile stereotypes. Stereotypes may be defined as distortions of observable fact. So, the Chinese saw the Occidental nations as greedy, dishonest, coarse and brutal. This was not surprising in view of the behaviour of European

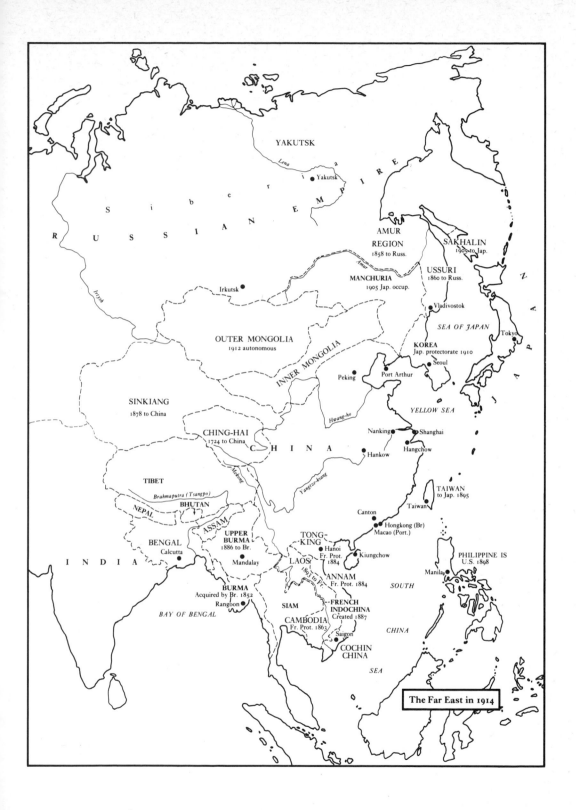

YAKUTSK

R U S S I A N   E M P I R E

S i b e r i a

Lena

•Yakutsk

•Irkutsk

Irtysh

AMUR
REGION
1858 to Russ.

SAKHALIN
1905 to Jap.

MANCHURIA
1905 Jap. occup.

USSURI
1860 to Russ.

Amur

•Vladivostok

OUTER MONGOLIA
1912 autonomous

INNER MONGOLIA

SEA OF JAPAN

•Tokyo

KOREA
Jap. protectorate 1910

•Seoul

SINKIANG
1878 to China

•Peking

•Port Arthur

Hwang-ho

YELLOW SEA

J A P A N

CHING-HAI
1724 to China

C H I N A

Nanking•

•Shanghai

•Hangchow

•Hankow

TIBET

Brahmaputra (Tsangpo)

Mekong

Yangtsz-kiang

TAIWAN
to Jap. 1895

NEPAL

BHUTAN

ASSAM

UPPER
BURMA
1886 to Br.

TONG-
KING

•Taiwan

Canton•

BENGAL

Calcutta•

•Mandalay

LAOS

Hanoi
Fr. Prot.
1884

•Kiungchow

Hongkong (Br)
Macao (Port.)

I N D I A

1863 to Fr.

ANNAM
Fr. Prot. 1884

PHILIPPINE IS
U.S. 1898

•Manila

BURMA
Acquired by Br. 1852

Rangoon•

SIAM

FRENCH
INDOCHINA
Created 1887

SOUTH

BAY OF BENGAL

CAMBODIA
Fr. Prot. 1863

•Saigon

CHINA

COCHIN
CHINA

SEA

The Far East in 1914

sailors and soldiers. The word 'loot' entered the English language at the time of the Opium War, as a borrowing from Hindustani; and every European force in China became notorious for looting – by officers as well as ordinary soldiers. Confucian doctrine treated links between nations as analogous to family ties. They must be either paternal or filial – dominant or subservient. In speaking of foreigners as 'barbarians' the Chinese (and Japanese) did not necessarily convey contempt, but rather viewed them as filial petitioners, seeking admission to the Oriental family. Hatred for the white men, as distinct from indifference, burgeoned when the foreigners proved to be asserting their own claims to dominance; the insult to Oriental pride was prodigious.

European inroads certainly hastened the collapse of the Manchu realm. But its internal weaknesses were undeniable. The Chinese reacted in various ways: clandestine struggles at the court of Peking, programmes for reform, outbursts of xenophobia – and outright rebellion. The first great surge of discontent was the revolt of the Taipings in southern China. Here, as in India, the infiltration of alien ideas helped act as a catalyst. The founder of the Taipings was Hung Hsiu-ch'uan, an ambitious, intelligent man with a grudge. He had failed to pass the state examinations that offered clever but poor Chinese their only avenue to power and prestige. Shut out from the civil service, a prey to delirious fantasies, Hung had a revelation in 1843. In a vision, an old man in a palace had given him a sword with which to kill devils. When he left the palace, he was accompanied by another man, called 'Elder Brother'. Now, a re-reading of a Christian pamphlet convinced Hung that the old man was God; 'Elder Brother' was Jesus Christ; and he was the younger brother of Jesus, designed by God as the scourge of God's enemies on earth – namely, all worshippers of false religions and in particular the Manchu Emperor. Hung's 'Society of God Worshippers' thus adapted elements of Christianity for Chinese purposes. Anti-foreign in being anti-Manchu, messianic, egalitarian, able to embrace members of sundry secret societies such as the White Lotus sect, the God Worshippers recruited far and wide. By 1851 Hung was known to his followers as the Heavenly King. Five of his associates were elevated to lesser ranks of kingship. They declared war on the Manchus, proclaiming a new *T'ai-p'ing* dynasty, the 'Heavenly Kingdom of Great Peace'. In the next two or three years they overran much of southern and central China. Their armies were strictly disciplined and boldly led. Opium, alcohol and tobacco

The Taiping Rising in its closing stages – a scene of death following the capture of North Fort in 1860 from the Taiping rebels.

were forbidden. The pigtail, introduced into China by the Manchus, was abolished. Women were guaranteed equality with men. Wherever they found a temple the Taipings, as iconoclastic as Cromwell's troopers, smashed pictures, idols and even ancestor-tablets.

The movement lasted for another ten years. But they were years of decline and disillusion. The Taipings brought not peace but a sword. Burning and massacring, forgetting their promises of land-reform, split by feuds between 'kings' who increasingly looked like traditional warlords, provoking hatred and resistance, galvanizing the Manchus into military exertion, alienating Europeans at first inclined to back them, the Taipings slumped into destructive, overweening chaos. The end came in 1864, with the storming of the opulent Nanking palace of Hung. In the holocaust, he committed suicide by swallowing gold leaf – an imperial gesture. Several of the wives that Christ's younger brother had decreed for himself killed themselves around his grave in the palace garden.

197

The fate of China was naturally of intense interest to the Japanese. Japan too had an Emperor, presiding over his court in the ancient temple-city of Kyoto. But in the mid-nineteenth century, his authority was nominal. Some historians have described Japan as a feudal society, since the monarchy was weak and considerable power was vested in the heads of local clans, especially in the west. The comparison is, however, only approximate. For one thing, central government was controlled not from Kyoto but from Edo (Tokyo) by the Tokugawa dynasty. This was sometimes known as the 'Bakufu' or 'tent government' because it had been military in origin. The head of the Bakufu was the 'Shogun' ('Tycoon' in Westernized form), a title roughly equivalent to 'Generalissimo'.

Commodore Perry of the US Navy meeting the Japanese Imperial Commission in 1854. His arrival heralded the end of the Japanese policy of isolation and a growing realization that modernization along Western lines could enable Japan to resist Western expansion in Asia.

The initial policy of the Shogunate was to exclude all interlopers. The 'Don't Think Twice' edict of 1825 was a summons to drive out and possibly wipe out foreign intruders. This was modified in 1842, to a ruling that foreign ships might be provisioned in case of need, though foreign individuals must not be permitted to land. Contact with the West, as we have seen, was restricted to a small Dutch agency in Nagasaki. Further modifications began to be recommended. A positive argument was that of the scholar Sakuma Shōzan, who taught himself Dutch and became impressed by Western learning. More negatively, the Bakufu reasoned that the Japanese would be no more able than the Chinese to exclude all foreign influence. Prudence and wisdom suggested that the Japanese ought therefore to absorb Western skills in order to become *militarily* strong, not merely to resist invasion but eventually to make war overseas.

The arrival of the United States in the form of Commodore Perry's ships in 1853 presented the problem in immediate guise. He could be fobbed off for a little while. But when he returned the following year, in greater strength, something definite had to be decided. Since his ultimatum rested upon superior force, the Shogunate had no alternative but to open two ports to the Americans, and no way of refusing the prompt demand by Britain, Russia, France and Holland for similar concessions. Beyond that, the Shogunate attempted compromise, steering between the extreme doctrines of *joi* ('expel the barbarians') and *kaikoku* ('open the country'). Naval vessels were laid down; Japanese technicians travelled abroad to study warfare and weaponry. Scholars tried to familiarize themselves with relevant portions of Western culture. A later instance is a Japanese edition of *Robinson Crusoe*, recommended in the preface as a work revealing how 'by stubborn determination an island can be developed'.

But the middle road was hard to find. Some Japanese in Yokohama and other ports profited from the dramatic increase in overseas trade. The livelihood of others was dislocated. Through an error, gold was undervalued in Japan; foreigners doubled their investment by exporting gold coin, with potentially catastrophic consequences for the national economy. Foreigners and Bakufu, both regarded as symptoms of Japanese degradation, were attacked in the streets. The Emperor now began to make himself heard as a critic of Bakufu policy. If it were continued, he announced, 'The national glory which has lasted for thousands of years will be utterly tarnished.' He captured the mood of a great many Japanese.

'Revere the Emperor! Down with the Bakufu!' appeared as a slogan. Gaining in confidence, he issued an imperial edict in 1863 that all foreigners were to be expelled within twenty days. The intensity of popular sentiment inhibited the Shogunate from repudiating his seemingly rash interference.

Sure enough, the Western powers stood their ground. During the next two years there were several displays of naval power by British, American and French ships, including the bombardment of two Japanese ports. In 1865, the arrival in Osaka Bay of a combined Western fleet forced the Emperor to yield. Thereafter *kaikoku* triumphed, at least on the surface. For Japan, the significance of these clashes was that the Emperor had triumphed over the Bakufu. He was admired for taking a strong line against the Occidentals, and again for adopting a new policy when this became inevitable. He had swung the nation behind him. The reign of the Tokugawas was over; he was about to resume his ancient throne as the Emperor Meiji. Hence the emphasis in 1868, when he formally took control, that this was a 'restoration'. In order to master the new, Japan was reinstating the old.

If this puzzled Europeans, it make excellent sense to nearly all groups in Japanese society. Edict after edict emerged from the imperial court, which at the Restoration moved from Kyoto to the former Bakufu headquarters in Tokyo. The Japanese grasped that so long as the inner core of national culture was preserved, modernization was not an expression of helplessness in face of Western aggression but a means of furthering Japanese national goals – not forgetting expansionism. The Emperor was at pains to stress democratic innovation. In his 'Imperial Oath' he proclaimed that public opinion was to be consulted and that absurd or restrictive customs would be discarded. He also managed to weaken clan sectionalism. The true emphasis was on unity and efficiency; reforms were means to ends. The bustle was nevertheless highly impressive. The old clans were replaced by prefectures. The local *samurai* armed bands gave way to a new imperial army; in 1873 a military-service law required all males to begin three years of conscription at the age of twenty. The system of taxation was drastically revised on modern principles. A Code of Education (1872) introduced the notion of schooling for all, with a resultant astonishing rise in literacy. The written language was rapidly changed; formal, semi-Chinese characters and expressions gave way to vernacular Japanese. Newspapers appeared in quantity. For most occasions, Western dress supplanted traditional Japanese costume. Japanese industry mushroomed, spreading out from the initial preoccupation with military production into all the areas of modern technology from mining to banking. Here too, government involvement was fundamental. There was some transfer into private hands, yet still obeying the central Meiji injunctions.

Here and there, the Emperor risked serious dissent. His early insistence that he was the hereditary high priest of the only genuine Japanese religion, Shintoism, took too little note of Buddhism and other deeply held forms of faith and had to be modified. On the whole however he succeeded in orchestrating ancient and modern. Clan-leaders accepted the prefecture system in the recognition that they as individuals would still qualify for appointment, and so retain authority. The *samurai* warrior-class were mollified by the incorporation of their *bushido* (code of honour) into the spirit of the imperial army. By 1889, when a new constitution was issued, the Emperor was clearly at the head of affairs. The motto *'Fukoku Kyōhei'* ('Rich country – strong army!') was coming to fruition. He was able to produce the constitution by fiat; parliamentary involvement, let alone criticism, was minimal. The Emperor, so said the constitution, was the heir of an eternal dynasty, a new Sun-King, 'sacred and inviolable'.

Attitudes to the West were dualistic. Europeans were apt to ridicule the Japanese as polite little imitators, apeing Western mannerisms with no proper comprehension. This was a misconception. So is the historians' temptation to equate modernized Japan with Bismarck's Germany as a nationalistic, oligarchic society, superimposing industrialism on a militaristic base. So it was, in part. But Japan was a special Oriental society, cherishing historic ambitions and profoundly resenting Western power and many aspects of Western culture. The Japanese passion was to beat the West at its own game, in order that Japan might set the rules for a different national game. Japan studied the rest of the world to avoid mistakes others had made. Apart from one Rothschild loan, floated in London in anticipation of conflict with Russia, the Japanese avoided dependence on foreign capital; the Emperor had no wish to be trapped as the Egyptian Khedive had been. Japanese xenophobia in fact increased as the nation grew more prosperously Westernized – partly as a backlash, partly as an expression of self-assurance. One indication was the drive to restate the 'Japanese national essence', for instance through the *Nihon Kōdō Kai* ('Japanese Morals Society'). Another, the first sign of expansionism, was a Perry-like expedition to Korea in

A battle in Korea during the Sino-Japanese War of 1894–5. Japan's adoption of Western techniques ensured her triumph and led to the establishment of Japanese control over Korea.

1876, to 'request' the resumption of diplomatic relations; a treaty of commerce was secured. A third manifestation was the mounting annoyance at European treaties exacted from Japan in her more vulnerable days, and a determination that they should be re-negotiated. War with China in 1894 and with Russia in 1904–5 gave spectacular proof of Japan's military prowess, and brought enormous satisfaction to the Japanese, mitigated only by exasperation that the Western powers were interfering to rob the victor of

her spoils. The final years between 1905 and 1916, the period of the 'Yellow Blessing', appeared to be vindicating all that the Meiji restoration symbolized: progress, prosperity, power, respect from those nations that had so presumptuously thrust themselves upon east Asia. In 1914 the Japanese joined the Allies in the war, not as India had done in a dependent role, but on her own terms, for national advantage.

Japan is the exception to the rule that the Western nations of

Tz'u-hsi, Dowager Empress of China, and the Emperor, receive the wives of the foreign ministers of the Great Powers in Peking in 1899. Chinese hatred of the Europeans, and Tz'u-hsi's own intrigues, resulted in the terrible Boxer Rising against the European intruders.

the late nineteenth century could mould the world in their own interests. China's misfortunes were another story. Yet here too, the West for a variety of reasons, including mutual jealousy, stopped short of complete penetration. Far less coherent than Japan, much less ably governed, China was still a formidable country, as much strengthened as weakened by traditional sentiment. After the failure of the Taipings came forty years of turmoil: anti-foreign demonstrations, punitive expeditions by European forces, payments of indemnities, the surrender of commercial spheres to importunate outsiders. There was no Manchu revival comparable to the Meiji restoration, though the dynasty was still able to display extraordinary personal ascendancy in the shape of an ennobled concubine, the Empress Dowager Tz'u-hsi. Otherwise, the Manchu court was too deformed to command respect. After the Taipings, the next demonstration of Chinese national feeling, the secret society of Taoists known as the 'Boxers' or 'Shadow Boxers', seems yet another aberration. Ferociously xenophobic, the Boxer risings of around 1900 might seem to resemble other pathetic and futile displays from dying societies – for example, the Sioux Ghost Dance cult of North America. The Boxer rebellion, though encouraged by the Empress Dowager, was suppressed by the Europeans, who having relieved their besieged legations in Peking, went on to sack the city in the barbarian fashion attributed to them. The lesson to be drawn from the episode, however, by a new generation of Chinese nationalists, as typified by the Westernized leader Sun Yat-sen, was that the Manchus were on their last legs. If they were helpless in face of foreigners, they were helpless also in face of any determined push to drive them out and form a new government. The Boxers had supported the Manchus as the rulers of China; 'Exterminate the Foreigners' had been their cry. Yet ever since the Taipings, the Manchus too had been viewed as foreigners; they were merely less foreign than the white men. Nationalist feeling could be harnessed against them.

So it proved. In 1911 the Manchus fell, almost without a struggle. Sun Yat-sen was China's new head. Once more, events were to re-enact the immemorial tale: loss of direction at the top, intervention by strong men, the lures of corruption, the centrifugal pull of warlord-domains. The lessons though were still valid; only the application was wrong. China must be for the Chinese. The old must become new.

The execution of Boxer leaders in China, May 1901. The suppression of the rising sounded the knell of the Manchu dynasty. Henceforth nationalist Chinese would look elsewhere for their leaders.

The contrast between the fates of China and Japan symbolized the dilemma facing Asia under the pressure of Westernization. At the beginning of the nineteenth century, both were resolutely opposed to contact with the West; Japan had the advantage of being an island as against the huge, sprawling land-mass of China, a country which could be held together as a nation only by a strong central authority. But in China, the central authorities were not sufficiently in control to unite the nation against foreign influence: the battles to prevent foreign intrusion were in vain. China never Westernized, and never fundamentally altered the traditional view that the West was barbarian. Japan also resisted the intrusion of foreign ideas; yet, eventually, by accepting the process of development on Western lines, many of the traditional aspects of Japanese culture were sacrificed. The sacrifice was successful, and Japan made the transition to a modern Westernized state, in a distinctively nationalist form. The Japanese took from Europe what they required: technical expertise from the British and Germans, commercial contacts from France and the Netherlands. Yet they maintained an independent stance, accepting from Europe only what they required. The fruits of this policy were their victory over Russia in 1904–5, and the extension of the Japanese Empire to the mainland. Like the willow, they had bent in the wind and survived; like the oak, China had broken.

Part Three

Aspirations and Angers

8 The Human Empire: Western Sensibility

The End of our Foundation is the knowledge of Causes, and secret motions of things; and the enlarging of the bounds of Human Empire, to the effecting of all things possible.

Francis Bacon, New Atlantis, *1626*

It was the age of science, new knowledge, searching criticism, followed by multiplied doubts and shaken beliefs.

John Morley, Recollections, *1917*

Shapes of the Age

Interpretations of the period 1848–1917, at least in its cultural aspect, vary very widely. Some historians view the era as having begun confidently but ended in discord and bewilderment. They can cite the memoirs of people who remembered their mid-century childhoods as idyllically, perhaps soporifically calm, and drew a contrast with the turmoil of adult life in which everything was change and confusion. In Britain, one might say, the splendours of the Great Exhibition of 1851 yielded in the 1870s to the protracted agricultural miseries of the Great Depression. All creeds, political, social, economic, cultural, were challenged, despaired of, contradicted by rival systems. Interpreters who discern a decisive shift from stability to instability are apt to fasten upon particular moments when they think the bottom fell out of the old order. One suggestion is the year 1870. The year of Dickens's death, it has been taken as a dividing-line between early and late Victorianism in Britain; a traumatic shock for France, because of the Franco-Prussian War and the Paris Commune of 1871; a new beginning for Germany and Italy as unified nation-states. For America, 1865 provides an obvious demarcation, since it saw the end of the Civil War and the start of the postwar boom that has been variously described as the 'Brown Decades', the 'Gilded

Age' and the age of the 'Great Barbecue'. Others point to the 1880s, when imperialism began to preoccupy the major powers. Roger Shattuck's account of the *avant-garde* in France, *The Banquet Years*, dates the phenomenon from the prodigious funeral of Victor Hugo in 1885. Others again regard the 1890s as the 'watershed' decade of modern history. The American Henry Adams, half-amused and half-appalled by the tendency of each successive scientific discovery to produce not enlightenment but further mysteries, chose 1900 as the date when 'the continuity snapped'.

Men alive in mid-century, if they were sensitive, felt that their times were already out of joint and confessed to a Hamlet-like inability to decide how to remedy matters. This is the tone of much of Tennyson's early verse, including *In Memoriam* (published in 1850) and *Maud* (1855), and pre-eminently that of Arthur Hugh Clough and Matthew Arnold. 'There never yet', said John Ruskin in *Modern Painters* (1856), 'was a generation (savage or civilized) who . . . so woefully fulfilled the words "having no hope, and without God in the world", as the present civilized European race.' If Friedrich Nietzsche was the first to insist emphatically that God was dead, the demise was touched upon as a possibility, in playful or sombre fashion, by a number of Europeans of the previous generation. Clough's *There is No God* –

> And almost every one when age,
> Disease, or sorrows strike him,
> Inclines to think there is a God,
> Or something very like him –

resembles Ernest Renan's famous sceptic's prayer, 'O God, if there is a God, save my soul, if I have a soul.' The complaint, as Arnold voiced it, was that mankind was caught between two worlds, one dead, the other powerless to be born; or, in the jingle of a poem by the American author James Russell Lowell:

> Men feel old systems cracking under 'em;
> Life saddens to a mere conundrum
> Which once Religion solved, but she
> Has lost – has Science found? – the key.

Underneath the soul-sickness was social injustice. Life was tolerably comfortable for people, according to Charles Kingsley in 1848, unless they happened to be 'Dorsetshire labourers – or Spitalfields weavers – or colliery children – or marching soldiers – or, I am afraid, one-half of English souls this day.' Material progress was being bought at a terrible price. The ostensible

210

spread of democracy was accomplishing little. The possession of a vote was an infinitesimal privilege. Worse still, it might merely hasten the coming of a mass-society in which questions of taste and morality were regulated by majoritarian appetites. Was democracy to entail what Herman Melville called a 'dead-level of rank commonplace'? Was the age losing its shape, and life losing all higher purpose? Against the notion of energy could be set the nineteenth-century alarm at the spread of *ennui*, listless depression, nervous exhaustion, paralysis of will in the face of impending catastrophe.

For our general purposes the shapes of the age can be thought of as the main themes that dominated the columns of the quarterly and monthly magazines, and that filtered down – by turns angrily, derisively, admiringly – into the weeklies and the daily newspapers. A logical sequence is to consider first the natural sciences, which enjoyed an astounding prestige; then the social sciences, including history and sociology, which tried to proceed on similar lines; then art and literature, which sometimes imitated the natural and social sciences and sometimes spurned them. Problems of religious faith were posed by all these developments. Finally, we can consider how far natural or supernatural certitude was undermined during the last twenty or thirty years before 1917.

The Marvels of Science

'Science', said the Prince Consort in commending the Great Exhibition of 1851, 'discovers laws of power, motion and transformation.' The task of industry, he added, was to apply these laws to 'the raw material'. Prince Albert's vocabulary is typical. Discovery, laws, power, motion, transformation: at least until the 1890s, such words were endowed with a sort of urgent awe. The high importance and the practical relevance of scientific endeavour were almost axiomatic.

This was true even where the inquiry dealt with remote eras and seemingly abstruse hypotheses. The most spectacular instance is the work of Charles Darwin, an English biologist who at the outset of his career thought he might become a clergyman. He drew upon his cultural heritage in other, more particular ways. Long before the end of the eighteenth century, astronomers had revealed the immensity of the universe. Somewhat later, geologists had come to realize that the earth must be far older than was specified in the conventional, biblical cosmology. Instead of a

Charles Darwin, a cartoon by F. Waddy (1873). Explorer, biologist and author, Darwin advanced a theory of evolution that challenged ideas which had been accepted for centuries.

few thousand years, time must be reckoned in millions of years. Moreover, the fossils analyzed by men like William Smith in England and Georges Cuvier in France were of extinct species. It had been previously supposed that every living form had been created simultaneously and continued to exist in a 'great chain of being'. By the early nineteenth century, geologists tended to accept instead the notion of 'catastrophism'. According to this the world had undergone a series of gigantic upheavals, each producing its own forms of life – a sequence dubbed 'progressionism' by contemporary biologists. Catastrophism could still be reconciled with the Mosaic theory of creation outlined in the book of Genesis; for the latest catastrophe in the series was taken to be that of the age of Noah. Naturalists such as Jean Lamarck, or Darwin's own grandfather Erasmus Darwin, conceded that the chain of being was not entirely static. There was an improvement in species, moving toward an ultimate perfection. But in their thinking, the divine machine still presupposed the Divine Mechanic; and they explained progressive change among different species as a quasi-religious, inherent impulse toward their own betterment.

The next stage leading toward Darwin's *Origin of Species* (1859) was the doctrine of 'uniformitarianism', brilliantly expounded by Darwin's close friend Charles Lyell in *Principles of Geology* (1830–2). Uniformitarianism denied the catastrophic theory of creation: the same causes now acting upon the world had existed since earliest times, the sequence was unbroken. If so, if God was not the all-explaining cause, then how and why had everything happened? In what ways was the development of man linked with that of other species? Geological speculation blended with other types of inquiry: Darwin's fieldwork in South America, correspondence with like-minded scientists, familiarity with the writings of Lyell, Alexander von Humboldt, and Robert Chambers (*Vestiges of Creation*, 1844; actually the work of a Scottish amateur but rumoured to have come from the pen of Prince Albert). Public interest was stimulated by polemical reviews and sermons, as rival theories clashed. Several men – Lyell himself, the French botanist Augustin de Candolle, and pre-eminently the English naturalist Alfred Russel Wallace – were on almost the same trail as Darwin. In a number of instances, they appear to have resisted the implications of the argument, and so to have closed their eyes to a hypothesis that now looks unavoidably obvious. Indeed Darwin's leisurely, almost lethargic pace of research may have concealed deep hesitations. He tried to leave the problem of human species out of the picture altogether in the *Origin*, and did not fully discuss it until 1871, when he published *The Descent of Man*.

The Descent of Man

Darwin's achievement lay in bringing forward the idea of 'natural selection' to explain the evolution of species. His reading of

Malthus gave him a clue. Malthus maintained that human population was expanding at a greater rate than the food required to sustain it. Candolle, quoted by Lyell, said that vegetation too had to compete for light and soil: 'All the plants of a given country are at war with one another.' And Lyell, noting how healthy growths choked out the less vigorous, spoke of the 'struggle for existence'. The well-known Darwinian phrase 'the survival of the fittest' was in fact coined by Herbert Spencer. Darwin took such hints, analogies and metaphors and, with a mass of corroborative detail, made out of them the thesis indicated by his full title: *On the Origin of Species by Means of Natural Selection, or the Preservation of Favoured Races in the Struggle for Life*. He insisted that there was variation within species: what was done by means of deliberate breeding within a few animal-generations could clearly be accomplished by 'natural selection' over enormous periods of time. The struggle for existence eventually extinguished some species: those that survived did so by dint of adaptation to the environment. Life, originally confined to a few simple forms or perhaps to one only, had diversified with splendid richness, the higher forms imperceptibly gaining on the lower, with man the highest of all. And the process would continue so long as the planet endured, in majestic efficacy.

A quarter of a century later, the biologist Thomas H. Huxley called the *Origin* 'the most potent instrument for the extension of the realm of natural knowledge' since the publication of Newton's *Principia*. The initial reception was by no means unanimously favourable. Some scientists, including Darwin's old tutor and the astronomer Sir John Herschel (who said the *Origin* was 'the law of higgledy-piggledy'), were hostile; a few, such as the Swiss-born Louis Agassiz of Harvard (a former pupil of Cuvier) never accepted evolutionism on Darwin's terms. As might have been expected, the clergy were prominent among Darwin's critics. The most notorious attack was delivered by 'Soapy Sam' Wilberforce, Bishop of Oxford, at the 1860 meeting of the British Association for the Advancement of Science. Wilberforce, relying upon oratorical tricks, asked Darwin's ally Huxley whether he was related to an ape on his grandfather's or on his grandmother's side. According to Lyell, Huxley replied with devastating seriousness that, given the choice of an ancestor between an ape and 'one who having received a scholastic education, should use his logic to mislead an untutored public, and should treat not with argument but with ridicule the facts and reasoning adduced in support

A satirical view of
evolution, from the
Illustrated Times (1863).
Darwin's theory began a
furious debate which
involved scientists,
theologians, and even
prime ministers.

of a grave and serious philosophical question, he would not
hesitate for a moment to prefer the ape'. The American scientist
John William Draper, who was present at the Wilberforce-Huxley
encounter, later published a *History of the Conflict between
Religion and Science* (1874) which was placed on the *index ex-
purgatorius* of the Roman Church. In truth, however, Darwinism
was quickly assimilated into intellectual discourse.

Another comfort to be derived from science was the conviction
that each advance aided progress on some other front. The more
knowledge, the more enlightenment. Thus Darwin had drawn
upon geology, paleontology, botany, embryology: reciprocally,
many fields could draw upon evolutionism, or felt they might.
Hence Marx's offer, politely declined, to dedicate *Das Kapital*
(*Capital*) to Darwin. Scientists of every colouration were fellow-
workers in a vast communal enterprise. In practice, like the
explorers who competed for priority in reaching the sources of
the Nile, or the North or South Pole, they were capable of frenetic

jealousy. Not many behaved as impeccably as Darwin and Wallace, in clarifying the record and giving one another credit. But this was the ideal. Science was felt to be a fraternity, perhaps a friary, dedicated to the service of mankind. Humility in performing small or laborious tasks was enjoined not only as a moral need but because a great part of scientific discovery consisted in breaking down a problem into its components. The method involved division of effort: analysis must precede synthesis. During the last few decades, these two words have acquired special associations. A person referred to in the 1970s as an 'analyst' would probably be taken to be a psychoanalyst, whereas the nineteenth century would assume he was a chemist. A century ago, 'synthetic' would be used either neutrally or in a complimentary sense, to describe an effort at system-building. By the 1970s, at least in popular usage, it has come to mean 'artificial' – probably a cheap substitute for the real thing.

Men working in the laboratories of, say, the 1870s were well aware of the practical applications of their realm of test-tubes and microscopes. Whole new industries grew from their experiments. But they were also buoyed up by the prospect of hitting upon fundamental laws that would furnish a new cosmogony. As with Darwinian evolutionism, the investigations of chemists and physicists built upon earlier hypotheses, if only in some cases to overturn them. Chemistry, organic and inorganic, wrestled with the atomic theories of scientists such as John Dalton and Amadeo Avogadro in an attempt to grasp the inmost, microscopic structures of a macroscopic universe. Julius Meyer, Dimitri Mendeleev and others produced periodic tables of the elements based on atomic weights. A perfect instance of the rational magic attributed to science was Mendeleev's insistence that three blank spaces on his chart must necessarily be filled by elements as yet undiscovered. Sure enough, his prediction was borne out by the subsequent discovery of gallium (1874), scandium (1879) and germanium (1885).

Power, motion, transformation: physicists in mid-century were fascinated by these, and by the interrelationship of heat, light and energy. Significantly, a batch of new word-coinages beginning with 'thermo-' date from this point in time. 'Thermodynamics', the study of the connections between heat and mechanical energy, is one example. Julius Mayer and James Joule were among the scientists who were, in the 1840s, independently trying to establish a mechanical equivalent for heat. Out of this climate of research came Hermann von Helmholtz's formulation (*Uber die Erhaltung der Kraft* [*The Conservation of Energy*], 1847) of a 'new universal law of all natural phenomena', now usually known as the First Law of Thermodynamics. 'It asserts', he said, 'that the *quantity of force which can be brought into action in the whole of Nature is unchangeable*, and can neither be increased nor diminished.' The word 'force' was replaced by 'energy' as being more precise. A few years later, William Thomson, Lord Kelvin, pursuing a different line in step with such physicists as Rudolf Clausius, announced his Second Law of Thermodynamics. This accepted the first law, of the conservation of energy, but stressed the dissipation of energy in the universe – a process that Clausius later called 'entropy'. While the total sum of energy remained constant, the amount of useful energy was being diminished through the conversion of useful into non-useful energy. These were theories rather than empirical demonstrations; indeed Helmholtz's paper was rejected by Poggendorff's great *Annalen der Chemie* (*Records of Chemistry*) as being too speculative. But their validity was soon apparent. Helmholtz, James Clerk Maxwell and the idiosyncratic Heinrich Rudolf Hertz (who suggested that the concept of force was unnecessary: space, time and mass were the true determinants): such scientists offered a solution to almost all the mysteries that had puzzled their predecessors. The early nineteenth century had been preoccupied with the steam-engine. They turned to the new sources of energy, electricity and electromagnetism. In this they were very much men of their time. Wilhelm Liebknecht, on a visit to London in 1850, found Karl Marx bubbling with excitement at the idea that, despite the temporary failure of the revolutions of 1848, 'natural science was preparing a new revolution. King Steam, who had revolutionized the world in the previous century, was coming to the end of his reign, and another, incomparably greater, revolutionist would take his place, the *electric spark*.' Marx urged his friend to go and look at 'a model of an electric machine which pulled a railway train', on exhibit in Regent Street. The scientists were unwittingly introducing an economic transformation, which must inevitably bring about a political revolution.

Such thoughts were foreign to Maxwell and other scientists. What they had in common with Marx was an extraordinary proud elation. To seek was to find: they were the privileged forerunners, travelling in new realms that gleamed before them like slopes of virgin snow. They embodied in their own careers the energy they sought to elucidate. They and many of the theorists in other fields were, one may say, human dynamos – the most productive scholars of any era in world history, harnessing themselves to the great apparatus of Knowledge. For them, if not for the mass of mankind with whom Marx concerned himself, labour was apparently never laborious.

The outcome for Maxwell and his colleagues, by about 1890, was an almost complete new scientific *Weltanschauung* (global philosophy). Light and electro-magnetism had proved to be related forms of wave-emotion, differing basically in wave-length. Energy was conceived as dual: that of 'matter' in motion, of which heat was an instance, or else of such phenomena as light and magnetism, which they called 'ether'. Not everything was yet explained. Nor did every scientist agree with every other; Kelvin, for instance, was initially resistant to Maxwell's propositions on electromagnetism. But there was fairly widespread conviction that everything within natural science could ultimately be explained within the framework that had been established.

The Science of Man

History was an ancient branch of literature. Around the middle of the nineteenth century, fresh claims began to be made on its behalf. The novelist Flaubert declared that science and history were the 'two muses of modern times'. Whether history was or might become a science in its own right was a different question. Henry Thomas Buckle, producing the first volume of his *History of Civilization in England* (1857), upbraided his colleagues for refusing to generalize. He himself hoped 'to accomplish for the history of man something equivalent, or at all events analogous, to what has been effected by other inquiries for the different branches of natural science'. The actions of men, 'being determined solely by their antecedents, must have a character of uniformity'. Looking back from the vantage-point of 1894, the American historian Henry Adams revealed how much he had been stirred by Buckle's challenge: 'Those of us who read Buckle's first volume . . . , and almost immediately afterwards . . . read *The Origin of Species* . . . , never doubted that historians would follow until they had exhausted every possible hypothesis to create a science of history.' Surely no scholar 'with a spark of imagination or with an idea of scientific method can have helped dreaming of the immortality that would be achieved by the man who should successfully apply Darwin's method to the facts of human history'.

The general public liked the big sweep of various historians who, fortunately for their readers, did not always practise the forbidding detachment they preached. The French historian Fustel de Coulanges warned his audience that 'Patriotism is a virtue and history a science, and the two should not be confounded.' But in this he was unusual. A good deal of historical scholarship was implicitly nationalistic. The reader could experience a glow of gratification on finding that his forebears had been men and women of such calibre, and on reflecting that, even so, he was vastly more civilized than they. History pedigreed and flattered him. He came of the finest stock and belonged to the best of nations.

If the professional historians avoided biography, there was general agreement that everyone, not forgetting children, could benefit from the example of greatness. Those who found Carlyle's biographies of Oliver Cromwell and Frederick of Prussia hard going could turn to more popular works such as Agnes Strickland's *Lives of the Queens of England* or J. G. Lockhart's *Life of Sir Walter Scott*, or to diaries and memoirs, or to a host of historical novels – Alexandre Dumas's *The Three Musketeers* (1844), Charles Kingsley's *Westward Ho!* (1855) and *Hereward the Wake* (1866), the Leatherstocking tales of James Fenimore Cooper, Charles Dickens's *A Tale of Two Cities* (1859), Joseph Scheffel's *Ekkehard* (1857), Charles Reade's *The Cloister and the Hearth* (1861) or perhaps Robert Louis Stevenson's *Kidnapped* (1886) and *Catriona* (1893).

Kierkegaard said: 'Life can only be understood backward but it must be lived forward.' Most of Queen Victoria's contemporaries were prepared to gird themselves for the tasks of tomorrow. But they needed the past, whether for enlightenment, decoration, consolation, precept or romantic charm. The serious scholar insisted with Fustel de Coulanges that 'history is not entertainment but science.' The writings of William Stubbs, Hippolyte Langlois or Heinrich von Sybel might never reach the attention of the magazine-reading public. Discussions of feudal tenure or of fine points of canon law might seem arid in the extreme. This was what Nietzsche (*Vom Nutzen und Nachteil der Historie*, 1874) termed 'antiquarian' – the pious accumulation of knowledge about the past simply because it was the past. Yet pedants, popularizers and public alike readily accepted that history was of value in enlarging man's horizons. The scholar could justify even the

Auguste Comte, the
French philosopher, who
was the first to coin the
word 'sociology'.

minutiae of his research as a legacy for succeeding generations of
historians who might perceive connections that had eluded him.
Along with ordinary folk, he could subscribe to the opinion of Dr
Johnson that 'Whatever makes the past, the distant, or the future,
predominate over the present, advances us in the dignity of
thinking beings.' Scholarship was progressive because man was
progressing.

The achievements of social science between 1830 and World
War I were extraordinary, and perhaps those of sociology were
the most impressive of all. Historians might say that sociologists
either specialized in documenting the obvious or else theorized
in vacuo, and that the middle ground between dull fact and cosmic

utterance was often empty. Sociologists could retort that most historical writing was nothing but a chronological string of facts. Moreover they did not regard as true sociologists those generalizers such as Auguste Comte and Herbert Spencer whom critics loved to pounce upon. Professional sociologists of the later nineteenth century were willing to admit that Comte and Spencer had over-reached themselves. Comte, who had in any case borrowed his ideas on the need for a 'positivist' (scientific, non-supernatural) approach to society from Saint-Simon, could be dismissed as naïve, although he continued to be revered in some Latin countries, especially in South America. His amalgam of statistics and benevolence did not wear well. What he first called 'social physics' and then 'sociology' (the term is his invention) was never sharply defined. His Law of the Three Stages – theological, metaphysical, positive – through which mankind was supposed to progress was intriguing, but became blurred with his elaborate scheme for a 'religion of humanity'. Rosy affirmations replaced detached observation. Several objections could be made to Spencer, including his all-out hostility to almost every form of controlling activity by the state. The principal accusation is, however, that Spencer carried the analogy between social and biological organisms to the point of absurdity within his grand evolutionary, survival-of-the-fittest scheme. For example, he compared means of transport with the circulation of the blood, and nerve fibres with telegraph wires, in far more than a metaphorical sense. Biological and indeed cosmological evolution was offered as a proof of human progress. Everything in the universe, for Spencer, moved from incoherent homogeneity to coherent heterogeneity. Nebulae were nebulous: solar systems, a later evolution, were systematic. In human existence, society improved as it grew more complex.

Yet Comte and Spencer were vastly admired in their day, by scientists among others. And rightly; for they were magnificent orchestrators of the welter of information and hypothesis. There was a Faustian boldness in their *summa*. Each in his way believed that social science was a moral science. This doubleness, present also in Marx and Engels and other nineteenth-century searchers after ultimate truth, ennobled their work in the act of formally weakening it. To the objection *'non sequitur'*, 'it does not follow', they answered: in time it will. The spirit is that expressed by Browning:

> Ah, but a man's reach should exceed his grasp,
> Or what's a heaven for?

The mood of the next generation of social scientists was less euphoric yet also infused with a kind of poetry. Whether a particular scholar was conservatively or radically inclined in his political and economic views, there is a basic assumption underlying a score of spendid books in different fields. The cardinal idea is that the world has changed, and man must wrestle with the consequences. In a way, nineteenth-century scholars shared the nostalgia of the ordinary citizen for the past, in particular the medieval past. Medieval history and society were subjected to an intense yet also oddly affectionate scrutiny. These researches posited a fundamental difference between medieval and modern conditions. Generally, they agreed that the break had been caused by the rise of middle-class capitalism and technology.

A few examples illustrate the power of this symbolic contrast upon the minds of the age. In the *Communist Manifesto* of 1848, Marx and Engels maintained that the triumph of the bourgeoisie 'has put an end to all feudal, patriarchal, idyllic relations. . . . It has resolved personal worth into exchange value ... The bourgeoisie has stripped of its halo every occupation ... hitherto looked up to with reverent awe. It has converted the physician, the lawyer, the priest, the poet, the man of science into its paid wage labourers.' They went on: 'Constant revolutionizing of production, uninterrupted disturbance of all social conditions, everlasting uncertainty and agitation distinguish the bourgeois epoch from all earlier ones. . . . All that is solid melts into air, all that is holy is profaned, and man is at last compelled to face with sober senses his real conditions of life and his relations with his kind.' This picture had already been presented in somewhat different form by Hegel and Comte among others. Comte's utopian new positivist order almost re-invented the groups and rituals of medieval Christendom, minus the Christianity. In *Les Ouvriers Européens* (1855), Pierre Guillaume Frédéric Le Play, concentrating upon basic family types instead of feudalism, contrasted the unstable family characteristic of decadent periods such as his own with two other stable patterns, one archaic and the other, the 'stem' family, to be found in various healthy, semi-traditional societies.

With Sir Henry Maine's *Ancient Law* (1861), the examples are taken from jurisprudence. But the contrast is strikingly clear. It is between societies or eras relying upon 'status' and 'ascription', and those defined by 'contract' and 'achievement'. The 'status'-'contract' typology quickly came into use among scholars in other fields. A few years later, in 1868, the first volume of O.

Gierke's *Das Deutsche Genossenschaftsrecht* likewise sketched a contrast between the organic, decentralized medieval world and the atomized, centralized nation-state of the modern world: in short, between partnership *(Genossenschaft)* and competitive individualism *(Herrschaft)*. In *Ancient Society* (1877) by the American sociologist Lewis Henry Morgan, a work that Engels used for his *Origin of the Family*, the distinction is between *societas* (a community of kindred) and *civitas* (the political state, where roles are defined by class and property). Here, as in Maine, we go back beyond medieval society. But the basic theme is the same: once there were real communities, now there are only loose conglomerates. It is finely presented by the German sociologist Ferdinand Tönnies in *Gemeinschaft und Gesellschaft* (*Community and Society*, 1887), as a transition from the countryside to the city, from the feminine to the masculine, from the vocation to the job, from solidarity to libertarianism. None of these is a lament, as such, or a plea of the sort made by William Morris for a restoration of medieval guild-life. They are not sentimental. But they are still among the best analyses ever made of the conditions of dynamic society, poised between commitment and indifference, between the programmatic breeziness of some of the out-and-out evolutionists and the gloom of late nineteenth-century pessimists. The great social scientists – we should add to the list Max Weber, Emil Durkheim with his concept of *anomie*, Georg Simmel, Vilfredo Pareto, and perhaps the English journalist Walter Bagehot (*Physics and Politics*, 1876) and the sardonic American Thorstein Veblen – made an extraordinary effort to rise imaginatively above what Marx and Engels called false consciousness, so as to understand the instincts and principles by which humanity operated.

Systems in Chaos

It is too simple to state that until about 1890 systems were being founded, while after 1890 they were being confounded. As we have seen, complexity and introspection can be traced back to the beginning of the century. In mid-century Arthur Schopenhauer could observe that 'To the palpably sophistical proofs of Leibnitz that this is the best of all possible worlds, we may seriously ... oppose the proof that it is the worst of all possible worlds.' Nor did ambitious thought-construction cease, in the natural or the social sciences.

Sigmund Freud,
'discoverer and inventor
of an entire new
conception of mankind'.

Nevertheless, there was a change, for a number of associated reasons. Historians of science usually take 1890 as the moment at which 'classical' gave way to 'modern' physics. A perhaps excessively precise date would be 1895. In that year, Wilhelm Röntgen of the University of Würzburg, experimenting with cathode rays, discovered that in certain circumstances a form of radiation was produced that could penetrate almost any material. These emanations he named X-rays. The next year, in Paris, Henri Becquerel found that uranium salts gave off radiation even when shut in a drawer; they affected some photographic plates kept in the same drawer. Following up this clue, in 1899 Pierre and Marie Curie isolated two new elements, polonium and radium – each more radioactive than uranium. During the next few years, scientists working in Montreal, in Cambridge (England) and in Copenhagen, concluded that radiation was caused by discharges from unstable atoms; and they went on exploring the atomic microcosm. Meanwhile, at a meeting in Berlin held in 1900, Max Planck introduced his 'quantum' theory to explain a problem in radiation. His theory was that energy, hitherto regarded as quite different from matter, was entropically dispersed in units or 'quanta', not in a continuous stream. Energy had been conceived of as moving in waves: now its structure, like that of matter, might be atomic. The intelligent layman Henry Adams, trying to grasp the import of these phenomena in the course of a visit to the Paris Exposition of 1900, confessed total bewilderment. He could make approximate sense of classical physics, but not of this new universe 'which had no common scale of measurement with the old. He had entered a super-sensual world, in which he could measure nothing except by chance collisions of movements imperceptible to his senses, perhaps even imperceptible to his instruments.'

The search for the congruences of incongruity, already embarked on by sociologists and anthropologists, was the special province of psychology. The philosopher Henri Bergson predicted in 1901 that the major task of the twentieth century would be 'to explore the unconscious, to investigate the subsoil of the mind' by means of fresh techniques. He was not yet acquainted with the work of the Viennese doctor Sigmund Freud, who was both discoverer and inventor of an entire new conception of mankind. Freud met the old and ailing William James on a visit to America in 1909, and was moved by James's parting words: 'The future of psychology belongs to your work.' By then, Freud had come a long way, by careful and sometimes hesitant stages, in face of considerable opposition. An early interest in hysteria (then treated as a disorder confined to women) led to work with J. M. Charcot in Paris and collaboration with Josef Breuer in Vienna. Freud experimented with various ways of dealing with nervous diseases: hypnosis, narcotics, the infant technique of psychoanalysis. Himself a prey to neurasthenia, he meditated on his own symptoms. His tendency to dream stimulated him to interpret the dreams of his patients. The realization that hysteria was displayed by men as well as women heightened Freud's interest in sexuality. At first he believed that only adults wove sexual fantasies. By degrees, he became convinced that sexuality was prominent in the sub-conscious minds of children, and even of babies. When he began to publish his findings (*The Interpretation of Dreams*, 1900; *The Psychopathology of Everyday Life*, 1904; *Three Essays on the Theory of Sexuality*, 1905), the great bulk of the medical profession, not to speak of the general public, either ignored him or denounced him as a lunatic and a purveyor of filth. Freud won recognition among a small cosmopolitan band during the next decade – hence the invitation to lecture in the United States, together with his Zurich follower of that time, Carl Gustav Jung. His essential work was in print by about 1910. But its immense significance was not generally perceived.

In retrospect, we can see how his theories fitted in with the turn-of-the-century theorizing about the apparent irrationality of mankind, and with the growing sexual candour of at least some art and literature: Edouard Manet's *Déjeuner sur l'herbe* (1863) and the drawings of Aubrey Beardsley in the 1890s, the novels of Emil Zola, Leo Tolstoy's *Anna Karenina* (1873–6) and *The Kreutzer Sonata* (1889), Theodore Dreiser's *Sister Carrie* (1900), and some of the plays of Eugène Brieux, Henrik Ibsen, August Strindberg and George Bernard Shaw are random examples. In Freud's and all these other cases, the immediate popular reaction was disgust, expressing itself often in cloacal images: the subsoil of the mind was apparently associated with nightsoil. The official reaction was sometimes censorship (the initial decree in Russia concerning *The Kreutzer Sonata*) or prosecution (the fate of the London publisher of Zola). The educated public, however, strove to be open-minded. 'Is Zola immoral?' was a typical theme for debate in German circles during the 1880s.

Movements in literature and the arts deserve to be looked at more closely. As one might expect, they reveal a sequence of concerns comparable to those of the natural and social sciences, with a fairly distinct shift of sensibility in the 1890s. There are obvious differences; in fact aphorisms such as 'Art is *I*: Science is *We*' make them seem diametrically opposite. In this view the arts are individualist and inspirational, the sciences collective and formal. The sciences – or more commonly Science – served often enough as a whipping-boy for those who felt that society was being treated too much as an organism or a machine. One serious aspect of the trend to 'scientism' was that some sociologists tended to explain *all* human behaviour as socially determined. Their models presupposed that the very existence of social forms guaranteed their rightness ('Whatever is, is best'), so that unconventional attitudes on the part of individuals were either of no account or else threatened the natural equilibrium of the community. In practice, however, there was no dramatic clash between Art and Science in the middle decades of the nineteenth

Déjeuner sur l'herbe, by Manet – 'growing sexual candour'.

century, and artists and scientists shared elements of sensibility. The parallels are clear from the literature and painting of the period, at least by those who prided themselves on being advanced. 'Realism' was their watchword. As the historian Ranke endeavoured to depict in the past only what had actually happened, so writers of fiction vowed to avoid the unhealthily fictitious. In the preface to their story *Germinie Lacerteux* (1865), Edmond and

Jules de Goncourt announced that by means of 'analysis and psychological research', the novel was becoming 'contemporary Moral History'. Having undertaken 'the studies and the obligations of science, it can demand the liberties and freedom of science'. Zola was even more explicit in *Le Roman expérimental* (*The Experimental Novel*, 1880). He based his entire defence of realism (or 'naturalism') upon another book about scientific experiment by the celebrated medical theorist Claude Bernard, including the notion that 'the originality, the inventiveness, the genius' of an experimenter was not incompatible with but actually arose from careful observation. Hence, 'If the experimental method leads to knowledge of physical life, it may also lead to knowledge of passional and intellectual life. It is only a question of gradation ... from chemistry to physiology, and then from physiology to anthropology and sociology. The experimental novel comes at the end.' So the novelist may be an exemplary observer, and by implication the highest form of observer. Science culminates in art. A similar dedication to accuracy, a similar effort to remain detached from the subject, characterized the work of realist painters. An extreme instance is Claude Monet's rendering of his wife Camille on her death-bed (1879). Professional instinct, he confessed, made him analyze the subtle flesh tints on her face: 'Even before I had the idea of setting down the features to which I was so deeply attached, my organism automatically reacted to the colour stimuli, and my reflexes caught me up in spite of myself. . . .' One cannot quite gather whether Monet is condemning or praising himself – the latter, to judge from the scientific vocabulary.

Realism and naturalism, like many another movement in the arts, ultimately raised more problems than they solved. In literature the determination to be truthful impelled authors to abandon elaborate plots and wedding-bell finales, intrusive moralizing and artificial dialogue. 'The field of art', N.G. Chernyshevsky argued in an admirable treatise (1853), 'is not limited to beauty in the aesthetic sense of the word ...; art reproduces everything in life that is of interest to man.' 'Take eloquence and wring its neck!' (*'Prends l'éloquence et tords lui son cou!'*) was the pithy recommendation of Paul Verlaine. A logical development, launched by the Goncourts and soon followed by Zola and by Flaubert in his story *Un Coeur simple (A Simple Heart)*, was to deal centrally with the lives of poor people, as was done by such painters as Gustave Courbet and Jean-François Millet. Another obvious duty for the conscientious realist was to aim at verisimilitude. The English artist William Holman Hunt went all the way to Palestine to find an authentic setting for his *Scapegoat*; Edgar Degas's sculpture *La petite danseuse (The little dancer)*, which created a sensation in 1881 with its 'frightful realism', was clad in an actual bodice, shoes and silk hair-ribbon. A further step was to paint in the open air instead of in the studio. Yet another was to make use of photography, for 'sketching' purposes and sometimes for the accidental novelties of composition it suggested. The most shocking obligation of the realist, for his audience, was the stripping away of artifice and euphemism. The nude became naked. In conventional poses, said Degas, the nude was coyly conscious of being looked at: his naked women were absorbed in their own affairs – 'It is as if you looked through a keyhole.' The introduction of 'sordid' themes into art and literature – denounced on the very score of keyhole-peeping – meant not only that people such as prostitutes should be depicted but that there must be no moralizing about vice and virtue. These, according to the critic Taine, were mere 'products' like vitriol and sugar.

So far, so good, for the realist/naturalist. But verisimilitude lay dangerously close to the burnished virtuosity of the academicians. To paint subjects without a 'moral' intention was to risk insipidity; this happened to the Impressionists, once the public got over its first disapproval of their bright simplified canvases and began to find them pretty. Or the choice of subject itself became a moral decision, and then a stereotype; despite what the artist may have intended, ordinary poverty – 'the man with a hoe' – acquired an aura of heroism, turning people into the People. In the field of design, William Morris and others introduced a conception of sincerity, respect for function and truthfulness to materials, that led away from 'realistic' patterns toward simplicity and abstraction. Painters similarly began to concern themselves with the problem that three-dimensionality on a two-dimensional surface was an illusion, possibly a deceit. One effort at a solution, stimulated by the enthusiasm for Japanese prints, was to paint in flat planes. The next stage, pioneered by Paul Cézanne and then by Georges Braque and Pablo Picasso, was to abstract the subject-matter into basic geometrical shapes: hence Cubism.

All these and more considerations excited and yet perplexed the creative imaginations of the late nineteenth century. For an increasing number, realism lost its glamour. If human activity was predetermined by external, 'scientific' factors, the prospect was bleak, and there was less and less room for sensibility. Yet science itself was revealing that the universe was infinitely mysterious, and that the mystery was nowhere more profound than in the human psyche. Within the mind, said the poet Gerard Manley Hopkins, there were abysses, 'frightful, sheer, no-man-fathomèd'. The search for reality was not abandoned but it was given fresh emphases with the recognition that subjective truth was at least as important as objective truth.

Riddles of the Universe

The result in the decades immediately preceding World War I was a fantastic *mélange* of styles, contradicting and superseding one another. Middlebrow taste lagged behind, still attached to more traditional notions of beauty, craftsmanship and the like, though willing to tolerate some innovation here and there – especially in matters of decoration and architecture if, as with Art Nouveau, they did not appear too outrageous; for these were fashions, and it was understood that fashions in dress and *décor* were meant to be somewhat sensational, and ephemeral. There was thus a certain popular sanction for the idea of 'originality', conceived of rather as theatricality.

The arts and sciences kept more or less in step with one another – if we can apply such a metaphor to a period when there were so many movements, each marching to its own music. At any given moment, the tastes of the main body were a long way behind those of the *avant-garde*. Indeed, the more outrageous members of the *avant-garde* would have denied that they had any commission to scout on behalf of the mass of society. The mass was by definition the enemy, or at any rate a herd incapable of finer feelings. The dislike was of course mutual. Nevertheless, in retrospect we can pick out features common to the successive generations. Until about 1890, even making allowances for the time-lag between conventional and unconventional attitudes, and for the different nuances of one nation from another, we can see that in all fields intellectual and aesthetic styles were generally consonant. Rare individuals resisted the *Zeitgeist* (Spirit of the Times) so violently that they may seem to be out of their time. Yet – Nietzsche is an instance – their very resistance was to formulations *of the time*. This is not to decry their originality, but to stress that nay-sayers can be understood to the full only in the context of the yea-sayers

Opposite: La petite danseuse by Degas, criticized by contemporaries for its 'frightful realism'.

230

The Viaduct at L'Estaque,
1882–5, by Paul Cézanne,
one of the pioneers of
Cubism.

233

Woman with mustard-pot,
1910, by Picasso.

of their era. And it is worth repeating that however conventional
the bulk of citizens were, the spirit of the age obliged them to give
assent to the principle of originality, even though demonstrations
of it might puzzle or enrage them.

Until about 1890, then, the common element – as in 'classical'
physics – was an attachment to rational inquiry. This was so
powerful that it undercut and modified the arguments of those
who by temperament or profession (notably churchmen) were
antagonistic. True, there was no lack of controversy over religious
doctrine. But much of the anguish came from believers who feared
their own unbelief, or people struggling to hold positions they
suspected were no longer tenable. Authority was represented by
the State rather than the Church, and heresy was defined in
political rather than religious terms. The most serious challenges

234

to organized religion were not over doctrine but over jurisdiction, as in the *Kulturkampf* between the Pope and Bismarck. The conflict date gained its name from the fact that what was at stake were two alternative views of German society: Bismarck's harsh, Protestant North German/Prussian tradition, and the counter culture of the predominately Catholic south of Germany. In fact the struggle was largely of Bismarck's own making, and one of the few battles which he lost. Pius IX denounced the errors of 'liberalism' and 'rationalism' in his encyclical *Quanta Cura* (1864). But, quite apart from the offence he gave to liberal Catholics as well as Protestants, his Syllabus of Errors was an attempt to shore up ecclesiastical prerogative, above all in Italy, in the face of what he took to be the almost overwhelming dictatorship of the state. The papal counterattack, exemplified in the Vatican Council of 1869–70 and its proclamation of the dogma of papal infallibility, was in large part a defensive reaction to the rationalist climate of the age.

After 1890, sensibility diversified to include the concerns we identify as 'modern' – though of course from the perspective of the 1970s, these too have acquired a patina of antiquity: anti-traditionalism generates its own tradition. In fiction and drama, naturalism remained the dominant mode; ironic, personal and vernacular elements appeared in the poetry of writers as diverse as Thomas Hardy, Jules Laforgue and T. S. Eliot. But there was a new fascination with the irrational, the exotic and esoteric – with private symbols rather than with exterior systems. As physicists of the 1890s began to stumble upon relationships between matter and ether, so the Symbolist poets of the period dreamed of elusive correspondences between words, colours and music. The rational seemed to engender the irrational, or to become indistinguishable from it. The craving for the absolute was pursued privately, mystically – whether in the form of revived Catholicism or theosophy or the special, organized American variant of Christian Science, or even in diabolism. The poet W. B. Yeats was among other things a numerologist; so was Freud's one-time friend the nose-and-throat specialist Wilhelm Fliess, who convinced himself that the figures twenty-eight and twenty-three, because of their connection with the number of days in the menstrual cycle, embodied some immense buried insight. In several respects, the post-1890 years could be called mystified.

9 Left, Right and Centre: Reform or Revolution?

The laws of the production and distribution of wealth . . . are the most beautiful . . . of the natural laws of God. . . . They call on each nation with silent bidding to supply of its abundance that which the other wants; and make all nations labourers for the common store; and in them lies perhaps the strongest natural proof that the earth was made for the sociable being, man.

Goldwin Smith, inaugural lecture as Regius Professor of History, Oxford, 1859

The liberalist of today has this advantage over antique or mediaeval times, that his doctrine seeks not only to individualize but to universalize. The great word Solidarity has arisen. Of all dangers to a nation, . . . there can be no greater one than having certain portions of the people set off from the rest by a line drawn – they not as privileged as others, but degraded, humiliated, made of no account. . . . Anything worthy to be call'd statesmanship in the Old World, . . . does not debate today whether to hold on, attempting to lean back and monarchize, or to look forward and democratize – but *how*, and in what degree and part, most prudently, to democratize.

Walt Whitman, Democratic Vistas, 1871

Along with the constantly diminishing number of the magnates of capital, who usurp and monopolize . . . , grows the mass of misery, oppressions, slavery, degradation, exploitation, but with this too grows the revolt of the working class, always increasing in numbers, and disciplined, united, organized by the very mechanism of the process of capitalist production itself. . . . Centralizations of the means of production and socialization of labour at last reach a point where they become incompatible with their capitalist integument. This integument is bust asunder. The knell of capitalist private property sounds. The expropriators and expropriated. . . .

Karl Marx, Das Kapital, Vol. 1, 1867

The revolutionary is a man under vow. He ought to occupy himself entirely with one exclusive interest, with one thought and passion: the Revolution. . . . He has only one aim, one science: destruction. . . . Between him and society there is war to the death, incessant, irrecon-

236

cilable. . . . He must make a list of those who are condemned to death, and expedite their sentence according to the order of their relative iniquities.

Revolutionary Catechism, *in Nechaev's possession when arrested in Switzerland in 1872.*

Lessons of 1848

Revolutions of one kind or another broke out in most parts of Europe during 1847–8. The first manifestations, in Switzerland, Denmark, Italy and then France, were libertarian and euphoric. New constitutions were demanded, and granted or promised with surprising ease. Louis Philippe abdicated in France; so did the King of Bavaria. Statesmen of the old guard – François Pierre Guizot in Paris, Prince Clemens Metternich in Vienna – were toppled from office. The early months of 1848 were 'the springtime of the people'. How good it was, exlaimed the French woman radical George Sand, 'to fall asleep in the mud and waken in the skies'.

As her remark suggests, many people were taken by surprise. Events swept them along. A whole continent seemed to be in the grip of an amazing contagion that ignored frontiers and dynasties.

The liberal revolutions of 1848 alarmed absolutist monarchs all over Europe. This Punch cartoon shows their plight, all in the same small boat, named the 'Ancien Régime'.

Many of the 1848 revolutionaries were young students – the mass risings have been dubbed 'a revolt of intellectuals'.

The red flag of international brotherhood waved on the barricades of Paris in February. Historians have noted that in the previous November, Marx and Engels, attending a Communist congress in London, were commissioned to prepare their epoch-making *Manifesto*. Yet if a new world was in the making, the signs and portents were visible enough. Perturbed by the activities of constitutional reformers in Switzerland, Metternich in that same month of November 1847 described the country as a 'volcano' and predicted that 'The foreign body which will cause it to erupt is the radical element.' Torn between alarm and fascination, Alexis de Tocqueville used the identical image two months later in the course of a speech in the French Chamber of Deputies.

238

The working class, he said, were aroused. 'Ideas flow through their breasts that will shake the basis of society: they say that everything above them is incapable and unworthy of governing; that the distribution of goods to the profit of some is unjust.' Such ideas must lead sooner or later to upheaval. 'We are sleeping on a volcano. . . . Do you not see that the earth trembles anew? A wind of revolution blows, the storm is on the horizon.'

Observers such as Tocqueville might feel that the scenario had already been written in 1789 and thereafter. The red flag was after all a Jacobin symbol. There had been an abortive Russian rising of the 'Decembrists' in 1825, and any number of minor peasant risings. Exiled Russian intellectuals – Alexander Herzen, Michael Bakunin – were hobnobbing with other trouble-makers in Geneva, Paris, Brussels and London. There had been commotions in Italy, Poland and Spain. A revolution in Paris had brought Louis Philippe to the throne in 1830, and there had been serious political and industrial riots in Paris and Lyons. In Scotland and northern England, working-class discontent had found expression in the Chartist movement. The bad harvests of 1845–7 had spread misery through Europe; in Ireland half the population was starving.

Radical theorists therefore had plenty to go on. And they had been active wherever they were allowed to spread their doctrines. In France, Louis August Blanqui revealed himself an uncompromising follower of the old insurrectionists Gracchus Babeuf and Buonarroti. Forever on the run, or on trial, or in jail, or briefly at the forefront of events, Blanqui was a sinister and repulsive figure to those who opposed him. Tocqueville, who saw Blanqui in 1848, recorded that he had a 'sickly, wicked . . . expression, . . . the appearance of a mouldy corpse; . . . he seemed to have passed his life in a sewer and to have just left it'.

What happened in France, as Marx and Engels subsequently showed with piercing insight, was essentially repeated in other countries. The problem was how far the revolution could and should be pushed. Ruling monarchs and their senior ministers were generally unpopular. There was a sentiment spread fairly widely through the lower and middling orders of society that favoured a diminution of central authority, perhaps to embrace republicanism. Nationalist zeal in Germany, Austria-Hungary and Italy easily merged with constitutionalist and libertarian programmes. But there was also a deepseated fear of lawlessness, mob-rule, 'socialist' control. The attachment to private property proved as desperate an ideology as any opposite theory of a levelling nature, and with far more and more powerful support. In France, only one in five of Blanqui's thirty million were urban workers. The other twenty-five million rural and small-town peasants and artisans had no enthusiasm for a truly egalitarian experiment. The Irish peasantry, despite an ancient habit of resistance, could muster no more than a flicker of revolt in 1848. Throughout Europe, when it came to a collision between socialism (real or imagined) and what might be called constitutional democracy, the middle classes backed away. The red flag yielded to the tricolour. In the words of Frederick William IV of Prussia, 'soldiers are the only cure for democrats'.

So in Paris, the carefree triumphs of February led to the horror of June 1848. The National Workshops were closed down; a popular rising was crushed in four days of gunfire and atrocities. Liberals like Alphonse de Lamartine, recently so full of fine talk, were now involved in the suppression, and the *petit-bourgeois* civilians enrolled in the National Guard showed no mercy for the men on the other side of the barricades. When the shooting ceased some fifteen hundred were dead, including four generals, the Archbishop of Paris and an unknown total of workers who had been shot or bayonetted as prisoners. Herzen and his family, living through these dreadful days in Paris, faced the dispiriting aftermath. The bloodstained dawn 'lighted up a scene of fearful desolation. Half of our hopes, half of our beliefs were slain, ideas of skepticism and despair haunted the brain and took root in it.'

The reaction was typical of Europe's intelligentsia. The people's springtime had been blasted. The Chartist movement had fizzled out in England. Risings in Cracow, Vienna, Madrid, Prague, Frankfurt ended in ignominy. At Frankfurt and elsewhere, the parliamentarians lost themselves in procedural mazes, earning contempt from once-admiring workers and once-frightened kings. Where resistance was more heroic, as in Vienna and in Hungary, the counter-revolution was the more severe. The Austrian capital remained under martial law for five years after 1848. In Paris the let-down was cruelly ironical. The Second Republic used its lately-acquired universal manhood suffrage in December 1848 to vote overwhelmingly for Louis Napoleon as its new president. Three years later, by means of a plebiscite, he imposed himself as head of state, and in another twelve months was proclaimed Napoleon III, ruler of the Second Empire.

The Liberal Affirmation

France was the country that sought to explain things. Words such as 'communism' and 'socialism' and 'individualism' entered the English language *via* French. The very terms 'left' and 'right', as guides to political ideology, derived from the seating arrangements in the French legislature. Blanqui's economist-brother, the respectable Adolphe Blanqui, is credited with coining the expression 'industrial revolution'. But Britain was the country that introduced the industrial revolution. Capitalism, a dominant bourgeoisie, an exploited urban proletariat: these were special features of British society. Engels's experience of the Lancashire textile-town of Salford, on which he based his *Condition of the Working Class* (1845), shaped Marx's conception of capitalist evolution. If the teachers of the first half of the nineteenth century were predominantly French, the classroom lay across the Channel in Britain.

Why then, despite some initial alarm, was there no real attempt at a British revolution in 1848? Disraeli was only one of many writers of the period who admitted that Britain was divided into two nations – rich and poor. The life of the poor in Glasgow, Manchester, Leeds or London was grim. J.C.Cobden's *White Slaves of England* was the not-unjustified title of an American book of the period, which asked why philanthropists in Britain were so ready to condemn black slavery in the United States but so blind to the plight of their own industrial serfs. More or less radical working-class organizations had existed there for several decades. Laws and prejudices were repressive enough to arouse anger, yet not so severe as to inhibit all discussion. When even conservative spokesmen conceded the evils of the factory system, why did the lid not blow off? When a similar fate later overtook the United States, why did neither country generate a vigorous radical movement?

Several answers can be offered, though some may seem merely to heighten the mystery. In the case of Britain, the first point is that together with the malady, Britain invented the rationale for industrial capitalism in the shape of liberal or classical economics. The essence of this doctrine was utility. Production and distribution obeyed iron laws, binding upon the manufacturer no less than upon his workers. Market forces determined profit, wages, rent. Employers were often willing to admit that the result bore harshly upon the working man – or woman or child. Wages might well permit subsistence only at the most meagre level. That was unfortunate, but unavoidable; for the manufacturer claimed that he could not survive in a competitive market unless, like his rivals, he pared costs with ruthless efficiency. The justification was that the whole nation benefited. Wealth circulated; the poor were becoming less poor. That Britain was outstripping other nations in Europe was taken to prove the argument: this together with the fact that the United States was making giant strides in productivity. The conclusion was that private enterprise and minimal government interference were the best guarantors of prosperity. Centralized government on the ancient European model was oppressive as well as inefficient. The British, and the Americans, prided themselves on their practical humaneness. In their own eyes, they *were* more philanthropic than other peoples. They did not as a rule lock men up in droves for their political opinions; they did not maintain a state censorship; they did not maintain a selfish, irresponsible aristocracy. A liberal economy might allot rewards and punishments as summarily as some absolute monarch. But the outcome was fair and logical. The idle poor suffered, as they must in any real, conceivable society. The respectable, temperate, church- or chapel-attending poor gradually improved their standard of living as they deserved to do. Courageous and hardworking manufacturers pioneered along the industrial frontier, enriching not merely themselves but the rest of mankind, and strengthening the ranks of the upper class through intermarriage. The aristocracy furnished the nation with leaders – in politics, religion, landowning, the armed forces – and on the whole performed these tasks competently, at least by the test of comparison with ruling groups in other countries. The Anglo-American nations, in their own eyes, were common-sensical, sturdy, progressive.

It is true that the articulate British workingman of 1850 would probably demur at the accuracy of this picture, and that many Americans would have resisted the view that the two nations were closely comparable. But strong common links did exist. Property was sacred in the Anglo-American value system, and to some extent throughout the Western world. What it signified is admirably expressed in the *Letters to an Old Comrade* that Herzen addressed to Bakunin in 1869:

The denial of private property as such is nonsense. . . . Love of his land is as deeply rooted in the peasant of the West as is the idea of communal possession in the Russian peasant. There is nothing absurd in this. Property, particularly the ownership of land, has represented to the man of the West his emancipation, his independence, his dignity, and constituted an idea of the highest civic importance.

Confiscation of one's own property, either by private exploitation or by the state, was therefore regarded as an outrage. Hostility to such tendencies, while it might be based mainly on individual greed, could appeal to an ideology of individual liberty whose origins were not ignoble. So long as this creed remained powerful, there was little room in Britain or the United States for the radical propositions that were being advanced in continental Europe. Violent, confiscatory or conspiratorial programmes were detested – and, more importantly, ridiculed or ignored. Thus, by the 1860s there were two major political parties in each country: the Liberals and Conservatives (or Tories) in Britain, the Democrats and Republicans in the United States. Neither was appreciably 'statist' or 'collectivist'. There was a Radical Republican wing, some of whose members in the aftermath of the American Civil War wished to crush the power of the plantation 'aristocracy' by redistributing their lands among ex-slaves and poor whites. The wing and the scheme however soon disappeared; for the consequences of confiscation of property would have been too serious for the American polity as a whole. After all, it had taken a major civil war to bring the Union to the point of confiscating the Southerners' property in other men – the Negro slaves. President Lincoln himself would have preferred to end the war by a negotiated peace in which the slaveholders were compensated for the loss of their human chattels. The private-enterprise ethic encouraged a different outcome.

It would be wrong to insist that liberal capitalism led inevitably to a two-party system in which each party was notably 'centrist'. This did not happen in Canada; and in Australia and New Zealand semi-socialist doctrines became prominent in national politics earlier than in Britain. Nor, to reiterate, does it follow that the British and American outlooks were identical. Trade-unionism in Britain, already firmly grounded after a decade of effort, acquired full legal status in 1871, with the TUC (Trades Union Congress) as the Central Parliament of Labour. Whereas the TUC concerned itself with parliamentary representation almost from the beginning, the equivalent American Federation of Labor (established in 1886) was reluctant to commit itself to either main party, let alone to sponser a new party on class lines. On the other hand, thanks in part to immigration, there was more violence and

CORMICK
REAPER AND MOWER
HICAGO R.R.
NO SMOKING
STRIKE
BRATED

extremism in American than in British labour history during the late nineteenth century. Anarchist groups, mostly recruited from German-born workers, were active in the big cities. In 1886 Chicago was the scene of the 'Haymarket massacre', in which a bomb was thrown into a column of police, and eight anarchists were charged with incitement to murder. In 1901 Leon Czolgosz, a self-styled anarchist, assassinated President McKinley. America was the home of the IWW (Industrial Workers of the World), founded in Chicago in 1905 by Eugene V. Debs, 'Big Bill' Haywood and others. The IWW's militant manifesto announced that:

Universal economic evils ... can be eradicated only by a universal working-class movement. . . . A movement to fulfill these conditions must consist of one great industrial union embracing all industries. . . . It must be founded on the class struggle, and its general administration must be conducted in harmony with the recognition of the irrepressible conflict between the capitalist class and the working class. It should be established as the economic organization of the working class, without affiliation with any political party.

The IWW, concentrating upon migrant workers, dockers and Western miners, spread its net as far as Australia. British movements seemed tame in comparison. In general, unions there were preoccupied with what Engels called 'laborism' as distinct from 'socialism': that is, with specific issues of pay and working conditions. Or they took the parliamentary route. This was a slow, frustrating process. Two miners, for instance, were elected to the House of Commons in 1874. By the end of the century, there was still only a handful of Labour spokesmen at Westminster, working uneasily in affiliation with the Liberal party and overshadowed by its chilly condescension. The nature of American presidential politics meant that *ad hoc* third parties could seize upon the excitement of the contest and at least make a showing. In 1892 the candidate of the short-lived People's or Populist party secured a million votes, or 8·5 per cent of the total vote. In 1904, 1908 and 1912 Debs ran as Socialist candidate. In 1912, despite obvious handicaps, 6 per cent of the voters rallied to him, giving him nine hundred thousand popular votes.

It is also true that the vigour of American protest had some influence upon British behaviour. The most notable example is *Progress and Poverty* (1879), a book by the Californian Henry George whose proposal for a 'single tax' upon land-ownership greatly impressed such early members of the semi-socialist Fabian Society (1884) as George Bernard Shaw. 'He struck me

Opposite: The 'Haymarket massacre'. On 5 May 1886 a bomb was thrown into Haymarket Square where thousands of Chicago workers were protesting against the shooting of strikers the day before. A policeman was killed instantly and the police opened fire on the crowd. In the general panic more policemen and a considerable number of workers were killed. Eight anarchists were arrested and four were executed after their trial before a prejudiced judge and jury. The anarchist movement in America gained its first martyrs. Painting by Flavio Constantini.

dumb', said Shaw, who heard Henry George speak in London in 1884, 'and shunted me from barren agnostic controversy to economics.' The imaginative writings of Edward Bellamy (*Looking Backward*, 1888) and, somewhat later, of Jack London (*People of the Abyss*, 1903; *The Iron Heel*, 1907) and Upton Sinclair (*The Jungle*, 1906), likewise made an impact across the Atlantic.

Nevertheless, the two countries preserved an essential similarity of attitude to social questions. Radical programmes remained on the fringe. Henry George himself was not a socialist, but rather an old-style Jeffersonian. Fabian socialism was cautious in the extreme, in accordance with the supposed traits of the Roman general Fabius Cunctator: 'For the right moment you must wait, as Fabius did most patiently, when warring against Hannibal, though many censured his delays; but when the time comes you must strike hard, as Fabius did, or your waiting will be in vain, and fruitless.' This brand of reformism, together with H. M. Hyndman's SDF (Social Democratic Federation) and the Socialist League with which William Morris busied himself for a while, struck foreign radicals as curiously anaemic and amateurish. Though Keir Hardie, the inspirer of the ILP (Independent Labour Party), was a socialist and most of his associates would have said the same, the red ties they sported at their first conference in 1893 did not prevent them from pouring scorn on 'hard-brained chatterers and magpies of Continental revolutionists'.

Engels was active in stimulating such movements, together with Marx's son-in-law Edward Aveling. But Marx himself had died obscurely in 1883. The opening volume of *Das Kapital*, published in Germany in 1867, was not translated into English until 1887, though a Russian translation had come out in 1872. Bernard Shaw, one of the first to study the work, was obliged to read a French version at the British Museum.

Given such outlooks, and the general indifference or hostility of the Anglo-American public to 'Continental revolutionists', one can begin to see why there was so great a divergence between the European mainland and the highly industrialized, liberal-minded offshore civilizations. As British and American people saw matters, there was no reason to adopt foreign ideologies. A frontal attack on private property could only undermine the fabric, with calamitous results. Gradual reform was the correct strategy. To some extent this was a lesson explicitly learned from Bismarck's Germany: welfare capitalism diminished unrest. In post-

The masthead reads:

The Labour Leader

A WEEKLY RECORD OF SOCIAL AND POLITICAL PROGRESS.

Ring out a slowly dying cause, | Edited by | Ring in the valiant man and free,
And ancient forms of party strife; | **KEIR HARDIE.** | The larger heart, the kindlier hand;
Ring in the nobler modes of life, | | Ring out the darkness of the land,
With sweeter manners, purer laws. | | Ring in the Christ that is to be.
| | —*Tennyson.*

No. 26. Vol. V. New Series. | (Registered at the G. P. O. as a Newspaper.) | SATURDAY, SEPTEMBER 22, 1894. | (Sent to any Address for 1s per quarter.) | PRICE ONE PENNY.

The Labour Leader of 22
September 1894, edited
by Keir Hardie, shows
bloated Capital grinding
Labour into the ground
during the strike of
Scottish miners.

Bismarckian Germany the impressive growth of the SPD (Social
Democratic Party) seemed to confirm the wisdom of moderation,
and of reform *via* parliamentary processes. So did the German
trade-figures. But even without the German example, Britain and
the United States would probably have reached the same conclusions. No doubt some of the rich were idle. The average
capitalist, however, believed that he worked hard for his money.
One American defence, the 'gospel of wealth' propounded by the
multimillionaire Andrew Carnegie, was that the rich man had a
responsibility to give away most of his capital for educational
purposes that would stimulate other members of the community
to improve their lot through self-help.

Since the liberal affirmation lacked a precise doctrinal framework, it could be continually modified without unduly shocking
its adherents. So the very word 'liberalism', in its political context,
shifted from outright *laissez-faire* to a fair measure of 'statism' or
'collectivism'. Not everyone approved the change. There were
fierce attacks in both countries on legislation restricting hours of
work, providing old-age pensions, or imposing taxes on income

Tolstoy, the Russian novelist and humanitarian, who wrote: 'Property is the root of all evil; and now all the world is busy with the distribution and protection of wealth.'

and inheritance – all of which could be interpreted as threats to individual liberty. The case against what he took to be galloping collectivism is eloquently presented in the long introduction to the second edition (1914) to A. V. Dicey's *Law and Public Opinion in England* (1905). Dicey suspected that 'The combination of socialistic and democratic legislation threatens the gravest danger' – not least because in his view, socialism and democracy were logically incompatible.

Nevertheless, the America of Theodore Roosevelt and the Britain of Asquith and Lloyd George seemed ready to accept an unprecedented degree of government control. They did so largely in the name of nationalism – certainly far more than in the name of socialism. Strong nations, it was agreed, needed to be governmentally strong. Government must promote trade and overseas expansion as well as internal harmony. In this light we can grasp why reformers of the Shaw variety supported the government in the Boer War, and in the next decade revealed an elitist appetite for demonstrations of power, together with a certain disdain for the man in the street. A parallel response is evident in the style of Americans of the 'Progressive' era, between 1900 and 1916. As Roosevelt insisted after the presidential election of 1912: 'The Progressive party owes no small part of its strength to the fact that it not only stands for ... measures of social and industrial reform, but ... also for the right and duty of this nation to take a position of self-respecting strength among the nations of the world. . . .'

In short, the liberal affirmation amounted to a conviction, sometimes libertarian, sometimes aggressive and sometimes complacent, that there was an inseparable connection between individual freedom and national wellbeing. Though qualified and occasionally shaken between 1848 and 1916, this persisted as the majority opinion – even among citizens whose personal freedom and wellbeing might look pitifully small.

Freedom and Overthrow

Among the apostles of liberalism, Herbert Spencer was a convinced opponent of the state. In *Social Statics* (1850), he dismissed almost the whole apparatus of state control or supervision. The state, he said, should have nothing to do with education, or poor laws, or banks, or health legislation, or even postal services. Oddly enough such extreme *laissez-faire* often resembles the tenets of the extreme wing of radicalism, in the form of anarchism.

Anarchism in its simplest or mildest form exalts the first person singular at the expense of any collective 'we' – especially where this we is remote, impersonal, bureaucratic, as was commonly felt to be the characteristic of the state. Individualist anarchism is a gentle, ancient creed, inherent perhaps in early Christianity. The wish is for men to live simply. A Thoreau, believing that a person is happy in proportion to the number of things he can do without, has much in common with, say, the great Russian author Count Leo Tolstoy as revealed in such works of the 1880s as the wonderful short story *The Death of Ivan Ilich* and the impassioned essay *What Is To Be Done?* The story portrays a conventional man's dying discovery that his entire life has been without meaning. The essay argues that this is true of almost every facet of modern existence, where people are either glutted or emaciated. For Thoreau as for Tolstoy, private property is a snare. A man's only real property, says Tolstoy, is himself; all else, as Ivan Ilich learns too late, is 'imaginary':

Property is the root of all evil; and now all the world is busy with the distribution and protection of wealth. . . . Men are accustomed to think that property is something really belonging to men, and for this reason they have called it 'property'. We speak indiscriminately of our own house and our own land. But this is obviously an error and a superstition. . . . property is only the means of utilizing other men's labour. And another's labour can by no means belong to me.

In the words of the *New Testament*, 'Go and sell that thou hast, and give to the poor, and thou shalt have treasure in heaven.'

Perhaps such testimony came easily to Thoreau and Tolstoy. Thoreau's mid-century New England was a peaceful, uncomplicated place. Land was cheap; no one within his ken was bloatedly rich, or destitute. The state made few demands upon him. His sole anti-governmental protest, apart from a little writing and lecturing, was a refusal to pay poll-tax in support of the Mexican War, of which he disapproved. The only punishment meted out to him was a night in jail. Few if any eyebrows were raised at the implications of Thoreau's claim to be his own judge and jury: 'The only obligation which I have a right to assume is to do at any time what I think right.' Things were less relaxed in Tolstoy's Russia. But then, when he decided to renounce his estates and his wealth, he was already well into middle age, and so admired and famous that his eccentricities were indulged.

The difficulties came when anarchist doctrine appeared to offer a direct challenge to authority. Personal abnegation was all very well; if a man chose to live like an ascetic hermit, so be it. What though if he was not content to be a quietist: if his writings gave offence to authority: if he sought to combine with others, and to declare war upon the state instead of waiting for it to wither away in God's good time? Then the troubles began. And from this comes the popular conception of the anarchist, not as a gentle undemanding creature but as a maniac, a wrecker, a conspirator with a bomb hidden in his coat. With the *Revolutionary Catechism* of Bakunin-Nechaev (the authorship is unknown) we have entered another realm than that of Thoreau and Tolstoy, or for that matter one of the founding fathers of European anarchism, Pierre-Joseph Proudhon.

The anarchist case has a rational basis, even where 'propaganda of the deed' seemed to amount to no more than senseless killing of innocent people. There was a violent rhetoric, which may have had an effect on people wholly unconnected with anarchist organizations. Peter Kropotkin, of almost saintly personal habits,

Opposite: Six anarchists executed in Barcelona, 1894. The belief in the coming revolution bred anarchist movements in almost all Western countries.

apparently sensed no contradiction between these and his call for 'permanent revolt by word of mouth, in writing, by the dagger, the rifle, dynamite. . . . Everything is good for us which falls outside legality.' The nub of the anarchist case was that the overwhelming, repressive weight of established society left no other recourse but violence. Governments were already intolerable in Russia and elsewhere. If their response to deliberate terrorism was yet more savage repression, so much the better in hastening the inevitable catastrophe. The only way to make an impression was to scare people out of their wits. At least the experience might make them ask some questions, instead of sealing themselves off in their privileged enclaves.

The more reactionary the country, the more extreme the radical response. To the ceaseless question, *What is to be Done?* – the title of a novel by N. G. Chernyshevsky (1863), and also in deliberate echo of a trenchant little guide by Lenin to revolutionary organization (1902) – the answer in a land such as Russia tended either to be a despairing shrug or a wildly conspiratorial scenario of violence. Imprisonment or exile were other paired alternatives. Nikolay Chernyshevsky was held prisoner for over twenty years, mostly in Siberia, for quite constructively critical opinions expressed in his writing. He was no anarchist, but his estimate of the bloody collapse of the 1848 risings in Europe made him detest authoritarianism. 'Far better anarchy from below than from above.' Such a man – later a folk-hero to Russian Marxists for his uncompromising honesty – could envisage a more specifically constructive role for anarchism, in the tradition of Babeuf and Proudhon, but with special reference to Russia. The feature of Russian life admitted by Occidentalists and Slavophils alike to be unique was the *mir* or village commune. On this local unit of intimate, organic comradeship, a new Russia might be built. Or if not yet, then at any rate it could furnish a kind of analogy for the localized and secret cells in which anarchists like the romantic Bakunin and the implacable young Nechaev grouped themselves, with a mania for the clandestine that was a choice as well as a necessity. Nechaev was utterly unscrupulous, as Dostoevsky indicated in his hostile novel *The Devils*. Yet like the anarchists in other countries – Errico Malatesta in Italy, or Sebastian Faure in France – Nechaev displayed the utter fearlessness of the genuine zealot. Years of suffering in jail before his final wretched death in 1882 did nothing to break his spirit. Violence bred a new selflessness and a new hagiography. Nechaevism helped to generate an

Opposite: The assassination of President Carnot of France, the victim of an Italian anarchist, in 1894. Painting by Flavio Constantini.

252

amazing Populist, or perhaps rather Nihilist movement in which young male and female intelligentsia by the score volunteered for whatever task was assigned to them in the grand mysterious encompassment of the impending Revolution. A terrorist league like the *Narodnaya Volya* (People's Will) acquired an extraordinary linguistic resonance. The same words appeared in different contexts: *narodniki* was the Russian name for the Populists. And the state retaliated with ever-more efficient countermeasures after the assassination of Alexander II. The *Okhrana*, a special secret police, were one manifestation – or, to revolutionaries, infestation.

Except for Russia, where it was not unchallenged by theorists of the left, and for France, the main anarchist strength lay in the Roman Catholic countries of the Mediterranean. One feature that separated a Bakunin from a Tolstoy was the former's contempt for religion. Anti-clericalism as an element of radicalism was almost absent in Britain and the United States. There, the local schoolmaster probably went to church on Sunday, and the urban intellectual who was not religiously inclined simply stayed at home. In France, Italy and Spain teacher and priest frequently symbolized angrily disparate ideologies. Leo XIII's conciliatory encyclical *Rerum Novarum* (1891) did something to offset the illiberal tone of Pius IX's *Syllabus Errorum* (1865). But anticlerical feeling was intense among radicals and workingmen, and the Church was with some reason regarded in these countries as a reactionary ally of reactionary régimes. Protesting that the dead hand of the past weighed intolerably upon them, insurgents turned to anarchism – borrowing their ideas from Bakunin, who had once sojourned in Naples, and from other renowned rebels. Lacking a strong liberal heritage, and relatively tardy in industrializing, radicalism in Spain and Italy took on an agrarian flavour. By the early 1870s, Spanish anarchism numbered some fifty thousand agricultural workers, chiefly in the south. Later it spread among the northern urban workers of Catalonia. Every now and then, towns and villages exploded in extraordinary fury, wreaking their anger on priests and nuns in a way that foreshadowed the bloody civil war of the 1930s.

A more solid development, however, was the industrially-based syndicalist movement which originated in France and Belgium. The genius of this growth during the 1890s was the young Frenchman Fernand Pelloutier. Syndicalism recognized that the anarchism of the 1870s, with its emphasis on conspiratorial

Opposite above: Bloody Sunday. A painting by N. Vladimirov which shows the Russian troops opening fire on the workers in St Petersburg, January 1905.

Opposite below: An early twentieth-century poster shows a familiar British reaction to the growth of the Socialist movement.

255

violence, had failed to accomplish much in the Mediterranean countries. More attracted by orthodox Marxism, and also drawing upon the older co-operative notions of Proudhon, it solved a number of problems for militant, unionized workers who were unimpressed either by parliamentary reformism or by the flamboyant and counter-productive 'propaganda of the deed'. In the guise of anarcho-syndicalism, it appealed to workers who cherished their local units and yet wished to band together for bold collective action. The principal syndicalist idea was workers' control, to be attained by means of 'direct action' through a simultaneous general strike. The effectiveness of well-planned strike action, though on a modest scale, had been noticed in the United States and was now adapted into the European

Cover of *Almanach du Père Peinard*, the most widely-read of French anarchist magazines.

256

philosophy. Syndicalism became the ruling programme of the principal French trade-union federation, the CGT (Confédération Général du Travail). Under its influence, 1 May was selected as a day on which to attempt a one-day strike or demonstration in all countries. This was tried out in 1890 with fair success, especially in France and Italy. The hope, never very precisely formulated, was that after some rehearsals – comparable with army manœuvres – the syndicalists could bring about a total stoppage of work on an international scale. This would lead to 'war' with capitalism, whether literally or figuratively, and to the capture of power by the unions.

Syndicalism was handsomely international in approach, as was stressed at the Anarchosyndicalist conference held in Amsterdam in 1907. The French delegates explained: 'Syndicalism does not waste time promising the workers a paradise on earth, it calls on them to conquer it. . . .' But, ominously for the future, it was already evident that Germany's powerful trade-union movement was unable or unwilling to subscribe to the syndicalist plan. And a voice from the past, that of the ageing anarchist Malatesta, wearily dismissed the general strike as 'pure utopia': a radical illusion no better founded than those of the previous half-century, including 1848 and the abortive Paris Commune of 1871.

The Marx-Engels Formulation

Karl Marx and Friedrich Engels, it is worth repeating, were two Germans who spent most of their adult lives in England – Marx until his death in 1883, Engels until he too died twelve years later. Theirs is one of the most remarkable partnerships in all history. They were temperamentally very different, yet except for rare moments maintained the closest harmony. One explanation is that they were men of exceptional integrity, devotees to a common cause of which they never wearied. Another is that Engels, while himself highly intelligent and versatile, never doubted that Marx was a genius. Because of that conviction, he was ready to labour at the horribly uncongenial tasks of the family textile business in grimy Lancashire; to find money to shore up Marx's precarious finances; to scribble newspaper articles on behalf of Marx; to collaborate with him on a mass of work beginning with the *Communist Manifesto* of 1848; and to toil over the complex material, including the unpublished portions of *Das Kapital*, that required posthumous editing and publication.

Karl Marx, the revolutionary whose work provided a theoretical basis for the communist movement.

Only the intensest faith could have sustained them. Outwardly their story was of endless disappointment and frustration. They had to watch the failure of almost every socialist and revolutionary enterprise. They had to endure not only neglect in Britain, but misunderstanding, misrepresentation and outright scurrility from men like Bakunin. They had to be scholars, ranging over world-evolution with the visonary detachment of a Charles Darwin (to whom Marx attempted to dedicate the first volume of *Das Kapital*), yet also to hector and cajole small meetings of wildly diverse individuals in anonymous committee rooms. They never lived to see the outcomes they predicted. They had to reckon with the possibility that some of their critics might be right: the victory of the proletariat might never occur, or only on terms and in places far removed from their analyses. They were like architects, drawing immense cityscapes at rickety

Friedrich Engels, close friend and colleague of Marx, and co-author of the *Communist Manifesto*.

tables by inadequate light on paper liable to tear at a touch.

The Marxian faith however remained intact. Basically what upheld Marx and his second self Engels, apart from a fine and resilient intellect, was the certainty that they had hit upon an absolute truth. Not for them the terrible reversals and self-doubts that beset so many of their contemporaries. Their task was to refine and extend the truth they had uncovered, much as Darwin's labour consisted in verifying and documenting his essential idea on natural selection. The world was their laboratory. Nothing, past or present, was without potential value. Flexible within their central doctrine, they could rest serenely sure that every fresh political or economic event was of utility in illustrating what Marx called 'scientific socialism'.

The fundamental idea of Marxism, explained in the *Manifesto* and elaborated in many different directions in subsequent years,

259

was the class-struggle. Others before him, Marx said in 1852, had drawn attention to differences of class and to economic grievances in history. His originality consisted in emphasizing the necessary element of class-*consciousness*, and in insisting that economic modes ('materialism') were the ultimate determinants. Or as Engels summarized Marxism, in his preface to the 1888 English edition of the *Manifesto*:

The fundamental proposition ... is that in every historical epoch the prevailing mode of economic production and exchange and the social organization necessarily following from it form the basis upon which it is built up, and from which alone can be explained, the political and intellectual history of that epoch; that consequently the whole history of mankind (since the dissolution of primitive tribal society, holding land in common ownership) has been a history of class struggles, contests between exploiting and exploited, ruling and oppressed classes; that the history of these class struggles forms a series of evolutions in which, nowadays, a stage has been reached where the exploited and oppressed class – the proletariat – cannot attain its emancipation from the sway of the exploiting and ruling class – the bourgeoisie – without, at the same time, and once and for all, emancipating society at large from all exploitation, oppression, class distinctions, and class struggles.

Since the economic mode disclosed and shaped successive patterns of society, Marx felt obliged to devise an economic interpretation of history. Since he conceived of class-roles as exploitative, he explained in detail (in *Das Kapital* and elsewhere) how the bourgeoisie exploited the proletariat. Since he and Engels were putting forward a comprehensive thesis of social evolution, past, present and future, it was necessary to refute the contentions of other reformers and revolutionaries. He was thus challenging the habitual viewpoints of historians, classical economists and a miscellany of liberals, conservatives and radicals. In general, the tone adopted by Marx and Engels in public writings was dispassionate, almost to the edge of pedantry. Their sharpest language was reserved for rival theorists. This was not out of spleen, though of course they could not entirely suppress their personal emotions. It was rather because, while the bourgeoisie moved along pre-ordained paths and could not be expected to do otherwise, the theorists were in a position to influence the future – and so to retard and damage the emergence of the new social order. Hence the understandable irritation with which, especially in private correspondence or face-to-face encounters, Marx and Engels

poured scorn on the Lassallean or Bakuninist or Fabian heresies. It did not signify, they felt, whether such persons acted innocently or malevolently. The road to hell was paved with good intentions. What mattered was that the heretics were leading mankind astray.

At this moment in time, it could be said that Marx and Engels were intriguers. They had established the First International, the International Working Men's Association (IWMA) in 1864, as a result of encouraging contacts between British and French trade-unionists. At once they ran into the problem of reaching agreement between a welter of incompatible doctrines. The deaths of Proudhon in 1864 and Lassalle in 1865 eliminated some of the difficulties posed by French mutualism and German (or Lassallean) socialism. But Bakunin's Russia-centred anarchism presented a new and graver challenge. Perhaps at that stage, Marx still believed what the *Manifesto* stated: namely, that scientific socialism was destined to prove itself above all in Germany. He

First Congress of the First International at Geneva (1866). The goal of international communism was central to Marxist ideology, and was not modified until Russia developed the theory of 'socialism in one country'.

261

may still have retained some of his old, German disdain for lumbering, contorted Russia. Referring to Bakunin, he told Engels in 1869: 'This Russian wants to become the dictator of the European workers' movement.' After Marx was dead, a Second International was organized in 1889. Again it ran into troubles through internecine argument. But several things were becoming clearer. One was that Marxism was strongly planted in the middle of the uproar. Critical of and criticized by the reformists on the one side and the extremists on the other, it had weathered well and acquired a sturdy theoretical and practical bulk. Any kind of international workers' movement was bound to compromise if it was to hold together. Marxism now occupied the high middle ground.

The exposition of labour value and surplus value in the first volume of *Das Kapital* was highly ingenious. But the rough edges of the argument were never entirely rounded off in his subsequent work or that of Engels, who after all mainly provided a gloss on broad positions already asserted. Marx needed to demonstrate that the worker was in fact cheated of his labour by the capitalist. But if the worker were not so cheated, or less comprehensively exploited than Marx alleged – as the Fabians tended to suspect – did not this greatly weaken the force of the dialectic?

Marx and Engels were well aware of such criticisms, and devoted much time to answering them – invariably to their own satisfaction. Some criticisms lacked substance. Some assumed a rigidity in Marxism that Marx himself, and Engels, denied. They did not, Engels protested late in life, possess magical powers of divination. Human affairs were infinitely complex. Each society possessed peculiar features. No one blueprint could cover them all with exact relevance. Time and chance and particular circumstance meant that adjustments must be made. The truth of Marxism was a general truth. Its force lay in the applicability of this general truth to the precise local conditions of man as a social animal. Societies *were*, Marx and Engels remained certain, ultimately governed by their economic systems. Once this was understood, men had the key to detailed understanding of their history and their destiny. The essence of Marxism, distinguishing it from the timid reformers on the one hand and the rabid dreamers on the other, was a sort of bold reasonableness. Generally speaking, the history of the twentieth century has suggested that Marx and Engels had good reason for feeling that they were more correct than their contemporaries about the drift of world events.

262

Revisionism and Leninism

There was, nevertheless, a great deal more arguing to be done before Marxism could be put to the test. Two figures deserve discussion: Eduard Bernstein as the most perceptive of the 'revisionists' who could not accept Marxism as the whole truth, and Vladimir Ilyich Ulyanov, known to posterity as Lenin, who sharpened Marxism into a mobilization plan for the overthrow of Tsarist Russia. With Bernstein may be linked the Frenchman Jean Jaurès.

The best-known sentence from Bernstein's book *Evolutionary Socialism* was this: 'What is generally called the goal of socialism is nothing to me, the movement everything.' In other words, Bernstein as an able and upright German Social Democrat who had lived in England, came to think that there was an unavowedly weak utopian element in Marxian socialism. The important advance, surely, was toward social justice. To dwell upon the Marxist scenario for a classless society, in which the state had evaporated, was to mistake the programme for the process. In Britain and Germany, socialists were gaining strength. Strength for what? Not, said Bernstein, to bring about a remote millennium, but to lead fuller lives in the here and now. There was nothing vulgar or evasive in the actual, steady fulfilment of real goals: better wages, better housing, better education, more say in the running of politics and industry. He accepted much of Marxism, and was a close friend of Engels. Dialectical materialism as such, however, struck him more and more as mystification. There were weaknesses in German trade unionism. Some of these could and should be repaired. Some, notably the SPD's all-too romantic attachment to the Fatherland, which the pacifist Bernstein did not share, could hardly be remedied by reference to the sacred texts of Marxism. He was of course castigated as an enemy of socialism, a backslider and an opportunist. But he held his position, defending it with courage and eloquence, and with an ethical dignity that perhaps indicated a serious potential weakness in Marxism as interpreted by the rank and file of the movement. Socialism, Bernstein reminded his associates, is about *fairness*. Otherwise it risks being not signally superior to the capitalism it combats. Bernstein was not alone in arguing thus. The English law-professor A. V. Dicey made similar complaints. The power of Bernstein's contentions was that he knew what he was talking about. He was not proffering a rationale for the established order.

He was saying that capitalism was a corrupt institution, and that socialists must beware lest they be themselves corrupted.

Jaurès too was a socialist humanist, shot dead by a fanatic at the end of July 1914, shortly after making a speech that called upon the workers of Europe to prevent the world war from breaking out. Like Bernstein, he usually thought of himself as a Marxist, though with deeper reservations. 'Marxism', he said, 'itself contains the means by which it can be supplemented and revised.' He wanted men to live always 'in a state of socialist grace' – helping one another, lifting up the oppressed, drawing closer and closer to the truly good society without scheming for any sudden revolution. Bernstein was increasingly sceptical that the Marxist new day would ever dawn. Jaurès was confident that it would, but not so much all at once as organically, in the way that the world passes from winter to spring, imperceptibly at any given moment yet steadily and inevitably from week to week as the sun edges higher in the sky and the days lengthen. In implication, perhaps, he was hardly a Marxist at all. That he professed to subscribe to so much of the creed is not a sign of his confusion or hypocrisy, but rather a sign that by the end of the nineteenth century, Marxism was omnipresent in the socialist cosmos.

The tough-minded Lenin was a very different kind of man. His great achievement, in coming up through the proscribed and factious maze of Russian radicalism, was to hammer out a definite dogma and then to impose it on a significant number of his companions in Russia or in exile. On the way he educated himself in socialism, he travelled, he endured the almost statutory Russian experience of arrest and imprisonment, he wrote and translated, he combated first the Populists and then, after 1900, the Social-Revolutionary party – which then outnumbered his own Social-Democrat group. In 1900, he became one of the editors of an underground periodical, *Iskra (The Spark)*. In the first issue Lenin contributed an article that sketched his principal thesis: 'Not a single class in history has reached power without thrusting forward its political leaders, without advancing leading representatives capable of directing and organizing the movement. We must train people who will dedicate to the revolution, not a spare evening but the whole of their lives.'

Much of this had a familiar ring. Selfless zeal was not new among revolutionaries. What was new was the emphasis, which Lenin was steadily to reinforce, on leadership and instruction. Marx had tended to assume that the working class would educate itself as the truth became apparent, and that intellectual socialists such as himself would move openly among the workers, teaching and also learning. The workers would by and large generate their own leadership. Political consciousness, the actual mechanisms of leadership, were treated somewhat incidentally as by-products of the central economic doctrine, or even suspected as a diversionary activity.

Lenin disagreed. He did not expect capitalism to collapse from its own weaknesses. He did not believe oppression was enough to stimulate an effective opposition. He was convinced that political adroitness was a separate, indispensable skill. Russia's police-state condition, and perhaps his own temperament and the memory of an elder brother condemned to death for conspiracy, combined to persuade him that the organizing activity must be sophisticated, systematic, authoritative, and hidden. The vehicle was the Social-Democratic party. Within the party, Lenin's group must control events. Sure enough, in 1903 his followers at the annual convention secured a majority. The Russian word for majority is *Bolsheviki*. Thereafter the Bolsheviks, with Lenin tirelessly prominent in shaping policy, schemed to infiltrate, to proselytize, to discipline the inchoate mass of Russian workers. It was soon clear that the industrial workers, not the great rural mass, were the material to mould. More than a decade was to elapse before Lenin, exiled in Switzerland, saw his chance. Until then, the Bolsheviks and Mensheviks ('minority') were bitterly at odds. Trotsky, sometimes occupying an independent position, had a moment of amazing prescience when he said: 'The Party is replaced by the organization of the party, the organization by the central committee, and finally the central committee by the dictator.' But all that lay ahead in a future not even Lenin could read. In the years between 1903 and 1917, he was furiously active in the reconstruction of Marxist socialism into a strange mixture of seminar, inquisition and – some would say – mirror image of the dreaded *Okhrana*.

As late as January 1917, however, Lenin was far from sanguine. Exiled in Switzerland, in his late forties, at odds with most of the spokesmen for international or Russian socialism, he commented resignedly that 'we, the old, will probably not live to see the decisive battles of the coming revolution'. The Bolsheviks had soon lost their 1903 majority. Lenin had offended the Populist element who still put the main emphasis on the Russian peasant mass. He had exasperated Plekhanov, the venerable theoretician of Marxism. He had failed to persuade Trotsky (the name taken by the bustling, talented young Jewish intellectual Lev Bronstein), or Martov (another gifted Jew, Julius Cedarbaum). He was widely regarded in revolutionary circles as a fringe-figure, whose wrongheaded obstinacy was as conspicuous as his dedication to the cause. These were bad years, no less for the emigrés and the party cells than for the bewildered, alternately vacillating and brutal administrations of Tsar Nicholas II. Rapid industrialization was creating a sizeable and discontented urban proletariat, and also increasing the dissatisfactions of large numbers of peasants. The unpopularity of the war with Japan in 1904–5 suddenly brought matters to a head in 1905.

Lenin, far away from the centres of activity in St Petersburg and Moscow in this year of abortive revolution, was not able to play any personal part until the immediate opportunity was almost gone. Strikes and risings in the main cities, and peasant demonstrations, seemed to startle him almost as much as they did the Tsar's ministers. The emergence of local workers' councils or *Soviets* had not been foreseen by the editors of *Iskra*. The government's action, reluctant and disingenuous though it was, in establishing elected legislative parliaments or *Dumas*, was similarly disconcerting. Lenin was almost heartbroken when at the outbreak of the world war in 1914 the workers' movements in every country swung behind their national governments instead of uniting to defeat capitalism's latest – to him – cynical folly. He could hardly believe that dedicated Marxists such as Giorgi Plekhanov or Karl Kautsky, editor of *Neue Zeit*, would succumb then to nationalist fervour.

Nevertheless Russia was clearly on the brink of some immense upheaval, from any moment after 1905. It might be averted or minimized, as the Tsar and the Mensheviks hoped in their different ways, given policies that were both wise and firm. Opposition to the régime was after all, as the Tsar's spies correctly told him, divided and scattered. P. A. Stolypin, who became prime minister in 1906, smashed the second Duma and arrested every troublemaker he could lay hands on. With this typical gesture of repression went a new drive to permit peasants to acquire their own land. For Lenin this raised the alarming prospect that agriculture would become 'capitalistic'. But Stolypin was murdered in 1911; strikers in the Lena gold fields of Siberia were mown down by troops in 1912; and on the eve of the 1914 war there was a fresh wave of industrial strikes.

Workers' demonstration
in Moscow, 1905. In that
year the Tsarist
Government was forced
to make concessions
towards a more liberal
constitution, but these
remained largely
inoperative.

Lenin was still peripheral and unpopular. Only hindsight
enables us to single him out as the prime revolutionary figure of
Russian history. In the decade before 1917, Menshevik interpretations seemed generally more attractive, and possibly shrewder.
But there was a good deal of common ground between Bolshevik
and Menshevik. Both could see, for example, that the groundswell
of popular discontent in Russia was growing, not diminishing as
in some other countries. It was apparent that what Lenin called
'Great Russian chauvinism' antagonized the outlying portions of
the empire – Finland, Poland, Georgia. The structure was
ramshackle beyond repair. If setbacks in the war with Japan had
helped to precipitate the semi-revolution of 1905, what might not
happen if Russia's ill-prepared peasant armies were led into

Lenin, 1917 – the man whose qualities as leader, man-of-action and political theorist proved irresistible during the struggle for power in Russia.

disaster against the methodical German hosts in 1914? What must actually be done to organize and maintain a government, in the event of a collapse of Tsarist authority, was something neither Lenin nor his radical contemporaries were thinking much about. Understandably, they were more absorbed in the indications of disaster for the government of the 'little father' Nicholas II – with the end of the Romanovs rather than with the specifics of a new post-revolutionary bureaucracy.

10 War: Conception and Reality

Surely all must unite in condemning the Arbitrament of War. . . . But if War be thus odious, if it be the Duel of Nations, if it be the old surviving Trial by Battle, then must its unquestionable barbarism affect all . . . its machinery, . . . together with all who sanction it, and all who have any part or lot in it, – in fine, the whole vast System.

Charles Sumner of Massachusetts, 'The Abolition of the War System in the Commonwealth of Nations', 1849

An Anti-War Society is as little practicable as an Anti-Thunder-and-Lightning Society.

Criticism of Sumner by Jeremiah Mason, also of Massachusetts

This, my lord, princes and statesmen, is where in your wisdom you have brought old Europe. And when nothing more remains to you but to open the last great war dance – that will suit us all right.

Friedrich Engels, late in life

The Power of the Powerful

As with other aspects of the period, the shape of warfare was determined by the leading nations. It was the ultimate demonstration of power; and as with other questions, the problem of whether modern war was a proof of man's health or of a sickness that might prove fatal remained profoundly ambiguous.

What was beyond doubt was that the major conflicts were waged between, instigated by or fuelled by the European powers together with the United States and the new Oriental challenger, Japan. Even non-European contests derived their tactics and weapons from the dynamic nations. It was French military advisers who were called in to Westernize the Japanese army, and British guns that supplied the firepower for the new Japanese fleet. The sophisticated equipment deployed in such lesser struggles as the

War of the Pacific (1879–83), between Chile and Peru, was furnished by European or American arms manufacturers. So were the two ironclad battleships flying the Chinese flag and the Japanese cruisers that confronted one another in the Sino-Japanese War of 1894–5.

From the upheavals of 1848 to the great explosion of 1914, with the exception of the American Civil War of 1861–5, the big wars were – to reiterate – nearly all waged in Europe or with European participation. In the Crimean War of 1853–6 Russia faced the Ottoman Empire, Britain, France and Sardinia. In 1864 Prussia warred with Denmark, in 1866 with Austria; and in 1870–1, as the principal agent of the North German Confederation, the Prussians grappled with the French. Russia was again at war with Turkey in 1877–8. There were continuous upheavals in the Balkans, as in the Serbo-Bulgarian War of 1885. Spain and the United States were enemies in 1898. And so on.

All over the rest of the world, in quest of colonial empire, the soldiers and ships of the great powers engaged in adventures, conquests, punitive expeditions. The tally of what Rudyard Kipling called 'the savage wars of peace' seems endless. Now and then, a shiver of apprehension ran through the world's capitals, as the telegraph brought news from some corner of the empire that the white man's brazen magic had failed. Here or there, civilization's marching emissaries had succumbed to the barbarian hordes. Some probing column had overreached itself, and been overwhelmed and massacred. So with Custer's cavalry, wiped out by the Sioux Indians at Little Big Horn in 1876, or the terrible onslaught of the Zulus on a British expedition at Isandlhwana in 1879, or the killing of General Gordon at Khartum in 1885, or – most sensational of all – the rout of an Italian force of fifteen thousand men by the Abyssinians at Adowa in 1896. There were parlous moments, as when the Russian General Lomakin nearly lost his army in the campaign of 1879 against the Tekke Turcoman tribesmen east of the Caspian; or in 1885 when 'howling Dervishes' broke into a British square at Abu Klea. There was the special case of the Boers and the humiliation they brought to British pride on Majuba Hill (1881) and elsewhere. Here and there, too, in the remoter regions of the world, savage prowess was tenacious enough to win from the white man the basic boon of survival. This was the achievement of the Maoris of New Zealand, of the Araucanian Indians of South America and, to some extent, of the Pathans of Afghanistan.

Opposite above : The British return from the battlefield of Inkerman after their costly but victorious encounter with the Russians (1854); painting by Lady Butler.

Opposite below : The battle of Gettysburg, a painting by Philippoteaux. This bloody battle in 1863 cost over 20,000 casualties on each side. It proved a turning point, after which the Union gained increasing ascendance over the Confederate forces.

270

But white pride tolerated few such resistances. Warfare was a prime means by which the great powers defined their spirit to themselves and to the rest of mankind. Ultimately, their right to rule seemed psychologically to depend upon their will to secure lodgement in the most inaccessible fastnesses, no matter how fiercely or numerously defended, and to defy all efforts to dislodge them. They were in their own eyes lion-tamers, breakers of wild horses. In the Western psyche, the 'silent, sullen peoples' who constituted the white man's burden must be taught the lesson of imperial invincibility. What if the machine-gun jammed, the ammunition ran low, the column was surrounded, women and children were threatened by fates worse than death? These were the bad dreams of Western newspaper readers. But always, as a counter, came the assurance that the column would hold out, that relief was on the way, that superior courage and training and technology were talismanic. And in actuality the lesson almost always *was* taught. Sitting Bull, the warrior who disposed of Custer, was himself later shot dead, on the pretext that he was trying to escape arrest. This was in 1890, the last year in which American Indians offered armed resistance to their conquerors. The Zulus were crushingly defeated a few months after the Isandlhwana episode. The Dervishes were mown down in hundreds when the British reoccupied the Sudan. Russian troops scattered the Turcoman war parties.

Progress?

In the large wars of the era, complex lessons for the great powers were discerned. Was their military dominance a triumph or a disease?

On the side of optimism, it should be noted first that some European thinkers believed that warfare was about to disappear from the earth. Auguste Comte in France and Herbert Spencer in England were among the theorists of human evolution who felt the world was passing from the 'military' to the 'industrial' stage. Pierre Proudhon, in *La Guerre et la Paix* (*War and Peace*, 1861), argued that men had outgrown combat as they had outgrown religion: war had 'held its last assize' during the generation of warfare culminating in 1815. According to such grand formulations, war belonged to the primitive phases of the progress of the race. It had had its utility in developing resolution and man's capacity to act in groups. But now its functions were superseded

Opposite: Existence by Paul Nash. The horrors of trench warfare inspired artists and poets to capture the essence of the squalor, boredom and, of course, the perils, of life at the Front in the First World War.

273

Custer's last stand, Little Big Horn, 1876. The famous Sioux victory was one of those instances where 'the white man's brazen magic failed'.

by subtler, more socially relevant impulses. 'War is on its last legs', said Ralph Waldo Emerson in a lecture in 1838; universal peace was 'as sure as the prevalence of civilization over barbarism, of liberal governments over feudal forms'. The French poet Victor Hugo expanded this vision in his eloquent address to a peace conference held in Paris in 1849. 'A day will come', he predicted, 'when the only battlefield will be the market open to commerce and the mind opening to new ideas. . . . A day will come when those two immense groups, the United States of America and the United States of Europe, shall be seen in the presence of each other, extending the hand of fellowship across the ocean.' Economists and businessmen interested in free trade echoed the idea that the extension of world commerce made the nations increasingly dependent upon one another. Each benefited from the capital, labour and markets of the others. Prosperity was indivisible. In short, as John Stuart Mill maintained (*Political Economy*, 1848), 'It is commerce which is rapidly rendering war obsolete.' So thought Richard Cobden and John Bright, the

274

leaders of the Anti-Corn Law League in Britain, and a number of Frenchmen including Michel Chevalier and Frédéric Bastiat. At the Paris peace meeting, and at successive conferences in Frankfurt, London, Edinburgh and elsewhere, delegates from western Europe and the United States condemned war as a wasteful anachronism and urged that governments should learn to disarm and to arbitrate.

Outright pacifism of the Quaker variety kept alive until 1914 – and of course thereafter. It produced eloquent spokesmen in the United States, like Elihu Burritt (the 'learned blacksmith') and Jane Addams (the founder of the famous settlement house in Chicago). Austria produced the redoubtable Baroness Bertha von Suttner, whose novel *Lay Down Your Arms* (1889) was translated into several languages and had an importance for the pacifist movement analogous to that of Harriet Beecher Stowe's *Uncle Tom's Cabin* for the abolitionists of the 1850s. Unlike abolitionism, however, pacifism never became widely accepted.

If war could not be prevented, steps could at least be taken to make it less frightful. Appalled by the sufferings of the French, Austrian and Italian wounded on the battlefield of Solferino (1859), a young Swiss spectator named Jean-Henri Dunant laboured to establish the Red Cross as an international organization. Dunant and other Swiss colleagues brought about the Geneva Conventions of 1864 and 1868, and secured agreement from most of the governments of the world to abide by codes to govern medical care for the wounded, and reasonable treatment for prisoners. Other initiatives brought about some clarification of the rules of war at sea, especially those relating to blockades and to the thankless situation of neutral countries.

Peace was an ideal everybody was willing to subscribe to in theory. Disarmament and arbitration, in moving closer to actual policy, commanded much more qualified assent. But they seemed goals possibly attainable, where total pacification remained a dream. About a hundred disputes between nations were in fact referred to international arbitration between 1850 and 1914. The prime instance was the Geneva Settlement of 1872 of sundry differences between Britain and the United States, which led to the payment of damages of $15,500,000 by Britain for having allowed British-built ships to prey upon Northern commerce during the American Civil War. In the next few years, the German Emperor was among the adjudicators of other Anglo-American disputes. After 1900, an international court located at The Hague arbitrated squabbles between the United States and Mexico, France and Germany (over Casablanca), Britain and Russia (over the 'Dogger Bank' incident of 1905, when Russian warships fired mistakenly on British trawlers mistaking them for Japanese torpedo boats. The Russian Baltic fleet was sailing to the Far East, to replace the Russian fleet destroyed by the surprise Japanese attack on Port Arthur in 1904). The Swedish inventor of explosives, Alfred Nobel, gave publicity to the goal of peace by providing in his will for awards to suitable recipients. Thus one of the nineteen peace prizes distributed between 1901 and 1913 went to Bertha von Suttner. Another, more questionably, was awarded to the American President, Theodore Roosevelt, for mediating in the Russo-Japanese War and for helping to arrange the Algeciras conference (1906) to settle European colonial disputes.

Nobel himself, before his death in 1896, was moving toward the hope that the great powers would discover that war was the worst possible way of deciding an issue. This idea was developed at vast length and with compelling documentation by the Polish-born banker-economist Ivan S. (Jean de) Bloch, the sixth and final volume of whose *Le rôle de la guerre (The Role of War)* was published in 1898. Among his readers were the officials surrounding Tsar Nicholas II. Few military men in other countries took him seriously. War between well-equipped armies would be mutual massacre; the entire social fabric of the warring nations would, Bloch maintained, disintegrate. Some less lunatic expedient than war would have to be devised. For the young Englishman Norman Angell, the same stark truth was evident. War was *The Great Illusion* (1910): in a conflict between major powers, the outcome would reveal little distinction between victor and vanquished. Nobel's view was that the great nations would, initially at any rate, refuse to disarm; and they would be correct in wanting to preserve the authority of the state against the ominous approaching tyranny of the discontented 'dregs of the population'. The solution was to persuade the nations to recognize existing frontiers, and to pledge themselves to use their armies collectively against any power that broke the law of peace. Stability would thus depend upon intelligent self-interest.

At the end of the century, there were some signs that such hard-headed estimates were beginning to have an impact. It was the Tsar, alarmed by the huge, ever-increasing cost of armaments, who took the initiative in summoning the first Hague Peace

Conference of 1899. Twenty-six nations – those of Europe, and the United States, China and Japan – were represented; the delegates were as a whole reputable and eminent, not starry-eyed dreamers. They were, in Prince Scipio Borghese of Italy's charming phrase, *'un groupe du high-life pacifique'*. For two months, breaking into specialist committees, they discussed armaments, the laws of war and arbitration. The Hague World Court was an immediate outcome. A second Hague peace conference met in 1907; this one was attended by the Latin American nations as well. From then until the calamity of 1914, men of good will could convince themselves that the civilized world was in sight of a new order from which large-scale war had been excluded. Men were not only more humane than their ancestors, they were more practical. They could perceive that war was bad ethics, bad business, bad for the maintenance of society itself. In 1914, books and articles began to appear celebrating a century of peace – meaning a century of immunity from the immense conflicts of the revolutionary era.

For the many who were less sanguine, or less analytically prophetic than Bloch or Angell, the decades after 1848 could still be seen in a fairly cheerful light. One interpretation, implied in

The Hague Peace Conference, 1899. Summoned at the instigation of Tsar Nicholas II, the delegates discussed such matters as armaments, arbitration, and the laws of war.

277

Sir Edward Creasy's influential book *Fifteen Decisive Battles of the World* (1851), was that wars did often settle matters definitively, and wholesomely. Most citizens of the powerful nations believed most of the time that world history revealed a progressive evolution. The civilized nations had a right and a duty to arrange the affairs of the rest of the world. Military prowess ensured that they would succeed. Nationhood was itself a higher state than tribalism. In the act of aggregating themselves into nations, aspiring peoples – as in Italy and Germany – might be obliged to pass through the fiery furnace of war. Such wars were inevitable, just, beneficial. Moreover, wars could and should be swift. On this point, military men were even more emphatic than the general public. In retrospect, their contention seemed to be borne out. The Crimean and American Civil Wars had been wretched, dragged-out affairs. But in the view of an arch-professional like General Helmuth von Moltke, chief of the Prussian general staff in the 1860s, this was because they had been mismanaged. The real proof of the effectiveness of war, properly conducted, was that Prussia had defeated Austria in six whirlwind weeks, and had taken only about five months to compel the surrender of France's main armies in 1870–1. In 1898, three months sufficed for the Americans to finish off Spain – a 'splendid little war'. Efficiency, as the Prussians brilliantly demonstrated, was the key. Well-trained and well-armed troops, thorough staff-work to bring about swift mobilization and then an overwhelming concentration of force at a critical strategic point, dash and persistence in the actual battle – these were the ingredients for a truly professional victory. Was this not the proper view of humane conflict? The advocates of naval expansion who were to be found in all Western countries from the 1880s onward could urge the same point: nothing was cleaner, quicker, fairer to civilians, more irrevocable than a good crisp battle at sea – as in the two encounters by which the Americans sank two Spanish fleets, or the astounding annihilation by the Japanese of the Russian fleet in Tsushima Straits in 1905, from which only ten out of thirty-eight ships escaped.

Individual reactions to the notion of war were highly equivocal. Proudhon's *La Guerre et la Paix* waxes lyrical on the mystic glories of combat. John Ruskin, lecturing on war in London in the 1860s, told his audience that 'modern war – scientific war, chemical and mechanic war' was 'worse even than the savage's poisoned arrow'. On the other hand, his studies had taught him that 'all great nations learned their truth of word, and strength of

278

thought, in war; that they were nourished in war, and wasted by peace; ... trained by war, and betrayed by peace ...'. We have seen in Chapter 9 how apocalyptic visions of mass destruction underlay the arguments of radicals in the quarter-century before 1914. They were not alone. At different moments war commended itself to all sorts of people: to fretting conservatives convinced that their countrymen were being morally undermined by life in factories and banks, or by labour agitators; and to glowing young poets like Rupert Brooke, who could write in a 1914 sonnet:

> Now God be thanked Who has matched us with His hour,
>   And caught our youth, and wakened us from sleeping.
> With hand made sure, clear eye, and sharpened power,
>   To turn, as swimmers into cleanness leaping,
> Glad from a world grown old and cold and weary. ...

Throughout the period, then, men were able to contemplate war with varying degrees of optimism. It was diminishing. Or it was becoming more surgically adept in operation. Or it was an agent of progress. Or a cleansing medium for sick peoples and individuals.

Regress?

Some of these attitudes could easily be defined as pessimistic; and there were certainly observers who felt that in its continuing propensity for war, civilization was regressing rather than progressing. Technology, busied mainly with peaceful purposes between 1848 and the 1870s, became harnessed to warfare. The Great Exhibition of 1851 was praised as a monument to peace. Yet, even at the Crystal Palace, a prize was awarded to Krupp's of Essen for its exhibit of high-quality cast steel. In the 1867 Paris Exhibition, visitors were awed by a giant cannon on the Krupp stand – and this very gun was to bombard Paris a few years later. Nobel's peace awards derived their money from his work on nitro-glycerin and dynamite. Technology produced infantry weapons like the breech-loading rifle which greatly increased the firepower, accuracy and range of modern soldiers. Smokeless powder and rifled artillery were to have equally devastating consequences.

After 1870, each of these major armies on the European continent was quick to imitate the German pattern: a large, highly trained, very professional army, its ranks filled with

279

Krupp's Hall at the exhibition at Dusseldorf in 1902 displays the latest weapons of war.

conscripts held to service long enough to make them virtually indistinguishable from regular troops; sophisticated and deadly weapons for each branch of the service; vastly improved methods of signalling and communicating; an expert staff of intelligent energetic men; detailed plans for the use of the nation's railroads to bring men and supplies to their frontier posts. If this was 'militarism', in that it also tended to subordinate civil to military needs, the Germans as the acknowledged masters of military

280

science retorted that they acted out of stern necessity. Britain and the United States could do without peacetime conscription because they were safe behind sea frontiers. For the same reason, these two countries could spawn more peace societies than the rest of the world put together, and dwell sanctimoniously upon the advantages of arbitration. They were hypocritical, in German eyes, because they had their own form of belligerence – not 'militarism' but 'navalism'.

To judge from the behaviour of the delegates at the Hague peace conferences, the German *tu quoque* was justified. The discussions of 1899 supply abundant material for connoisseurs of national self-righteousness. Behind the scenes, the governments of the great powers were cynically contemptuous of the conference. None was prepared to forgo advantages already enjoyed, or to sanction proposals that might conceivably inhibit its future conduct. No nation already strong would countenance disarmament, or even cooling-off periods since these would enable other nations to make good their own deficiencies. Suggestions to prohibit the use of certain new weapons or techniques – air bombardment, gas-projectiles, expanding ('dum-dum') bullets – were accepted by most of the governments involved. The futility of such ratifications was soon apparent after the outbreak of the 1914 war. Their irony was apparent to the delegates when the British and Americans held out. On 'dum-dum' bullets, the British felt vulnerable because they had already been accused of using them in South Africa. On asphyxiating gases, the American dissent was expressed by the famous 'navalist' Captain (later Admiral) Alfred T. Mahan, whose writings on sea power had made him a world figure. Mahan was temperamentally a mild, retiring person, of conspicuous religious piety. As he subsequently put his position, with perfect historical soundness:

The objection that a machine of war is barbarous has always been raised against new weapons. . . . In the middle ages it was firearms which were denounced as cruel. Later, shells, and more recently, torpedoes. It seems to me that it cannot be proved that shells with asphyxiating gases are inhumane or unnecessarily cruel machines of war, and that they cannot produce decisive results.

I represent a people that is animated by a lively desire to make warfare humane but which nevertheless may find itself forced to wage war; therefore it is a question of not depriving itself through hastily adopted resolutions of means of which it could later avail itself with good results.

The Hague conference of 1907 was equally barren. As in 1899, no progress whatsoever was made toward disarmament. This time, the German delegates were the most palpably obstructive. But all were operating within the logic – internally strong – of national sovereignty, vital interests, national honour.

The Military Realm

So far, we have made little distinction between the civil and the military. The army of each nation had special attributes: each nation had the kind of army it wanted, or possibly the army it deserved. Yet the military realm was to some extent enclosed and separate. Each army was preoccupied with its own social and technical atmosphere. Beyond that, there was an international military realm. Soldiers were fascinated by other soldiers: what they wore, how much they were paid and otherwise rewarded, what weapons they carried, what formations they adopted and what ideas they had for winning wars. They attended one another's manoeuvres and were present in surprising numbers to watch one another's battles – whether for strictly professional reasons or because in service life it was the thing to do. George B. McClellan, the Union commander in the early part of the American Civil War, was an observer in the Crimea; John J. Pershing, the commander of the American forces in France, 1917–18, was present at the Russo-Japanese War. As armies developed in size and sophistication, during the pre-1914 decades, this scrutiny became more intense, more knowledgeable, more emulative. Victorious armies were paid the tribute of frank imitation. Up to 1870 most other nations copied French fashions of dress and nomenclature: the *képi* (peaked cap) was the most admired headgear. After 1870 Germany was the object of military plagiarism: the *Pickelhaube* (the Prussian spiked helmet) drove out the French *képi*. Service periodicals dated back to the 1830s; their quantity and quality vastly improved after 1870, and serious military men prided themselves on keeping abreast with the latest professional opinion from all parts of the world.

The spirit of the armies in which these men had grown up was, within the officer corps, aristocratic (the French army was a partial exception), unreflective and deeply conservative. Stultifying years in garrison or on parade were interrupted by occasional popular disturbances or – for the British and French – by experience in small wars overseas, against militarily inferior native opponents. This experience in India or Algeria put a premium on the primary military virtues – willingness to attack, confidence in the outcome – but did nothing to stimulate a more reflective approach. In most armies, the officer regarded himself as *par excellence* a gentleman; in Britain, until 1871, he purchased his own commission unless he belonged to the less socially admired artillery or engineers. He kept apart from the other ranks, who were recruited mainly from the rural population and the unemployed. Where enlistment was voluntary, as in England, it

was noticeably briskest in times of economic depression or at the onset of each winter when casual work became scarce. In continental armies like the French, selective conscription by lot produced a similar result: the well-to-do were permitted to hire substitutes, leaving the impecunious and unlucky to fill up the ranks. The cavalry were the most elegant branch, sartorially and in social prestige. In traditional conception, the cavalry charge was the climactic moment of a battle, the point at which the flower of the nation put the enemy to flight. Nowhere was military conservatism more engrained. A few exceptionally thoughtful soldiers began to suspect that the days of the dragoon and hussar were over; what could sabre or lance do against rifle and field-piece? Armies needed fast-moving riders for advanced reconnaissance. The American Civil War demonstrated the value of men on horseback equipped with carbines, who dismounted to fight. In the Franco-Prussian War, the French cavalry were shot to pieces when they attempted old-style charges. But the lessons were not learned. On both sides in the 1914–18 war, cavalry regiments waited and waited in vain for their big moment, unable to realize that it had gone forever.

   In the old armies, then, traditional assumptions prevailed. The tremendous innovation of the Napoleonic wars – the nation

Cavalry engagement during the battle of Gravelotte; painting by Aimé Morot. Campaigns in the Franco-Prussian War of 1870–1 demonstrated the diminishing usefulness of mounted cavalry.

AIME MOROT. 18??

in arms, the whole people surging against the enemy – was not an inspiration but a bogey to the officer corps of 1850. They did not trust and could not handle mass armies. Their ideal was a professional, long-service, army, the well-knit, firmly hierarchical standing army as it had existed for a century and more.

The shock, as we have said, came from new weapons and from new doctrines: from professionalism of an entirely different sort, from the application of analytical intelligence to the age-old problems of warfare. The Prussian army in 1870 made plenty of mistakes; it was still saddled with obtuse, self-willed old warriors in profusion. But Moltke and his new breed of staff officers were something else. If war was a clumsy, chancy business, their function was to do whatever could be done to diminish the element of uncertainty. The British, with their penchant for congratulating themselves upon calamities, ignored the appalling staff-work that had led to the Charge of the Light Brigade under Lord Cardigan and instead gloried in the sheer gallantry of the episode. To Moltke, a blunder of this nature was something to be eliminated. The extent of his success was staggeringly apparent in 1870. The new-style staff officer, it has been said, bore the same relation to the warrior of the old dispensation as a trained architect to a rule-of-thumb carpenter.

The events of 1870–1 appeared to prove that the German army was the best in Europe, and therefore the best in the world. Every other major army strove over the next forty years to reproduce the Prussian system. Military writing became strikingly more acute and speculative, and preparation for hypothetical wars more thorough and far-ranging. In the staff colleges of Europe, the military balance of power was estimated, one might say, to the last gramme, under laboratory conditions. Intelligent professionals were well aware that the emulative tendencies of modern armies might leave very little to choose between one side and the other. They also realized that the increased accuracy and range of battlefield weapons seemed to favour the defender far more than the attacker. Such considerations stimulated nations to form clearcut alliances. Of these the most crucial was the Franco-Russian alliance of 1893.

As with other armies, French military thinking was an odd blend of emotion and calculation. At its most visceral, the emotion involved a longing for revenge against the Germans, and a monarchist desire to re-establish the old steadfast union of king, church and army, as the means of restoring France, despite

285

republican bad faith and the nation's relative industrial and man-power weakness, to its rightful place among the great powers. At the other extreme of prudential calculation, the problem was how France might win a war against its formidable enemy Germany. The extremes met in the writings of Colonel Ardant du Picq, the author of a brilliant, passionate pamphlet published in 1880, posthumously (du Picq was killed in the 1870 fighting), and also of Ferdinand (later Marshal) Foch of the new French war college. Both men were struck by the importance of the moral factor. Modern battle, once committed, was a terrifying chaos: everything therefore depended upon the will to win of the individual soldiers. This idea drew sustenance from the evident readiness of the German troops in 1870 to 'march to the sound of the guns' without waiting for formal orders. It accorded with French temperament. It also helped to convince officers of Foch's generation that *élan* could overcome mass firepower, that morale mattered more than technology in the last resort. Foch, and followers such as Louis de Grandmaison, insisted that firepower actually aided the offensive, provided that the attackers outnumbered the defenders and that their weapons were at least as good. Their bullets and shells would deluge the defence (especially if the shells came from guns as effective as the French seventy-five millimetre '*soixante-quinze*' introduced in 1897). The will to victory, backed by the Schneider-Creusot armaments output, would carry the day.

German military thought placed somewhat less of a premium upon offensive exuberance. But the Germans too envisaged an offensive war in which enemy resistance would be crushed in a few months at most. This apparent overconfidence rested upon assumptions that were far from euphoric. As soon as the Franco-Russian alliance was concluded, Count Alfred Schlieffen, Moltke's successor as chief of staff, began to face the nightmare prospect of a war on two fronts, east and west. Moltke, pondering the possibility before the alliance became a fact, saw that it would be impossible for Germany to wage war with equal intensity on both fronts at once. His preference was for a holding action against France and a concentration of effort in the east to knock out Russia. Schlieffen, whose first plan was drawn up as early as 1894, reversed the preference: France was to be the primary target, in combination with a quick limited blow against the Russians in East Prussia. For the plan to work, though, the offensive in the west would have to be mounted with lightning decisiveness, so as to knock the enemy off balance and then rout him before he had time to mount his own inevitable offensive. A further consideration was that a long war was out of the question; the strains it would impose upon the economy and upon the German people would be intolerable.

Militarily, the German scenario was plausible, indeed perhaps irrefutable, given Schlieffen's premises. His scheme of operations did not differ in some fundamentals from the French 'Plan XVII', except in being rather more realistic and tactically shrewd. Yet at bottom, it was a gambler's stratagem, an all-or-nothing throw. The stakes were so high, and the influence of the military so predominant in Wilhelmine Germany, that the temptation to beat the clock, to rush headlong into war once it seemed imminent, was almost irresistible. In military necessity, the Germans were obliged to come perilously close to waging undeclared war – and to push their troops through neutral Belgium was a basic feature of the Schlieffen plan. True, the French general staff took for granted that the Germans might decide to violate Belgian neutrality. At some point in all this, military hardheadedness began to look like lunacy.

Navalism

The metaphysics of 'navalism' would eventually lead to a comparable, imperceptible transition from boldness into rashness, from insight into purblindness.

The process was reached by initially gentle stages. In the mid-nineteenth century, the world's navies consisted essentially of wooden sailing-ships. The shift from timber and canvas to iron and steam took several decades. At the beginning the British navy was as large as that of all the other powers put together. There seemed no strong reason to depart from old and tried weapons or methods of construction and propulsion. The innovating impulse came from France, first of all through experiments with guns that could fire shells instead of the solid round-shot of Nelson's day. In the 1840s, the gifted young naval officer Dupuy de Lôme, well in advance of his British colleagues, decided that steam would soon supplant sail as the primary means of propulsion: hitherto it had been regarded as an auxiliary source. Since the ship's engines would be both vital and vulnerable, he devised laminated iron armour at the waterline. Napoleon III was impressed, and hastened the construction of several armour-protected floating batteries for use against Russian forts in the Crimea. One of these managed to knock out a quantity of emplaced guns with practically no damage to itself. De Lôme's faith in both steam and armour seemed to be vindicated. As he remarked, an ocean-going ironclad placed among ordinary wooden warships would be as devastating as 'a lion in a flock of sheep'. He was rewarded with a senior position in the French Ministry of the Marine, and able to press forward at the end of the 1850s with the construction of what was intended to be an entire ironclad steam fleet ('ironclad' signifying sheets of metal some four inches thick, laid over a wood-built ship as a carapace). The first vessel of this

The battle of Mobile Bay, 1864. The American Civil War was a portent of the age of the armoured warship.

type was by orthodox standards a monster, of nearly six thousand tons. Now the British bestirred themselves. Their own ironclad answer, the nine-thousand-ton *Warrior*, was launched in 1861. For several years, the two nations competed briskly, introducing thicker armour and deadlier armament in leapfrog alternation, until the French defeat by the Prussians enabled their trans-Channel rivals to forge ahead and restore the old lead, though not quite on the same terms.

Meanwhile, the American Civil War supplied dramatic illustrations of what the new naval technology might portend. Having no navy of any kind, the Confederate South had to improvise. It quickly produced an ironclad, built on the hull of the captured Union USS *Merrimac* (rechristened the *Virginia*). Marauding in Northern coastal waters, the *Merrimac* caused consternation by sinking two unarmoured ships and killing 250 men of their crews for the loss of two men on its own side. The Union was able to counter with the just-completed *Monitor*. Their duel was inconclusive in that neither ship was able to disable the other. 'The clangor of that blacksmith's fray', said the American writer Herman Melville, echoed round the world. The entire nature of combat seemed to him altered by a single encounter:

> War yet shall be, but warriors
> Are now but operatives; War's made
>   Less grand than Peace,
> And a singe runs through lace and feather.

The subsequent performance of ironclads during the American Civil War was not quite so startling. Their engines were apt to break down or their turrets to jam. Even so, their imperviousness was almost unbelievable. In the Union attack on Mobile Bay in 1864 – itself, like the earlier capture of New Orleans, a remarkable lesson in audacity – the Confederate *Tennessee* faced a whole Union squadron. Though pounded at last into silence, it had only two men killed inside its iron chambers.

In the next twenty years, the ironclad became a standard feature of all navies, though a few wooden ships lingered on in the world's lesser fleets – including at that time the United States. Armour plating grew thicker and thicker, reaching the ultimate in cumbersomeness at twenty-four inches, around 1880. This was to offset the complementary increase in the penetrating power of naval guns, which by the 1880s were able to hurl sixteen-inch shells a distance of several miles. Naval technology advanced so rapidly and so variously that for a few years governments appeared uncertain how next to proceed. Some tacticians set store by new applications of the old idea of ramming enemy ships. Others began to toy with the notion of the submarine, which had appeared in primitive form during the American Civil War and which was introduced (with electric propulsion) into the British and French navies in the 1880s. Others again speculated on the possibilities of different types of mines, especially the 'automobile' torpedo invented by Robert Whitehead, an Englishman living in Fiume which was then part of Austria-Hungary.

Once more, the theoretical energy was supplied by the French, on this occasion by the restless naval officers of the *Jeune Ecole* (new school), anxious to press the claims of their arm of the service against those of the army, and to cut the rival British navy down to size. Their contention was that the day of the battleship was over. It could be bottled up by minefields, and sunk by torpedo-boats. Indeed, the day of Britain might be over; the island race was no longer self-supporting in food or in other materials, and so could be starved into submission. Large navies with large ships following orthodox methods had, it seemed, contributed very little to the major wars of the 1850s and 1860s.

The assertions of the *Jeune Ecole* were in themselves too radical to be taken very seriously. There was, nevertheless, something of a lull in the 1880s, largely because of British uncertainty over what to do next. The lull ended when the British, worried by their isolation among the coalescing alignments of the big nations, decided in 1889 to expand the navy according to the 'two-power' formula. Britain, that is, would maintain its navy so as to equal the strength in battleships of the two other largest navies in the world – those at that period of France and Russia. Though financially burdensome, the programme was technically feasible, since Britain also possessed the largest shipbuilding capacity in the world; and these shipyards could reap incidental benefits, in the new worldwide climate of naval expansion, by selling warships to lesser navies such as the Brazilian and the Japanese.

The rationale for this climate was supplied with amazing opportuneness in the following year, 1890, through the publication of Mahan's *Influence of Sea Power upon History*. Mahan's aim, in preparing a set of lectures for the United States naval war college, was to see whether there were any abiding principles governing naval warfare. His answer was an indubitable yes. The sea lanes of the world were vital highways; whoever controlled them had command of the sea; and any nation with the proper geographical location that established command was well on the way to becoming a world power. Stated thus, Mahan's thesis sounds either platitudinous or dubious. But in the 1890s it seemed novel and incontrovertible. Re-examining the histories of wars in which navies had been prominent, his contemporaries felt he had brought to light a whole neglected dimension of power and possibility. As a mark of British gratification, Mahan received honorary degrees from both Oxford and Cambridge in the same week. His fellow-countrymen, such as Theodore Roosevelt and Henry Cabot Lodge, determined to raise their own navy from comparative impotence to great-power status, quoted his words as holy writ. In Germany, William II, fascinated since boyhood by the grandeur of the British fleet, was vastly impressed.

The Russian fleet at Tsushima, May 1905. The third largest navy in the world, after Great Britain and France, Russia's Far Eastern fleet was to be largely destroyed in the Russo-Japanese War.

When he became Kaiser in 1888, the German fleet ranked fifth among the world's navies. William's immediate impulse was not to climb into higher place. Then and later, he considered himself an Anglophile – a grandson of Queen Victoria, for whom blood was thicker than seawater. His hope, through the 1890s, was that Britain could be brought into the Triple Alliance (Germany, Austria, Italy), in which case its naval strength would be of immeasurable importance.

But Britain remained aloof; the scramble for colonies grew more intense, and with it the conviction that seapower was necessary to sustain empire; in 1897 Alfred Tirpitz, a tireless advocate of naval expansion, was chosen by William II to be secretary of the German admiralty; and Tirpitz swiftly proceeded – with a certain amount of opposition from the German army but with the Kaiser's blessing – to push through the *Reichstag* the fateful Fleet Laws of 1898 and 1900. The intent of these was to construct a German navy second only to that of Britain. This, with the aid of further levies upon an uneasy but muted *Reichstag*, Tirpitz accomplished by 1914. Technically his achievement was extraordinary; ship for ship, his battle fleet was probably the best in the world. In other respects, the upsurge of German navalism was an act of consummate folly. The effect of the Fleet Laws was to set off a deadly naval race, and to convince the British that German aggressiveness was unbounded. The British, for their part, were perhaps obtuse in failing to grasp that their own

292

paternalistic supremacy at sea might irk other nations. They contributed to the race, half unwittingly, by launching a new all-big-gun battleship, the *Dreadnought*, in 1906, that rendered all other battleships, including their own, obsolete. They were dismayed by the German refusal after 1906 to entertain proposals for an easing-off of battleship construction. Above all, they were baffled, and with reason, by the Germans' abstract passion to create a formidable new fleet that could not be quite formidable enough to risk a major battle with the British. The consequence, at any rate, was to impel the British to strengthen their home fleet by withdrawing ships from the Mediterranean and elsewhere. This entailed reaching agreement with other non-hostile naval powers, and so drawing the British closer to quasi-alliances.

The Approach of War

It is not possible to measure out the proportions of blame attaching to the major European powers for the final outbreak of war in 1914. If expenditure on armaments were a reliable index, Britain and Germany were the most culpable, followed on the eve of war by Russia and France. Austria-Hungary and Italy were some way behind. But then, these figures are to a considerable extent a measure of relative national wealth. On some other scale of innate belligerence, small nations such as Serbia, Bulgaria and Greece would have to be weighed in the balance. If foreign policy were the key, then every *entente*, every alliance, secret or otherwise, was offensive in contemplating specific enemies – against which the army staffs had prepared elaborate contingency plans. It was also the product of fear – fear of being outmanœuvred and over-matched, fear of a surprise attack ('preventive war' in the euphemism of the attacker) of the kind launched by Japan against the Russians in Port Arthur in 1904. A weird blend of cerebration, fluke and hysteria shaped the alignment of the powers – aggravated of course by colonial rivalry. What was happening was not altogether unprecedented. Combat had been endemic in world history; greed rationalized as patriotism had long been a feature of the nation state. The difference was one of degree, and had to do with the unprecedented pace of change – of which the sudden introduction of the dreadnought was a symbol. Dynamism in power politics meant keeping a jump ahead of one's competitors; and this promoted extreme jumpiness.

In the most desperate phases of the 1914–18 war and afterward, blame for the catastrophe was usually laid at the feet of govern-ments, embassies, military juntas, arms manufacturers, inter-national bankers: scheming villains who had victimized the ordinary peace-loving citizen. Certainly, public opinion was manipulated, in the countries where popular sentiment was supposed to count. It was moulded by the press and by means of such propaganda organizations as the Navy Leagues that flourished in Britain, Germany, Italy and the United States. In countries like Russia, men were conscripted both literally and metaphorically.

Yet so far as we can estimate genuine opinion, the common man in Europe closely approximated the mentality of his rulers in

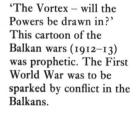

'The Vortex – will the Powers be drawn in?' This cartoon of the Balkan wars (1912–13) was prophetic. The First World War was to be sparked by conflict in the Balkans.

veering between arrogance and despondency, perplexity and assurance. Mass attitudes can be gauged for instance in the flood of fictional accounts of imaginary future years that began in 1871 with *The Battle of Dorking*. This plausibly detailed description of a successful German invasion of England was written by an engineer officer, Colonel Sir George Chesney, and stimulated an immediate rush of imitations – many of them, like his own tale, swiftly translated into other languages. Thus within months of the appearance of *The Battle of Dorking*, Edouard Dangin produced a French revenge-fantasy, *La Bataille de Berlin en 1875*, whose title is self-explanatory. In viewpoint, there was little to choose between military and civilian authors, though for obvious reasons army and navy officers were eager to make use of these fictions to plead the case for enlarged service expenditure and improved training. If anything, a more dispassionate tone prevailed in *The Great War of 189–* (1893), a collaborative forecast by the British naval officer Philip Colomb and a team of professional associates, than in the shrill pages of William Le Queux's *The Great War in England in 1897* (1894) which was devised in part as a circulation-raising stunt for the Harmsworth press. Some novels, such as Sir W. F. Butler's *The Invasion of England* (1882), Charles Gleig's *When All Men Starve* (1897), Gustav Erdmann's *Defenceless at Sea* (1900), and J. Bernard Walker's *America Fallen!* (1915), sought to scare their readers with bad dreams of defeat. Others were pure wish-fulfilment, like the novels by 'Danrit' (Emile Driant, son-in-law of General Boulanger) that specify French triumphs over Germany or Britain, or A. Niemann's *World War: Germany's Dream* (1904), which appeared in translation as *The Coming Conquest of England*.

Taken as a whole, this vast spread of popular literature suggests that for the dynamic nations, with the partial exception of the United States, the contemplation of the coming war exercised an almost morbid fascination. There was the absorption in sheer technology, the pride in imagined pre-eminence, the dread of supersession and obsolescence (to be obsolete was a crime, bringing inevitable punishment), the naïve willingness to believe in secret weapons, the chauvinistic suspicion of foreign intrigue and espionage. There was the bewildering kaleidoscope of conceived alliances and enmities. In most British stories of 1880–1900, France was the usual aggressor, after 1900 Germany. Yet apart from H. G. Wells, few of these fantasists showed any true awareness of the risk of doom. Even ambitious tales of world conflict ended with rosy visions of permanent peace – sometimes in British works like Louis Tracy's *The Final War* (1896) guaranteed by Anglo-American hegemony. In the vast majority of these imaginings, the war lasted no more than a few months. Theirs was a strangely sanguine apocalypse.

Expectation and Reality

As in fiction, so it was in professional expectation. 'The outcome of the next war will be decided in less than a month after the opening of hostilities' (General Bonnal, *The Next War*, 1906). This did not quite mean that the war would be over in a month. It meant that the general staffs had convinced themselves that speedy mobilization, set in motion before the actual declaration of war, would bring on a major battle almost immediately. Each assumed a victory for their own side, with winner-takes-all consequences as in a modern naval battle. Because a lengthy war was unthinkable, it was not thought about: the few realists who tried to do so in the French officer corps, for instance, were accused of being defeatist. Commandant Mordacq (*The Length of the Next War*, 1912) warned against the danger of a collapse of public morale if people were allowed to believe that everything would be over after the first great battle. But even he did not anticipate a war of more than about a year. Sir Edward Grey, the British Foreign Secretary, consoled the House of Commons on the eve of the nation's entry: 'If we are engaged in war, we shall suffer but little more' – through interruption of normal trade with the Continent – 'than if we stand aside.' By not invading Holland in 1914, the Germans expected to be able to maintain their world commerce *via* Dutch ports.

Each belligerent had its neat scenario. For the Germans, the Schlieffen-based sweep through northern France, with Paris as the autumn harvest. For the French, an unstoppable offensive in Lorraine, leading to the recovery of the lost provinces. For the Russians, a march through East Prussia and so to Berlin, coupled with another drive on Budapest. For the British, the gratification of a naval battle in the North Sea, and the annihilation of Tirpitz's dreadnoughts, followed by a crippling blockade of the helpless German coastline.

The German dream was almost realized. Belgium was overrun. In a month, the German advance guards could see the Eiffel Tower sticking up on the horizon. But then the timetable began

August 1914. Russian
trenches under attack
from artillery during the
battle of Tannenburg,
painting by Max Rabes.

to go wrong. At the climactic battle of the Marne, in early September, the French and the small British expeditionary force
staved off defeat and went over to the attack. Before Christmas,
the front was stabilized in a line of trenches zigzagging all the way
from the Swiss frontier to the Channel coast. On the Eastern Front,
Russian and Austro-Hungarian offensives had resulted in defeat
and disappointment. There were isolated naval actions between
British and German warships, but no sign of a major engagement.
This was not to come until the battle of Jutland, in 1916, but
even then it was broken off inconclusively.

For a while, it is true, the soldiers as well as their commanders
cherished the hope that the next big battle would be decisive.
When they spoke of Armageddon they still invested it with a
quasi-religious splendour – good and evil contending, as in the
Book of Revelations, in the last great 'battle of that great day of
God Almighty'. Reservists and volunteers were cheered and kissed
by enthusiastic crowds. The first soldiers' poetry of a Rupert

297

Brooke or a Siegfried Sassoon was full of youthful idealism. 'In the earlier months,' David Jones remembered, 'there was a certain attractive amateurishness, and elbow-room for idiosyncrasy.' Zeppelins and wire-and-canvas aircraft seemed insignificant when compared with the death-dealing aerial fleets of fantasy literature.

But every offensive was brought to a standstill, beaten by barbed wire, machine-guns and high explosive. The French army alone had nearly a million casualties (killed and wounded: the approximate ratio was one man killed for every five wounded) in 1914, and well over a million in 1915 – all this for a maximum Franco-British gain of three miles during that year. By 1916 the strain for both sides was almost intolerable. The Germans were winning against Russia, but the effort to sustain a two-front war was crippling. The tragic disillusionment of the French was movingly disclosed in Henri Barbusse's *Le Feu* (1916; published in English, 1917, as *Under Fire*). The terrible battles of 1916, on the Somme and around Verdun, were not 'battles' in the old sense but bloody nightmares spread out over weeks and months. On both sides, the men in the trenches began to hate the remote commanders, planning fresh offensives from far behind the lines; and to feel estranged from the comfortable, patriotic civilians at home. 'Every one talked a foreign language; it was newspaper language', said Robert Graves of England in 1916, after he had been sent home wounded.

The one thing the dynamic nations could not imaginatively encompass was stalemate. Movement was their medium. The generals who, faced with deadlock, could only regroup for another offensive have been castigated as stupid. But they were responding to the inner prescriptions of their era; they were not behind the time but exactly of it. One irony of the impasse on the Western Front was that competitive energy had raised all the main armies to the same level of staunch excellence: Armageddon was a draw. Another irony was that progress had apparently culminated not in a standstill but in something still worse: a regression. The mud-smeared infantry, hiding in burrows, looked like the denizens of a primeval swamp. In close combat they fought one another with clubs and spikes. The modern era prided itself upon documentation. But the deaths of many thousands of these men were anonymous; their shattered corpses had been deprived even of name, rank and number.

Epilogue

The world scene at the end of 1916 appeared to invert and caricature all the values that the dynamic societies had trusted in. Technology turned vile. Inventiveness produced high-explosive and poison gas. The lofty pretensions of the nation-state were invoked to encourage masses of men in one kind of uniform to slaughter men clad in a slightly different uniform. Dreams of a rebirth of old, chivalric, pre-commercial gallantries stirred some. Others were bored with bourgeois urban sameness. Instead they died in droves, butchered like cattle; and the incessant pounding of artillery created a terrain infinitely more monotonous than the streets of peacetime – a featureless lunar landscape, a waste packed with shell-craters. Hopes that all mankind could be brought together in peaceable assemblies, as in the ceremonies of the revived Olympic Games, were travestied on the main fronts of the war. There was a gathering of the tribes: contingents from Britain and France and Germany and Portugal and Belgium and Italy and Russia and Austria-Hungary, from Canada and Australia and South Africa and the United States, from Serbia and Greece and Turkey and India, came together into the terrible fraternity of the killing-grounds of the world conflict.

According to such a conception of the movement of events during our period, Western man had finally trapped himself in his own logic. He had confused quantity with quality, appetite with fruitfulness.

Capitalist society, it could be said, raised higher than ever before the injunction to accumulate, to compete, to surpass. Conventional religion continued to deplore the tendency, but with even less effect than in former ages. Property became associated with individuality, so closely that the two could not be separated. Personal prowess was equated with the imperative to be 'up and doing', as Longfellow put the matter. Increasing numbers of men, especially in business, held posts on the express understanding that they must endlessly improve. Year by year they must excel their own performances, and beat their rivals. The *Oxford Dictionary* gives 1883 as the date of the first printed usage of the expression 'breaking the record', in the sense of going one better than all previous bests. The rationale tended to regard record-breaking as an end in itself: the graph must always rise. When it dropped, as it fairly regularly did through the operations of the business cycle, societies were apt to panic because such depressions challenged their very basis. One did not have to be a Marxist to wonder whether there might not be something insensate in a process that affected national policies as well as individual strivings. What was the ultimate point of being 'go-ahead' (a significant nineteenth-century coinage) if to cease going-ahead was to court disaster?

In this view, then, the period 1848–1917 was all of a piece. The underlying assumptions of the dynamic societies were already formed. The next seventy years revealed the development of their ideology, with its belief in national and racial destiny, its competition for wealth and empire, its adoration of science. By the second decade of the twentieth century, the theory goes, the pressures had built up to an ungovernable extent. Or, to change the figure, the gods retaliated. Mankind got what was coming to it. One reason for the crash was that the stabilizing agencies themselves had little to offer. Traditional societies such as China were internally weak, and unable to withstand the dynamic forces. In the West, the argument for tradition too often sounded selfish or ridiculously diehard. The spokesmen for the *status quo* were obliged to claim virtues for it which they suspected it did not really possess. Middle-of-the-road thinkers sounded foolish or disingenuous by simultaneously applauding and deploring change. Even thoroughgoing radicals were liable to reveal themselves unwittingly as mouthpieces of their time. Thus Bakunin, enemy of the capitalist order, compounded his offence by being an atheist. But one of his contentions was curiously dynamic in style. He objected to the primal prohibitory myth of the exclusion from Eden. What else, he asked, could an intelligent man and woman do but acquaint themselves with the Tree of Knowledge?

The popular culture of the antagonists in the 1914–18 War indicates an almost uncanny sameness – more impressive in a way than the resemblances of previous decades, since conflict sealed the warring nations off from one another: neither side had much direct knowledge of what the other was feeling. Yet the postcard *Kitsch* of France and Germany duplicated almost precisely the same martial, religious and facetious images. Bosomy ladies symbolized Germany or Marianne. Angels and nuns watched over the wounded. Fritz or François, in his dugout, thought of his loved ones, and they of him. Babies announced their intention to grow up

WHO SAID GERMANS?

quickly and fight for the Fatherland or for *la Patrie*. This out-pouring of material might almost have come from a single establishment, operating perhaps in neutral, intermediate Holland or Switzerland, so interchangeably standardized was it.

Three qualifications need, however, to be stressed. The first is that if one set of attitudes pervaded the dynamic societies, and in turn infiltrated the rest of the world, this set contained sharp tensions or polarities. Nationalism was both centripetal and centrifugal. It drew societies together through unification, and dispersed them in obedience to the principle of self-determination. The spread of universal themes and techniques was countered by intense competition for cultural and economic primacy. Many men and women entertained high hopes of betterment, prosperity and peace. Some felt that Christianity would be the chief force for good; some found the instinct of fellowship, less spiritually expressed, in the international expositions that punctuated the era. One body of ideas insisted that industrial capitalism was as beneficent as it was irresistible. A contrary body of ideas maintained that industrial capitalism must be reformed or possibly destroyed because its power was so malevolent. In between these extremes was an abundance of different and differing notions.

First World War – British propaganda postcard. The war of words played a vital part in the development of attitudes and morale in all countries involved in the conflict.

301

From a close perspective, the world of 1848–1917 displayed an almost infinite variety, defying large generalization.

The second comment is that to present 1917 as the logical outcome of previous decades, ending on a notion of total collapse, is to fail to do justice to the toughness of the dynamic scheme. If the soldiers involved were tragic dupes, the majority failed to perceive this. Most of them went on fighting, with extraordinary tenacity. Russia disintegrated only after an appalling sequence of defeats. Ernest Hemingway's war-novel *A Farewell to Arms* depicts the Italian army, engulfed by the disaster of Caporetto. What he does not go on to make clear is that the Italians recovered and held their front. William Faulkner's novel *A Fable* deals with the mutiny in the French army of 1917. Again, however, the French held on despite war-weariness. As late as the spring of 1918, the Germans were still able to mount an offensive that almost brought them victory. One may argue that the values of these societies were inadequate or contradictory. What seems undeniable is that for millions of individuals the social cement continued to be extremely strong. If the Russian direction of the war had been only somewhat less flagrantly incompetent, it is perfectly possible that there would have been no revolution, or at least nothing on the lines of 1917–21. Lenin might have ended his days in Switzerland, and Stalin have remained unknown to history.

The old societies could be called repressive. Yet on the whole their members were willing sacrifices, buoyed up by attachments they did not take lightly. On its own terms dynamic society was very much a going concern. The machine-order, after all, was equipped with oiling-points, governors, safety-valves. Why should the pressures build up to explosion-point? There was nothing entirely fore-ordained in the evolution of the 1914–18 War. A peace might have been concluded by, say, the spring of 1915, leaving the advantage with the Germans. Some historians think that would have been not only a feasible but a desirable outcome.

The third observation is that seventy years is a long time. A great deal of change took place between 1848 and 1917. The period cannot be neatly chopped into short sub-periods of a decade or so. But we can discern a considerable transition, with the 1870s or 1880s as a dividing-line. Before it, British industrial and trading supremacy was conspicuous. Thereafter, the United States and Germany were coming to the forefront. Before the 1870s, steam and iron were the chief features of society. By the end of the

302

century, electricity and steel were important challengers. There was a transition from the old, somewhat haphazard acquisition of colonies to the so-called 'new imperialism'. There was a profound shift in science from 'classical' to 'modern' concepts, and in the arts and social sciences from objective to subjective approaches. Awareness of such changes was perhaps delayed among the ordinary citizens. But, like it or not, change was the very essence of their lives.

Bibliography

This is not intended as a full bibliography. It is simply a selection of some of the books that are still in print and readily available in the English language, and which I have found useful. Their own reading-lists provide further guidance. Some of the items are relevant to more than one chapter.

1 PROLOGUE: THE WORLD IN MOTION

Briggs, Asa, *The Age of Improvement* (London, Longmans Green, 1959)
—— (ed.), *The Nineteenth Century: The Contradictions of Progress* (London, Thames & Hudson, 1970)
Crankshaw, Edward, *The Fall of the House of Habsburg* (London, Longmans, 1963; Sphere, 1970)
Lyons, F.S.L., *Internationalism in Europe, 1815–1914* (Leyden, A.W. Sythoff, 1963)
Moore, Barrington, Jr., *Social Origins of Dictatorship and Democracy* (London, Allen Lane, The Penguin Press, 1967)
Morazé, Charles, *Les Bourgeois Conquérants* (Paris, Armand Colin, 1957); translated as *The Triumph of The Middle Classes* (London, Weidenfeld & Nicolson; New York, World, 1966)
Rae, John B. and Mahoney, Thomas H.D., *The United States in World History*, 3rd edn (New York, McGraw-Hill, 1964)
Schoenwald, Richard L. (ed.), *Nineteenth Century Thought: The Discovery of Change* (Englewood Cliffs, N.J., Prentice-Hall, 1965)
Taylor, A.J.P., *Europe: Grandeur and Decline* (Harmondsworth, Penguin, 1967)

2 MACHINES

Armytage, W.H.G., *The Rise of the Technocrats: A Social History* (London, Routledge Kegan Paul, 1965)
Bartlett, C.J. (ed.), *Britain Pre-eminent: Studies of British World Influence in the Nineteenth Century* (London, Macmillan; New York, St Martin's Press, 1969)
Faulkner, Harold U., *The Decline of Laissez-Faire, 1897–1917*, vol. 7, *The Economic History of the United States* (New York, Holt, Rinehart & Winston, 1951)
Giedion, Siegfried, *Mechanization Takes Command* (New York, Oxford, 1948)
Habakkuk, H.J., *American and British Technology in the Nineteenth Century* (Cambridge U.P., 1962)

Hobsbawm, E. J., *Industry and Empire: An Economic History of Britain since 1750* (London, Weidenfeld & Nicolson, 1968)

Kirkland, E. C., *A History of American Economic Life*, 4th edn (New York, Meredith, 1969)

Landes, David S., *The Unbound Prometheus: Technological Change and Industrial Development in Western Europe from 1750 to the present* (Cambridge U.P., 1969)

Middlemas, Robert K., *The Master Builders* (London, Hutchinson, 1963)

Morison, Elting E., *Men, Machines, and Modern Times* (Cambridge, Mass., M.I.T. Press, 1966)

Saul, S. B. (ed.), *Technological Change: The United States and Britain in the Nineteenth Century* (London, Methuen, 1970)

Taylor, Arthur J., *Laissez-Faire and State Intervention in Nineteenth-Century Britain* (London, Macmillan, 1972)

Turner, E. S., *The Shocking History of Advertising!* (London, Michael Joseph, 1952)

3 PEOPLE AND CLASSES

Armengaud, André, *Population in Europe, 1700–1914*, vol. 3, *Fontana Economic History of Europe* (London, Fontana, 1970)

Briggs, Asa, *Victorian People* (London, Odhams, 1954; Chicago U.P., 1955; Harmondsworth, Penguin, 1965)

——, *Victorian Cities* (London, Odhams, 1963; Harmondsworth, Penguin, 1968)

Cipolla, Carlo, *Literacy and Development in the West* (Harmondsworth, Penguin, 1969)

Green, F. C., *A Comparative View of French and British Civilization, 1850–70* (London, Dent, 1965)

Moller, Herbert (ed.), *Population Movements in Modern European History* (New York, Macmillan, 1964)

Mumford, Lewis, *The Culture of Cities* (New York, Harcourt, Brace, 1938)

Perkin, Harold, *The Origins of Modern English Society, 1780–1880* (London, Routledge, 1969)

Shryock, Richard H., *The Development of Modern Medicine* (New York, Knopf, 1947; London, Gollancz, 1948)

Sorlin, Pierre, *La Société Française, 1840–1914* (Paris, Arthaud, 1969)

Tobias, J. J., *Crime and Industrial Society in the Nineteenth Century* (London, Batsford, 1967; Harmondsworth, Penguin, 1972)

Wakstein, Allen M. (ed.), *The Urbanization of America* (Boston, Houghton, Mifflin, 1970)

Weber, Adna F., *The Growth of Cities in the Nineteenth Century* (New York, 1899; repr. Ithaca, Cornell U.P., 1963)

Weimer, David R. (ed.), *City and Country in America* (New York, Meredith, 1962)

Vannier, Henriette, *La Mode et Ses Métiers ... 1830–70* (Paris, Armand Colin, 1960)

4 NATIONS AND NATIONALISM

Baron, Salo W., *Modern Nationalism and Religion* (New York, Harper, 1947)

Curti, Merle, *The Roots of American Loyalty* (New York, Columbia U.P., 1946)

Gobineau, Comte de, *Introduction à l'Essai sur l'Inégalité des Races Humaines* (Paris, Nouvel Office d'Edition, 1963)

Hayes, Carlton J. H., *Nationalism: a Religion* (New York and London, Macmillan, 1960)

Helmreich, Ernst (ed.), *A Free Church in a Free State?* (Boston, D.C. Heath, 1964)

Kedourie, Elie, *Nationalism* (London, Hutchinson, 1960, 1961)

Kohn, Hans, *Prophets and Peoples: Studies in Nineteenth Century Nationalism* (New York, Macmillan, 1946)

——, *Pan-Slavism: its History and Ideology* (Notre Dame, Indiana, U. of Notre Dame Press, 1953; New York, Vintage, 1960)

——, *Nationalism: its Meaning and History* (Princeton & London, D. Van Nostrand, 1955)

——, *American Nationalism* (New York, Macmillan, 1957)

Robertson, Priscilla, *Revolutions of 1848: a Social History* (Princeton U.P., 1952)

Shafer, Boyd C., *Nationalism: Myth and Reality* (New York, Harcourt, Brace & World, 1955)

Snyder, Louis L. (ed.), *The Dynamics of Nationalism* (Princeton & London, D. Van Nostrand, 1964)

Sugar, Peter F., and Lederer, Ivo J. (eds.), *Nationalism in Eastern Europe* (Seattle & London, U. of Washington Press, 1969)

5 EUROPEAN SETTLEMENT AND IMPERIAL IMPULSE

Brunschwig, H., *French Colonialism, 1871–1914* (London, Pall Mall Press, 1966)

Chamberlain, M.E., *The New Imperialism* (London, Historical Association, 1970)

Fieldhouse, D.K., *The Colonial Empires: a Comparative Survey* (London, Weidenfeld & Nicolson, 1966)

Gann, L.H. & Duignan, P., *The Burden of Empire* (London, Pall Mall Press, 1968)

Gollwitzer, Heinz, *Europe in the Age of Imperialism, 1880–1914* (London, Thames & Hudson, 1969)

Henderson, W.O., *Studies in German Colonial History* (London, Frank Cass, 1962)

Kiernan, V.G., *The Lords of Human Kind: European attitudes towards the outside world in the Imperial Age* (London, Weidenfeld & Nicolson, 1969)

Koebner, R., *Empire* (Cambridge U.P., 1961)

Robinson R., & Gallagher, J., *Africa and the Victorians: The official mind of imperialism* (London, Macmillan, 1961)

Semmel, B., *Imperialism and Social Reform* (London, Allen & Unwin, 1960)

Taylor, A.J.P., *The Struggle for Mastery in Europe, 1848–1918* (Oxford, Clarendon Press, 1954)

Thornton, A.P., *The Imperial Idea and its Enemies* (London, Macmillan, 1959)

Williams, William A., *The Roots of the Modern American Empire* (New York, Random House, 1969)

Wright, Harrison M. (ed.), *The 'New Imperialism'* (Boston, D.C. Heath, 1961)

6 THE AMERICAN CONTINENT

Boorstin, Daniel J., *The Americans: The Democratic Experience* (New York, Random House, 1973)

Gerbi, Antonello, *The Dispute of the New World: the History of a Polemic, 1750–1900* (U. of Pittsburgh Press, 1973; first publ. Milan, Ricciardi, 1955, as *La Disputa del Nuovo Mondo*)

Grenville, J.A.S. and Young, G.B., *Politics, Strategy and American Diplomacy ... 1873–1917* (New Haven and London, Yale U.P., 1966)

Hanke, Lewis (ed.), *Have the Americas a Common History?* (New York, Knopf, 1964)

——, (ed.), *History of Latin American Civilization*, vol. 2: *The Modern Age* (Boston, Little, Brown, 1967)

Hartz, Louis, *et al.*, *The Founding of New Societies* (New York, Harcourt, Brace, 1964)

Kraus, Michael, *The North Atlantic Civilization* (Princeton & London, D.Van Nostrand, 1957)

Morton, W.L., *The Canadian Identity* (U. of Toronto Press & Madison, U. of Wisconsin Press, 1961)

Perkins, Dexter, *Hands Off: A History of The Monroe Doctrine* (Boston, Little, Brown, 1941)

Pike, Frederick B. (ed.), *Latin American History: ... Identity, Integration, and Nationhood* (New York, Harcourt, Brace & World, 1969)

Silberschmidt, Max, *The United States and Europe: Rivals and Partners* (London, Thames & Hudson, 1972)

Warner, Donald F., *The Idea of Continental Union: Agitation for the Annexation of Canada to the United States, 1849–93* (Lexington, U. of Kentucky Press, 1960)

Whitaker, Arthur P., *The Western Hemisphere Idea: its Rise and Decline* (Ithaca, Cornell U.P., 1954)

Womack, John, *Zapata and the Mexican Revolution* (London, Thames & Hudson, 1969)

Woodward, C. Vann (ed.), *The Comparative Approach to American History* (New York & London, Basic Books, 1968)

7 AFRICA AND ASIA

Akamatsu, Paul, *Meiji 1868: Revolution and Counter-Revolution in Japan* (London, Allen & Unwin, 1972)

Beasley, W.G., *The Meiji Restoration* (Stanford & London, Stanford U.P., 1972)

Brown, Delmer, N., *Nationalism in Japan, 1955* (repr. New York, Russell & Russell, 1971)

Embree, A.T., *India's Search for National Identity* (New York, Knopf, 1972)

Franke, Wolfgang, *A Century of Chinese Revolution, 1851–1949* (Oxford, Blackwell, 1970; first publ. 1957, Munich, R. Oldenburg Verlag, as *Das Jahrhundert der Chinesischen Revolution*)

Hibbert, Christopher, *The Dragon Wakes: China and the West, 1793–1911* (London, Longmans, 1970)

Irvine, Keith, *The Rise of the Coloured Races* (London, Allen & Unwin, 1972)

July, Robert W., *The Origins of Modern African Thought* (New York, Praeger, 1967; London, Faber, 1968)

——, *A History of the African People* (New York, Scribner's; London, Faber, 1970)

Kennedy, Malcolm, *A History of Japan* (London, Weidenfeld & Nicolson, 1963)

Middleton, Dorothy, *Victorian Lady Travellers* (London, Routledge, 1965)

Neumann, William L., *American Encounters Japan: From Perry to MacArthur* (Baltimore, Johns Hopkins U.P., 1963; New York, Harper Colophon, 1965)

Nutting, A., *The Arabs* (London. Hollis, 1964)

Oliver, R. & Atmore, A., *Africa Since 1800* (Cambridge U.P., 1967)

Sansom, George B., *The Western World and Japan* (London, Cresset Press, 1950, repr. 1965)

Seal, A., *The Emergence of Indian Nationalism* (Cambridge U.P., 1968)

Spear, Percival, *India: A Modern History* (Ann Arbor, U. of Michigan Press, 1961; repr. as *A History of India*, Harmondsworth, Penguin, vol. 2, 1965)

Steiger, George N., *China and the Occident: The Origin and Development of the Boxer Movement, 1927* (repr. New York, Russell & Russell, 1966)

8 THE HUMAN EMPIRE: WESTERN SENSIBILITY

Basalla, G., Coleman, W. & Kargon, R.H. (eds.), *Victorian Science* (Garden City, N.Y., Doubleday Anchor, 1970)

Bentley, Eric R., *The Cult of the Superman* (London, Robert Hale, 1947)

Cruickshank, John, *Aspects of the Modern European Mind* (London, Longmans, 1969)

Himmelfarb, Gertrude, *Victorian Minds* (London, Weidenfeld & Nicolson, 1968)

Hofstadter, Richard *Social Darwinism in American Thought* (revised edn., Boston, Beacon Press, 1955)

Holt, Elizabeth G. (ed.), *From the Classicists to the Impressionists: Art and Architecture in the Nineteenth Century* (Garden City, N.Y., Doubleday Anchor, 1966)

Houghton, Walter E., *The Victorian Frame of Mind, 1830–70* (New Haven & London, Yale U.P., 1957)

Hughes, H. Stuart, *Consciousness and Society: The Reorientation of European Social Thought, 1890–1930* (New York, Knopf, 1958)

Hurd, D.L. & Kipling, J.J. (eds.), *The Origins and Growth of Physical Science* (Harmondsworth, Penguin, 1964)

Ideas and Beliefs of the Victorians (London, Sylvan Press, 1949)

Jullian, Philippe, *Dreamers of Decadence: Symbolist Painters of the 1890s* (London, Pall Mall Press, 1971)

Moers, Ellen, *The Dandy:Brummell to Beerbohm* (New York, Viking Press, 1960)

Mosse, G.L., *The Culture of Western Europe* (Chicago, Rand McNally, 1961; London, John Murray, 1963)

Nisbet, R.A., *The Sociological Tradition* (New York, Basic Books, 1966; London, Heinemann, 1967)

Nochlin, Linda, *Realism* (Harmondsworth, Penguin, 1971)

Shattuck, Roger, *The Banquet Years: the Origins of the Avant-Garde in France, 1885 to World War I* (revised edn, New York, Vintage, 1968)

Williams, Raymond, *Culture and Society, 1780–1950* (London, Chatto & Windus, 1958; Harmondsworth, Penguin, 1961)

9 LEFT, RIGHT AND CENTRE: REFORM OR REVOLUTION?

Carr, E.H., *The Romantic Exiles* (1933; Harmonsworth, Penguin, 1949)

Caute, David, *The Left in Europe Since 1789* (London, Weidenfeld & Nicolson, 1966)

Fejtö, François (ed.), *The Opening of an era: 1848* (New York, Howard Fertig, 1966)

Feuer, Lewis S. (ed.), *Marx and Engels: Basic Writings on Politics and*

Philosophy (Garden City, N.Y., Doubleday Anchor, 1959; London, Fontana, 1969)

Fishman, W. J., *The Insurrectionists* (London, Methuen, 1970)

Gray, Alexander, *The Socialist Tradition: Moses to Lenin* (London, Longmans Green, 1946)

Hare, Richard, *Pioneers of Russian Social Thought* (2nd edn, New York, Vintage, 1964)

Hook, Sidney, *Marx and the Marxists: the Ambiguous Legacy* (Princeton & London, D. Van Nostrand, 1955)

Kennedy, G. (ed.), *Democracy and the Gospel of Wealth* (Boston, D.C. Heath, 1949)

Kochan, Lionel, *The Making of Modern Russia* (London, Cape, 1962; Harmondsworth, Penguin, 1963)

——, *Russia in Revolution, 1890–1914* (London, 1966)

Krimerman, L. I. and Perry, L. (eds.), *Patterns of Anarchy* (Garden City, N.Y., Doubleday Anchor, 1966)

Lichtheim, George, *Marxism* (2nd edn, London, Routledge, 1964)

——, *A Short History of Socialism* (New York, Praeger; London, Weidenfeld & Nicolson, 1970)

Pelling, Henry, *The Origins of the Labour Party, 1880–1900* (London, Macmillan; New York, St Martin's Press, 1954)

Shannon, David A., *The Socialist Party of America* (New York, Macmillan, 1955)

Viereck, Peter, *Conservatism from John Adams to Churchill* (Princeton & London, D. Van Nostrand, 1956)

Woodcock, George, *Anarchism* (New York, World, 1962; Harmondsworth, Penguin, 1963)

10 WAR: CONCEPTION AND REALITY

Brodie, Bernard, *Sea Power in the Machine Age* (Princeton U.P., 1941)

Bury, J. P. T. (ed.), *New Cambridge Modern History*, vol. 10, *The Zenith of European Power* (chs. 11 & 12)

Challener, R. D., *The French Theory of the Nation in Arms, 1866–1939* (New York, Columbia U.P., 1955)

Clarke, I. F., *Voices Prophesying War, 1763–1984* (Oxford U.P., 1966; London, Panther, 1970)

Craig, Gordon, A., *The Politics of the Prussian Army, 1640–1945* (Oxford U.P., 1955)

Earle, Edward, M. (ed.), *Makers of Modern Strategy* (Princeton U.P., 1952)

Falls, Cyril, *A Hundred Years of War* (London, Duckworth, 1953)

Hinsley, F. H. (ed.), *New Cambridge Modern History*, vol. 11, *Material Progress and World-Wide Problems* (1962, ch. 8)

Howard, Michael, *The Franco-Prussian War* (London, Hart-Davis, 1960; London, Fontana, 1967)

Huntington, Samuel P., *The Soldier and the State: The Theory and Politics of Civil-Military Relations* (Cambridge, Mass., Harvard U.P., 1957)

Millis, Walter, *Arms and Men: A Study in American Military History* (New York, Putnam's, 1956, Mentor, 1958)

Mowat, C.L. (ed.), *New Cambridge Modern History*, vol. 12, *The Shifting Balance of World Forces* (1968, chs. 6 & 7)

Ropp, Theodore, *War in the Modern World* (Durham, N.C., Duke U.P., and Cambridge U.P., 1959)

Vagts, Alfred, *A History of Militarism: Civilian and Military* (1937; revised edn, New York, Meridian, 1959)

Chronological Tables

1848	*Jan*	Revolution in Sicily
		Gold discovered at Coloma, California; gold rush begins
	Feb	Sir Harry Smith, British governor of Cape of Good Hope annexes territory between Orange and Vaal rivers
		Revolution in France; Louis Philippe abdicates; republic proclaimed
		Treaty of Guadeloupe Hidalgo ends war between Mexico and the United States
	Mar	Revolution in Berlin and Vienna
		Revolution in Venice, Parma, and Milan
		Sardinia declares war on Austria
		Outbreak of Second Sikh War in India
	April	Insurrection in Warsaw suppressed by Prussians
		French National Assembly meets
		Chartist petition presented to British Parliament
		Austrians suppress revolt in Cracow
		German National Assembly meets in Frankfurt
		Second revolution in Vienna; Emperor Ferdinand flees to Innsbruck
	June	Slavonic congress meets in Prague
		Austrians suppress revolt in Prague
		Bloody street-fighting in Paris; workers' revolt suppressed by General Cavaignac
	July	First Women's Rights Convention held at Seneca Falls, NY
	Aug	Austro-Sardinian truce at Vigevano
		Emperor returns to Vienna
		Boers defeated by Sir Harry Smith at Boomplatz
	Sept	Austria abolishes serfdom
	Oct	Third revolution in Vienna
		Conservatives capture Vienna; radical leaders executed
	Nov	French National Assembly promulgates republican constitution
	Dec	Louis Napoleon elected President of the French Republic
		Emperor Ferdinand abdicates in favour of nephew Francis Joseph
1849	*Jan*	British defeat Sikhs at Chilianwallah
	Feb	Rome proclaimed a republic under Mazzini
	Mar	Frankfurt Parliament promulgates constitution
		Zachary Taylor inaugurated as President of the United States
		Frankfurt Parliament elects Frederick William of Prussia as Emperor of Germany

	April	Frederick William IV of Prussia rejects imperial crown offered by Frankfurt Parliament
		Popular disturbances in Canada
	May	Guiseppe Garibaldi enters Rome at head of patriot forces
		French National Assembly dissolved
	June	German National Assembly moves to Stuttgart; soon dissolved by troops
	July	French take Rome and restore city to Pius IX
		Austrians restore Grand Duke of Tuscany
	Aug	Treaty of Milan between Austria and Sardinia
		Venice surrenders to Austria
1850	*Jan*	Henry Clay introduces in US Senate compromise resolutions to settle debate over extension of slavery to territories
		British seize Greek vessels at Piraeus in return for ill-treatment of a British citizen (Don Pacifico) at the hands of a Greek mob
	April	Clayton-Bulwer Treaty between US and Britain
	May	Universal suffrage abolished in France
	June	Louis Napoleon forbids political clubs and public meetings
	July	President Taylor dies; succeeded by Millard Fillmore
	Aug	Passage of Australia Constitution Act
	Sept	Clay's Compromise accepted by US Congress; Louis Napoleon restricts freedom of press
1851	*May*	Great Exhibition opens in London
		Gold discovered in Victoria and New South Wales
	Dec	Coup d'état of Louis Napoleon; rioting in Paris; many demonstrators killed by troops
		Austrian Constitution abolished
1852	*Jan*	Britain recognizes independence of Boer republic of Transvaal at Sand River Convention
		New French constitution gives Louis Napoleon dictatorial powers
	May	Treaty of London between Britain, France, Russia, Austria, Prussia, and Sweden guarantees territorial integrity of Denmark
	Sept	Duke of Wellington dies
	Nov	Cavour becomes premier of Piedmont
	Dec	Louis Napoleon becomes Emperor Napoleon III
1853	*Mar*	Franklin Pierce inaugurated President of US
	April	Russians claim right to protect Turkish Christians
	June	British and French fleets arrive at Basika Bay (Dardanelles)
	July	Russian force occupies the Danubian Principalities
	Sept	British fleet ordered to Constantinople
	Oct	Turkey declares war on Russia
	Nov	Turkish fleet destroyed off Sinope

	Dec	Gadsden Purchase; US obtains more territory from Mexico
1854	Jan	British and French fleets enter the Black Sea
	Feb	Convention of Bloemfontein constitutes second Boer republic, the Orange Free State
	Mar	Alliance between Britain, France and Turkey
		US Commodore Perry negotiates a commercial treaty with Japan
		Britain and France declare war on Russia; start of Crimean War
	May	Kansas-Nebraska Act passed by US Congress
	June	Austrian ultimatum to Russia
	Aug	Russia evacuates Principalities; occupied by Austrians
	Sept	Allied troops land at Crimea
		Allies defeat Russians at Alma River
	Oct	Sebastopol bombarded
		Allies defeat Russians at Balaclava (Charge of the Light Brigade)
		Ostend Manifesto proclaims that US would be justified in taking Cuba by force if Spain refused to sell
	Nov	Battle of Inkerman; Russians fail to break Allied encirclement of Sebastopol; great suffering among Allied troops during winter of 1854–5, Florence Nightingale organizes nursing services
1855	Jan	Sardinia joins Allies against Russia
	Mar	Tsar Nicholas I dies; succeeded by Alexander II
	Sept	Sebastopol falls
	Nov	Sweden allies with Britain and France against Russia
1856	Feb–March	Congress of Paris ends Crimean War
	May	Tasmania becomes a self-governing colony
		John Brown leads anti-slavery forces in the 'massacre' of Pottawatomie Creek, Kansas
1857	Mar	James Buchanan inaugurated President of the US
		Dred Scott decision by Supreme Court angers Northern feeling
	May	Outbreak of Indian Mutiny
	July	Massacre of Cawnpore
1858	Jan	Felice Orsini attempts assassination of Napoleon III
	July	Secret meeting between Napoleon III and Cavour at Plombières
	Aug	to plan unification of Italy
	Sept	First cable sent from Britain to North America
	Nov	Powers and territories of East India Company transferred to British Crown
	Dec	Indian Mutiny finally suppressed
		Ottawa becomes capital of Canada
1859	April	Austrians invade Piedmont
		France declares war on Austria
	May	Piedmontese victory at Palestro

	June	French and Piedmontese defeat Austrians at Magenta
		Austrians defeated at Solferino
	July	Preliminary treaty of Villafranca between France and Austria
		Cavour resigns
	Oct	John Brown leads raid on US arsenal at Harper's Ferry
	Nov	Treaty of Zurich confirms Villafranca
1860	*Mar*	Plebiscites in Tuscany, Parma, Modena, and Romagna in favour of union with Piedmont
	April	Plebiscites in Nice and Savoy in favour of union with Piedmont
		First Italian parliament meets in Turin
		Maori uprising in New Zealand
	May	Garibaldi and his Redshirts land in Sicily; take Palermo
	Sept	Garibaldi takes Naples
	Oct	Plebiscites in Naples and Sicily in favour of unification
		Garibaldi defeats Neapolitans on the Volturno
	Nov	Abraham Lincoln elected President of US
	Dec	South Carolina secedes from the US
1861	*Jan*	Frederick William IV of Prussia dies; succeeded by William I
	Jan-May	Mississippi, Florida, Alabama, Georgia, Louisiana, Texas, Virginia, Arkansas, Tennessee, North Carolina secede from the US
	Feb	Delegates at Montgomery, Ala. form the Confederate States of America
		Jefferson Davis elected President of the Confederacy; Alexander H. Stephens is Vice-President
	Mar	Lincoln inaugurated President of the US
		Serfs emancipated in Russia
		Kingdom of Italy proclaimed; Victor Emmanuel of Piedmont becomes first king of Italy
	April	Confederates capture Fort Sumter in Charleston, S.C.; start of the American Civil War
	June	Cavour dies
	July	Confederates defeat Federals (Union) at Bull Run
	Nov	General George B. McClellan appointed to command Federal forces
	Nov-Dec	*Trent* affair almost leads to war between Britain and US
	Dec	French, British, and Spanish troops land in Mexico to enforce payment of debts; beginning of Napoleon III's effort to found empire in Mexico
		Death of Albert, Queen Victoria's Prince Consort
1862	*April*	Battle of Shiloh, Tenn.; Confederates driven back
	April-July	Peninsular Campaign; Federal forces under McClellan finally driven away from Richmond by Confederates under Joseph Johnston and Robert E. Lee
	Aug	Lee defeats Federals under Pope at Second Bull Run

		Garibaldi, attempting to take Rome, defeated and captured at Aspromonte
	Sept	Lee defeated by McClellan at Antietam
		Bismarck appointed Chancellor of Prussia
		Lincoln issues preliminary proclamation emancipating slaves
	Dec	Lee and Stonewall Jackson defeat Federals under Burnside at Fredericksburg
		Indecisive battle between Bragg (Confed.) and Rosecrans (Fed.) at Stone River, Tenn
1863	*Jan*	Lincoln issues formal Emancipation Proclamation
		Insurrection in Poland; crushed by Russia and Prussia
	Mar	Opening of Schleswig-Holstein question between Denmark and Prussia
	May	Lee defeats Federals at Chancellorsville; Stonewall Jackson killed
		New Maori uprising in New Zealand
	June	French troops take Mexico City
	July	Lee defeated by Federals under Meade at Gettysburg
		Confederate stronghold of Vicksburg, Miss. surrenders to Federals under Ulysses S. Grant
	Sept	Rosecrans (Fed.) defeated by Bragg at Chikamauga, Ga
	Nov	Bragg defeated by Grant at Chattanooga
1864	*Jan*	Austro-Prussian ultimatum to Denmark
	Feb	Austro-Prussian forces invade Schleswig
	Mar	U.S. Grant created Commander-in-Chief of Federal forces
	April	Archduke Maximilian, supported by French, accepts Mexican crown
	May	Grant and Lee clash in the Wilderness, at Spotsylvania, and on the North Anna
	June	Grant checked at Cold Harbor, but besieges Lee at Petersburg
	July	Federals under Sherman take Atlanta
	Oct	Treaty of Vienna ends hostilities between Denmark, Austria, and Prussia. Denmark cedes Schleswig-Holstein
	Nov	Lincoln re-elected President of the US
1865	*April*	Lee evacuates Petersburg; surrenders shortly thereafter at Appomattox
		Assassination of Lincoln; succeeded by Andrew Johnson
	May	Jefferson Davis captured by Federals
		Last Confederate army surrenders in Louisiana; end of the American Civil War
	Oct	US demands withdrawal of French troops from Mexico
		Bismarck and Napoleon III meet at Biarritz; Napoleon promises French neutrality in approaching Austro-Prussian conflict
	Dec	13th Amendment to US Constitution – abolishing slavery – ratified

1866	*April*	Bismarck concludes defensive and offensive alliance with Italy
	June	Fenian raids on Canada
		Seven Weeks' War between Austria and Prussia begins
		Italy declares war on Austria
	July	Prussians defeat Austrians at Sadowa
		Italian fleet defeated by Austrians near Lissa
	Aug	Treaty of Prague ends Seven Weeks' War
1867	*Mar*	Last French army evacuated from Mexico
		Reconstruction begins in the American South
		Alaska purchased by US
	April	Formation of North German Confederation headed by Prussia
	June	Maximilian shot by Mexican patriots
		Austria-Hungary becomes a Dual Monarchy
	July	British North America Act establishes Dominion of Canada
	Aug	Second Reform Bill passed by British Parliament
	Nov	French and papal troops defeat Garibaldi's attempt to seize Rome at Mentana
1868	*Feb–May*	Impeachment and trial of President Johnson. Acquitted
	May	Outbreak of third Maori War in New Zealand
	June	14th Amendment to US Constitution – attempt to broaden civil rights – ratified
1869	*Feb*	15th Amendment – attempt to maintain enfranchisement of Southern blacks – ratified
	Mar	U.S. Grant inaugurated President of the US
	Nov	Suez Canal opened
1870	*June*	Leopold of Hohenzollern, relative of King of Prussia, accepts Spanish crown; France hostile to this; beginning of Franco-Prussian crisis
	July	Leopold induced to give up claim to Spanish crown, but William I refuses to give assurances to French that Leopold's candidacy will not be renewed (Ems Telegram)
		France declares war on Prussia
	Aug	French defeated at Mars-la-Tour and Gravelotte
		Irish Land Act passed; attempt to settle agrarian unrest in Ireland
	Sept	French under Napoleon III defeated at Sedan
		Revolution in Paris
		German armies besiege Paris
		Italian patriots enter Rome
1871	*Jan*	Paris surrenders
		William I proclaimed German Emperor at Versailles
	Feb	French National Assembly meets at Bordeaux; Thiers elected Chief Executive
		Preliminary treaty between Germany and France
	Mar	Uprising in Paris; start of the Commune

London Conference ends neutrality of the Black Sea

May Treaty of Frankfurt ends Franco-German War

'Bloody Week' in Paris; Commune suppressed

Aug Geneva Award settles claims of the US against Britain for allowing Confederate cruiser *Alabama* and other war-ships to be built in British yards

Thiers becomes President of French Republic

Nov Re-election of Grant as US President

1872 *Oct* Responsible government established in Cape Colony

1873 *Jan* Napoleon III dies

May '*Kulturkampf* Laws' passed in Germany against Catholic Church

Oct Alliance of the Three Emperors – Germany, Austria-Hungary, Russia

1875 *Nov* Britain buys Suez Canal shares

1876 *April* Royal Titles Act declares Queen Victoria Empress of India

May Turks massacre Bulgarians – outcry in western Europe

July Serbia and Montenegro declare war on Turkey

Nov Disputed election in US. Rutherford Hayes finally becomes President

1877 *April* Russia declares war on Turkey

Britain annexes Transvaal

Nov Russian victory at Kars

1878 *June-July* Congress of Berlin attended by delegates from Germany, Russia, Austria, Britain, France, Italy, and Turkey seeks solution to Near Eastern Question

Oct Passage of anti-Socialist Laws in Germany

1879 *Jan-July* Zulu War

Oct British invade Afghanistan

Nov Amnesty proclaimed in France for the Communards

Dec Boers proclaim independence of Transvaal

1880 *Oct* Outbreak of war between British and Transvaal

1881 *Jan* Boers defeat British at Laing's Nek

Feb Boers defeat British at Majuba Hill

Mar James Garfield inaugurated President of the US

Tsar Alexander II killed by terrorists; succeeded by Alexander III

April Treaty of Pretoria gives South African Republic independence under British suzerainty

Lord Beaconsfield (Disraeli) dies

July President Garfield assassinated; succeeded by Chester A. Arthur

1882 *May* Lord Cavendish, Chief Secretary for Ireland, murdered by Fenians in Phoenix Park, Dublin

Triple Alliance between Germany, Austria, and Italy

318

	July	British bombard Alexandria
	Sept	British occupy Egypt and Sudan
1883	*Nov*	British defeated by Egyptians under the Mahdi at El Obeid
1884	*Feb*	General Gordon sent by British government to Sudan
	Mar	Three Emperors, Alliance renewed
	Oct	Mahdi takes Omdurman
1885	*Jan*	Treaty of friendship between Germany and the South African Republic
		Mahdi takes Khartoum; Gordon killed
	Feb	Germany annexes Tanganyika and Zanzibar
	Mar	Grover Cleveland inaugurated President of the US
1886	*May*	Haymarket Square riot in Chicago
	July	First Home Rule Bill for Ireland defeated
	Dec	American Federation of Labor organized
1887	*April*	First Colonial Conference held in London
	June	Queen Victoria's Golden Jubilee
		Reinsurance treaty between Germany and Russia
1888	*Mar*	Emperor William I of Germany dies; succeeded by Frederick III
	June	Frederick III of Germany dies; succeeded by William II
1889	*Jan*	General Boulanger's *coup d'état* thwarted in Paris
	Feb	French Panama Company collapses
	Mar	Benjamin Harrison inaugurated President of the US
	April	Boulanger flees from France
	Oct	First Pan-American Conference in Washington
1890	*Mar*	Bismarck dismissed
	July	Sherman Anti-Trust Law passes US Congress
	Oct	McKinley Tariff Act passed
1891	*May*	Triple Alliance renewed for twelve years
1892	*Aug*	Franco-Russian military convention
	Nov	Cleveland re-elected US President
1893	*Jan*	Foundation of British Independent Labour Party
	Feb	De Lesseps, president of French Panama Company, fined
		Widespread financial and political scandal uncovered
	July	Outbreak of Matabele War
	Sept	British Parliament rejects second Irish Home Rule Bill
	Oct	Russian naval squadron visits Toulon; followed by Franco-Russian alliance worked out between Dec 1893–Jan 1894
1894	*Jan*	British occupy Matabeleland
	April	British establish protectorate over Uganda
	June	French President Carnot murdered
	Aug	Outbreak of Sino-Japanese War
	Nov	Tsar Alexander III dies; succeeded by Nicholas II
	Dec	Trial of Dreyfus; he is condemned and deported to Devil's Island

1895	*July*	Beginning of controversy between US and Britain over the border between Venezuela and British Guiana
	Dec–Jan 1896 Dr Jameson's raid against Transvaal
1896	*Jan*	German Emperor congratulates Kruger, President of Transvaal, for his success in suppressing Jameson raid (Kruger Telegram)
		Cecil Rhodes forced to resign as Prime Minister of the Cape Colony
1897	*Mar*	William McKinley inaugurated President of the US
	June	Queen Victoria's Diamond Jubilee
	June–July Second Colonial Conference in London
	Dec	Russia occupies Port Arthur
	Jan	Publication of Zola's '*J'accuse*' letter; Dreyfus Affair splits France
	Feb	Kruger re-elected President of South African Republic
	Mar	First German Naval Law passed, expands German Navy
	April	Outbreak of war between US and Spain
	July	French occupy Fashoda; Franco-British crisis
	Sept	British General Kitchener defeats Dervishes at Omdurman
	Nov	French evacuate Fashoda
		Germans secure preliminary concession for building a Baghdad Railway
	Dec	Treaty of Paris between US and Spain
1899	*May–July* First Hague Peace Conference
	Aug	Franco-Russian alliance extended
	Sept	Dreyfus pardoned
	Oct	Outbreak of Boer War
	Dec	British defeated by Boers at Magersfontein, Stormberg, and Colenso ('Black Week')
1900	*Feb*	Boers defeated at Paardenberg
		British Labour Party founded
		British garrison at Ladysmith relieved
	May	British garrison at Mafeking relieved
		Britain annexes Orange Free State
	July	European powers begin suppression of the Boxer Rebellion in China
		Humbert, King of Italy murdered; succeeded by Victor Emmanuel III
	Sept	Britain annexes Transvaal
1901	*Jan*	Queen Victoria dies; succeeded by Edward VII
	Sept	President McKinley assassinated; succeeded by Theodore Roosevelt
	Nov	Hay-Pauncefote Treaty gives US right to construct Panama Canal
		British break off negotiations over Anglo-German Alliance

1902	*May*	Treaty of Vereeniging ends Boer War
	June	Triple Alliance renewed
1903	*April–May*	Edward VII visits Lisbon, Rome, Paris
	Nov	Panama gains independence from Colombia
		Hay-Bunau-Varilla Treaty between Panama and US; US gains zone in isthmus for building a canal
1909	*Feb*	Japan declares war on Russia
	April	*Entente cordiale* between France and Britain
	Dec	President Roosevelt enunciates corollary to Monroe Doctrine enlarging scope for US interference in Western Hemisphere
1905	*Jan*	Japanese take Port Arthur
		Russian workers massacred in St Petersburg ('Bloody Sunday')
	Feb–Mar	Russians defeated by Japanese at Mukden
	Mar	German Emperor visits Tangier; initiates First Moroccan Crisis
	May	Russian fleet destroyed at Tsushima
	Aug	Tsar creates Imperial Duma (assembly)
		Anglo-Japanese alliance
	Sept	Treaty of Portsmouth, N.H. ends Russo-Japanese War
	Oct	General strike in Russia
	Nov	Sinn Fein Party founded in Dublin
	Dec	Workers' insurrection in Moscow
1906	*Jan–April*	Algeciras Conference ends Moroccan crisis
	Feb	Royal Navy launches *Dreadnought*; first all big-gun battleship
	May	German government decides to increase naval tonnage and plan for own *Dreadnought* class battleships
	Dec	Transvaal and Orange Free State granted self-government
1907	*Feb–April*	Edward VII visits Paris, Madrid, and Rome
	June	Second Hague Peace Conference meets
	Aug	Anglo-Russian *entente* established
1908	*Oct*	Interview with German Emperor in *Daily Telegraph* (London) suggests that Germans are hostile to British
1909	*Feb*	Franco-German agreement over Morocco
	Mar	William H. Taft inaugurated President of the US
	July	Bethmann-Hollweg becomes Chancellor of Germany
1910	*May*	Edward VII dies; succeeded by George V
	July	Union of South Africa becomes a dominion
1911	*April–May*	French advance in Morocco; Second Moroccan Crisis
	July	German gunboat *Panther* arrives off Agadir, Morocco
		Lloyd George's Mansion House speech; threat of war with Germany
	Aug	Franco-Russian military convention
	Sept	Russian premier Stolypin assassinated by revolutionaries
	Nov	Germany backs down over Moroccan question
1912	*Mar*	German Naval Bill increases Imperial Navy

		Alliance between Bulgaria and Serbia
	May	Alliance between Bulgaria and Greece
	Oct	Outbreak of First Balkan War: Greece, Bulgaria, and Serbia against Turkey
	Nov	Woodrow Wilson elected President of the US
	Dec	Triple Alliance renewed
		Armistice between Turkey, Bulgaria and Serbia
1913	*Feb*	Renewal of First Balkan War
	May	Treaty of London ends First Balkan War
	June	Alliance between Serbia and Greece against Bulgaria
		Outbreak of Second Balkan War: Serbia and Greece against Bulgaria
	Aug	Treaty of Bucharest ends Second Balkan War
	Oct	German-Turkish military convention
	Nov-Dec	Liman Von Sanders Crisis embitters Russo-German relations
1914	*Mar*	Suffragette riots in London
	April	Visit of George V and Foreign Secretary Sir Edward Grey to Paris
	June	Anglo-German agreement settles Baghdad Railway controversy
		Archduke Francis Ferdinand of Austria-Hungary assassinated by Bosnian nationalists at Sarajevo
	July	French President Poincaré visits St Petersburg
		Austria sends ultimatum to Serbia; followed by a declaration of war
	Aug	Germany declares war on Russia
		Germany occupies Luxembourg
		Germany declares war on France
		Germany invades Belgium
		Britain and Belgium declare war on Germany
		US declares neutrality
		Montenegro declares war on Austria
		Austria declares war on Russia
		Serbia declares war on Austria
		Japan declares war on Germany
		Germans capture Liège
		Germans defeat British and French (Allies) at Mons and Namur
		Germans under Hindenburg and Ludendorff defeat Russians at Tannenberg
	Sept	Battle of the Marne; Germans retreat in the west
		Germans defeat Russians at the Masurian Lakes
	Oct	Germans take Antwerp
	Nov	First Battle of Ypres
		Turkey declares war on Britain
1915	*Jan*	Battle of Soissons

	Mar	Battle of Neuve-Chapelle
	May	Italy declares war on Austria
		Lusitania sunk by German navy; many US lives lost; President Wilson sends protest note to Berlin
	July	US forces land in Haiti; establish protectorate
	Dec	Joffre appointed French Commander-in-Chief
		Haig appointed British Commander-in-Chief
1916	*Jan*	Spartacist Communist group founded in Berlin
		Allies evacuate Gallipoli
	Feb-Dec	Battle of Verdun
	April	Easter Rebellion in Dublin
	May	Italy declares war on Austria-Hungary
	June	British-German naval battle at Jutland
	July-Nov	Battles on the Somme
	Aug	Hindenburg appointed Chief of German General Staff
		Italy declares war on Germany
	Nov	Wilson re-elected
		Francis Joseph, Emperor of Austria-Hungary dies; succeeded by Charles
	Dec	Nivelle becomes French Commander-in-Chief
		Lloyd George forms War Cabinet
		Allies refuse Central Powers' peace offer

List of Illustrations

The author and publishers would like to thank the museums, agencies and photographers listed below for their help in supplying the illustrations and for permission to reproduce them.

Picture research by Penny Brown and Andrea Nelki.

Index

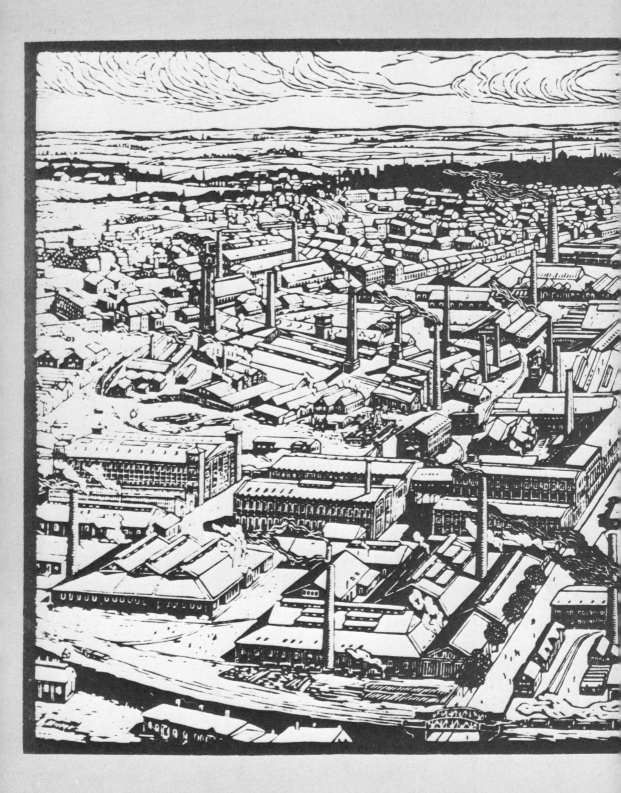